# Everyday Masculinities and Extreme Sport

For Colin Gibberd and his son, Fast Eddie

# Everyday Masculinities and Extreme Sport
## Male Identity and Rock Climbing

VICTORIA ROBINSON

Oxford • New York

English edition
First published in 2008 by
**Berg**
Editorial offices:
First Floor, Angel Court, 81 St Clements Street, Oxford OX4 1AW, UK
175 Fifth Avenue, New York, NY 10010, USA

Berg is the imprint of Oxford International Publishers Ltd.

**Library of Congress Cataloging-in-Publication Data**
Robinson, Victoria, 1959-
    Everyday masculinities and extreme sport : male identity and
rock climbing / Victoria Robinson. — English ed.
        p. cm.
    Includes bibliographical references and index.
    ISBN-13: 978-1-84520-136-4 (cloth)
    ISBN-10: 1-84520-136-1 (cloth)
    ISBN-13: 978-1-84520-137-1 (pbk.)
    ISBN-10: 1-84520-137-X (pbk.)
    1.  Rock climbing. 2.  Sports—Social aspects. 3.  Sports—
Psychological aspects. 4.  Masculinity. 5.  Men—Identity. I.
Title.

    GV200.2.R64 2008
    796.522'3—dc22                                        2008030293

**British Library Cataloguing-in-Publication Data**
A catalogue record for this book is available from the British Library.

        ISBN      978 1 84520 136 4 (Cloth)
                    978 1 84520 137 1 (Paper)

Typeset by Avocet Typeset, Chilton, Aylesbury, Bucks
Printed in the United Kingdom by Biddles Ltd, King's Lynn.

**www.bergpublishers.com**

# Contents

# List of Illustrations

## Figures

# Acknowlededgments

This book has been a long time in the making. Therefore, a number of people need to be duly acknowledged for enabling me to think through the issues around masculinities and 'extreme' sports. First, I am indebted to all the interviewees who engaged in a dialogue with me over sporting bodies, emotions and their love of rock climbing. Many of these interviews could be carried out because of funding given for the project from the Open University and the University of Manchester. At Berg, editors Kathryn Earle, Kathleen May, Julia Hall, Julene Knox, as well as Emily Medcalf in sales and marketing, have been patient and encouraging with me. Graeme Alderson, Rachel Dilley, Norman Elliott, Ian Heywood, Kathy Plate, Steve Robertson, Kaydee Summers and Sammy have alerted me to relevant material. Angela Meah and Sam Holland have usefully read and commented on the manuscript. Kath Woodward and Belinda Wheaton have given advice on individual chapters and, moreover, their own research on men and sport informs this study. Elizabeth Silva made pertinent suggestions on the initial outline for the book and David Morgan's help and comments have been invaluable. Nick Colton, Deputy Chief Executive Officer at the British Mountaineering Council, drew my attention to useful information, while Seb Grieve has graciously allowed me to use a number of his photographs. Thanks are due also to those climbers who appear in the images. Jenny Powell, at the University of Sheffield, transcribed the interviews with humour and empathy. A special mention should go to Jenny Hockey, who, with her characteristic intellectual and personal generosity, has discussed many of the issues herein with me, and read through the manuscript. I am also grateful to Richard Jenkins for asking me to edit a special edition of a journal on rock climbing, thus subjecting my work to further international influences. The final manuscript was in much better condition after the academic and climber, Terry Gifford, edited it in its later stages with care and precision, and made suggestions. He also introduced me to some inspiring rock climbing and mountaineering literature. Family and friends have had to forbear with me over the course of writing the book, especially my mother Sandra Robinson, and friends Maggie Murdoch, Sarah Pickles and Heather Symonds. Diane Richardson has always made time for our long-term friendship, whatever the circumstances of her own life. Further, Liz Stanley's recognition of the importance of the ideas of the mundane, the extreme and the everyday to my thinking, has been vital to the original conception of the study. The two people, above all, who have witnessed my writing of the book at an everyday level, when I was, at times, rather extreme myself, are my son, Eddie Joe Robinson, now aged thirteen, and Joe Picalli. Ed, I suspect, is very glad the book is finally finished, but, to his credit, not once did he ever say I should stop writing. He is my star. Joe has been an enormous help in too many ways to mention regarding the ideas and the images included here. However, I do want to note that his presents to me of exquisite boxes of chocolate (most notably from Betty's, York and Le Péché Mignon, Nice) have been much appreciated, and have sustained me when writing. I would also like to thank him for having both a rather fine mind which he has brought to bear in our discussions and, arguably, an even finer (climbing) body.

I could not have conceived of this book if I had not gone climbing, for the first time, with Colin Gibberd. I can't recall for sure but I think the sun was shining that day. Lastly, and with a delicious sense of completion, I should say that the responsibility for what is written here is, of course, wholly mine.

Victoria Robinson
Sheffield and Nice

# CHAPTER 1

# Introduction

Writers on gender issues all too often think they have found the "One True Source" of all the mischief.

R.W. Connell, 'Foreword', in L. Segal, *Slow Motion: Changing Masculinities, Changing Men*

Sport is, indeed, not the source for all such 'mischief', although it is *one* vital source. However, in thinking about how we might conceive of sporting masculinities in different ways we open up both masculinity and sport to new questions and areas for research. Specifically, this empirical study of the extreme sport of rock climbing in the UK investigates male identities by considering the routine *and* extraordinary practices and relations in a sporting culture. Furthermore, the wider context for sporting participation, defined as the everyday cultures and experiences outside of the sporting sphere, is also viewed as fruitful and necessary to explore. In this way, any potential shifts in masculinity and gender relations can be identified and finely scrutinized.

Theoretical and empirical work on alternative sports such as rock climbing, windsurfing, skateboarding, surfing and snowboarding to name but a few, has emerged from the 1980s to the present. Activities as diverse as Ultimate frisbee, adventure racing, extreme ironing and extreme skiing have also been referred to as alternative sports as the category has expanded and diversified. In this study, I will refer to the diverse body of this literature, which focuses especially upon European and North American writing, throughout this volume. I will also, in Chapter 3, explore the meaning and classification of extreme sports in detail. However, it is important to acknowledge initially that there are different terms that have been used to define such sports. There are also debates about which terms describe these sports better and capture the diversity of participants' experiences. For example, Wheaton (2000b and 2004b) uses the term 'life style sports'; 'whizz sports' is preferred by Midol and Broyer (1995); whereas 'extreme sports' is the definition used by Rinehart and Sydnor (2003); Lyng (1990, 2005) prefers the term 'edgework' to describe a number of diverse, high-risk activities, including sport, and these are seen as sites where norms and boundaries are transgressed. Other terms used, sometimes generically in the field and in this book, include the notions of 'risk sports', 'panic sports', 'alternative sports' or 'new' sports (see also Laviolette 2007).

Wheaton (2004b) points out that it is the meaning of these terms, not the terms themselves, which is most important. In her study of male windsurfers, she prefers the term 'lifestyle' because it is a description used by the participants themselves. Also, for her, it more fully encapsulates the cultures and identities inherent in a particular sport, as well as signalling the importance of the socio-historical context for such activities. The term 'extreme', Wheaton argues, has been incorporated into popular media discourses and this, it could be argued, serves to co-opt any radical elements of alternative sports. However, in later work (Wheaton 2007) she does accept that the label of 'extreme' can be useful to describe dominant aspects of the windsurfers' experience – for instance, their 'extreme' commitment'.

In my study I do use a notion of the 'extreme' both as a descriptive category of the sport of climbing, and as an analytical concept, which I go on to define in Chapter 2. This is partly because in participating in rock climbing (and mountaineering) as a risk sport, death or serious injury can be a potential hazard, unlike windsurfing, or a number of other alternative sports. Other commentators also continue to use the term 'extreme' when analysing a range of alternative sports, even when it is problematized. For instance, Rinehart and Sydnor (2003: 3) state, 'Though the cultural pop of a term like "extreme", when linked to sports, gives those sport forms a certain faddish panache, many participants are in for the long haul.' (See also Poole (2005) for a wider discussion of the term 'extreme' in relation to sport, among other issues.)

I am sensitive to the fact, however, that not all the participants in my research use the term 'extreme' to describe their climbing activities, even if others did. Some, as did Wheaton's interviewees, preferred to see rock climbing as a lifestyle that encompasses a whole way of living and existing in the world. Other, older, participants in my study started their climbing careers before the term 'extreme sports' even existed. I also, in different chapters, problematize the notion of 'the extreme' by examining how the mundane and the extreme world of climbing interact, over, for example, the life course. Additionally, rather than overstating the importance of these differences in terminologies to describe and analyse a range of new sports, Wheaton's (2004b: 3) point is useful to bear in mind: 'Despite differences in nomenclature, many commentators are agreed in seeing such activities as having presented an "alternative", and *potential* challenge to traditional ways of "seeing", "doing" and understanding sport.'

As well as a consideration of terminology, another aspect that has concerned those interested in sporting identities has been the tension between an emphasis on either the local or the global. Segal (2007) argues that the challenge for those involved with theorizing masculinity lies in a need to consider the complex, everyday realities of gendered lives, along with a continuing conceptualization of shifting female and male subjectivities. It is also, for her, crucial to recognize the importance of making such connections in both local and global contexts.

The latest phase of globalization can be seen to facilitate an increase in a variety of sports cultures (Maguire 1999). Global processes are now seen as characterized by the organization of diversity and not uniformity: '(n)ew sports such as windsurfing, hand-gliding and snowboarding have emerged and "extreme sports" have become the cutting edge for some devotees of peak experiences' (Maguire 1999: 87). Further, within globalization, Maguire sees the existence of extreme sports as evidence of resistance to globalization/Americanization through this pluralization process.

Extreme sports seem well placed activities to enable the exploration of how specific sport cultures are effected by the processes of globalization. Such processes are evident with the emergence of a world media system and an international sport system, which gives sport a global character, including the rise of the celebrity sports star, such as David Beckham (see Cashmore 2004 and Smart 2005). Rock climbing, in its specific UK features, reveals how a local sport responds in complex ways to these processes. I acknowledge these global processes here, for instance in a consideration of the increasing commercialization of extreme sports, including rock climbing, in Chapter 3. I also would endorse pleas for the continued importance of theorizing both masculinities (Connell 2005) and sport (Wheaton 2007) in relation to the global. However, my main focus is on the microrelationships and politics of a specific sporting culture and in that I am continuing in a long and established tradition of empirical and ethnographic study of localized cultures. I have also been mindful that this methodology has been subject to critical reflection on a number of aspects, for example, the view that such ethnographic analysis tends to suppress inconsistencies in the data, or debate on how a sense of 'authenticity' is produced by the researcher (see Clough 1992; Sparkes 2002).

## The Study

Theoretical work on rock climbing has started to emerge, especially in British, Australian and North American contexts (see for example, Donnelly and Young 1999; Lewis 2000, 2004; Kiewa 2001; Heywood 2002, 2006; Donnelly 2003; Dornian 2003; Robinson 2004 and 2007; Appleby and Fisher 2005; Abramson and Fletcher 2007; Dilley 2007; Gilchrist 2007; Plate 2007; Summers 2007).

Although my main focus in this book is on rock climbing, as a sport, it has some interesting parallels with, and points of departure from, other new sports. For instance, as Borden (2001) notes, skateboarding is a sport that produces space, time and self and which, for its practitioners '. . . involves nothing less than a complete and alternative way of life' (Borden 2001: 1). Many of the climbers I spoke to could be seen in these terms. However, skateboarding is seen as an urban phenomenon, whilst climbing, traditionally, is not. Nonetheless, with increasing numbers of climbers choosing to climb only at indoor climbing walls, often in big city locations, the sport can also be seen to be spatially fluid. Throughout this volume, I compare the experiences and sporting practices of my participants with others in diverse, alternative sports.

My main aim in carrying out the research that informs this book was to explore (extreme) sporting masculinities in everyday contexts. To realize this, I investigated how the sport of rock climbing is experienced and practised at the everyday level. The everyday world of male rock climbers that I have documented has been explored in this study as a 'largely taken for granted world that remains clandestine, yet constitutes what Lefebvre calls the "common ground" or "connective tissue" of all conceivable human thoughts and activities' (Gardiner 2000: 2). Moreover, Chaney's (2002) emphasis on how the everyday is present, not just as a set of structures or routines, but as a way of investing them with meaning has informed my research.

In particular, I wanted to identify any contradictions in men's embodied experiences so that potentialities in relation to shifting identities could be explored in detail. In so doing, I was concerned with what a critical consideration of the extreme (also characterized as the extraordinary) and represented by the activity of climbing with its attendant risks and potential danger, reveals about both static and changing masculinities. My interest was also in the possibilities of any reconceptualization of the boundaries of the extraordinary and the mundane, characterized by the wider, everyday worlds of the participants.

My chief research objectives were: to analyse a range of climbers' responses to the sport of climbing and its associated practices in relation to their own sense of a gendered identity across the life course; to assess how a climbing culture contributes to the production of difference in terms of diverse variables in relation to identity, including age and ability; to explore whether and how old and new male identities coexist and interact within the subculture of climbing; to theorise the culture of climbing in relation to gender relations, and to investigate men's sporting identities in the wider context of the private sphere of heterosexual relationships and the family, as well as the public sphere of work.

Key questions in formulating this research have been:

- How does the leisure activity of climbing relate to and produce everyday forms and practices of masculinity?
- How do the experiences of diet regimes and body practices such as training, male friendships and feelings of intimacy and vulnerability and expressions of sexuality inform an exploration of masculine subjectivities?
- How does greater numbers of women coming into the sport effect men's everyday experiences of gendered relations?
- How is men's sporting sense of themselves connected to and informed by their identities as fathers, partners and workers?
- How do life course changes influence how men conceive of and practice the sport of rock climbing?
- How does increasing commercialization of an extreme sport effect men's everyday sporting experiences and agency?
- How do sporting risks taken by men connect to their performances of masculinities?

For an initial pilot study, I conducted ten semi-structured interviews with British male rock climbers who have climbed worldwide. The climbers were from Yorkshire, Derbyshire, Wales and Dorset. All were white and in their twenties and thirties. Most of these climbers would be classified as elite climbers – those who could climb at a level of proficiency that many other climbers, if not most, could not attain. My main emphasis was on rock climbing, but some of the climbers were also mountaineers. Further, rock climbing shares some characteristics with mountaineering – for example, both are risk pursuits. However, there are also differences in terms of equipment used, the location of the activity and the intent of the participants – see Abramson and Fletcher (2007) for a more detailed look at these differences. I also make some distinctions between these activities throughout the study.

To extend the study, I broadened the sample by interviewing a wider range of male climbers in terms of age and motivations for climbing, including non-elite climbers, those who climbed infrequently or who no longer climbed, those who had lived and climbed abroad and also women. Thus, climbers could broadly be categorized as: professional (if sponsored to climb); those who were unemployed but whose life revolved, often on a full-time basis, around climbing pursuits; those who could be considered to be serious climbers but who were also in full-time work; those who climbed at the weekends; those who climbed only occasionally (for instance, on holiday); and those who no longer climbed (because of illness or a lack of interest, for example). In the study, if it is useful in illustrating a point, I indicate if a climber fits into one of these categories, but I do not always do this as individuals can cross over groups during a climbing lifetime or may not belong to any of them. I do, however, more often, indicate if a climber can generally be categorized as elite or not. Although the focus of the research is on men and masculinity, I thought it important to include the voices of women, so that the male climbers' narratives could be interrogated from an alternative standpoint. The interviews with women also allowed me to investigate the issue of gendered sporting relationships, in both public and private spheres, in more detail.

A number of the female interviewees climbed (sometimes but not exclusively with male participants), whereas others were the non-climbing, heterosexual partners of male climbers, mainly drawn from this study. In this wider sample, participants were also drawn from other parts of the UK, including the Lake District and Scotland. Thus, including the pilot study sample, I interviewed forty-seven people in total. Their ages ranged from 21 to 76 years. Of the thirty-three men interviewed, all were either climbers or lapsed climbers. Of the fourteen women interviewed, eight identified as climbers, whereas six female interviewees did not climb but were currently in a heterosexual relationship with a male climber. All the interviewees were white. All the male participants identified as heterosexual. In comparison, twelve female participants defined themselves as heterosexual and two identified as lesbian. The majority of participants would be classified as middle class, by either their education or occupation.

However, a very few of the male climbers in the 20–30 age group were unemployed and a significant minority of mid-life and older climbers spoke about having a working-class background and/or of having a contradictory class position, despite now having greater material wealth or an occupation that could be categorized as middle class. A small number of the elite climbers made a living from climbing, through sponsorship deals with equipment manufacturer, for instance. Other interviewees, across age, gender and elite/non-elite categories had jobs connected to the climbing or outdoors industry, for example, by working in outdoor pursuits shops, at indoor climbing walls, for climbing organizations, by being mountain guides or climbing instructors, or by working in the roped access industry (the latter which I specifically explore in Chapter 7).

Other participants had occupations that were unconnected to sport, including running their own business, or lecturing in universities, or were in full time education, or were retired. Further, the interviews were carried out during a period of over five years. This long timescale enabled me to account in depth for changes in the sport of climbing when the data were analysed, through, for instance, a greater commercialization or women's increased participation. Moreover, I was also able to gain a more detailed knowledge of some of the participants over this period, by observing them sporadically in sporting and social situations.

The greater preponderance of interviewees who either identified or could be classified as middle class, and the fact none of the male interviewees identified as gay or bisexual, together with the fact that all of my sample were white, illustrates the composition of UK rock climbing as a sport in general. As Rinehart and Sydnor (2003: 10) state, '. . . extreme sports are also mostly "white", "wealthy", and exclusionary'. To which I would add, they are also predominantly heterosexual in constitution. Participation in extreme sports therefore, Rinehart and Sydnor argue, demands that individuals have leisure time, funds and access to specialized sporting environments. Or, as Bourdieu (1986) notes, in relation to new sports, activists must be rich in cultural capital in the respect, for instance, of using and maintaining equipment, something that Goffman (1967) recognized earlier.

Recent figures from the British Mountaineering Council (BMC), the main organization in Britain for those interested in hill walking, climbing and mountaineering, are revealing in a number of these respects. This is specially because rock climbing is one of the fastest growing extreme sports in the UK. An equity survey (BMC 2006) of 10 per cent of the 63,000 members, which had a 17 per cent response rate, revealed that women's participation is now 25 per cent of all participation. This is an increase from the 16 per cent female participation recorded in a survey conducted in 2000. Further, 98 per cent of people who responded to the survey were white and this category is unchanged from the previous survey. Respondents who classified themselves as having a disability rose, from 1.4 per cent to 6 per cent. There was no data collected on class, or sexuality. This is interesting in itself and reveals, therefore, that what is considered to be the main priorities used to assess, or it could be argued, encourage, sports participation in climbing in the UK, is historically specific.

As a (lapsed) climber myself and by living in Sheffield – which has been identified as the central climbing city in the UK in terms of proximity to (dry)
climbing routes and of numbers who climb – as well as through having a male
partner who climbs, I had access to a wide variety of climbers for my study. They
included elite/non-elite climbers and different age and gender categories. I also
knew some of the interviewees personally (though not the majority.) I therefore
had insider access to part of my sample. This was especially relevant in locating
the elite participants for the study where outsider access would have made this
task harder, if not, in some cases, almost impossible. Furthermore, all the participants were made anonymous for the purposes of this study. This was
because, even though some interviewees had stressed they did not mind the possibility of being identified, others had asked for anonymity.

At times, I also used visual material as stimuli in the interview process. This
was either in the form of photographs that I had of others climbing, or photographs from climbing magazines, where some of the rock climbers I interviewed
had been featured. In doing this, I was mindful of Nettleton and Watson's
(1998) suggestion of the importance of visual prompts in using a range of
methods for accessing lay accounts of the body, as well as Benyon's (2002) stress
on the importance of the visual as a research method in accessing masculinities
and male subjectivities. The use of visual matter as stimuli in the interview
process met with varied responses. Some interviewees were not happy to talk
about their self-image either in photographs they had of themselves or pic-
tures/articles of themselves in climbing magazines. They were uneasy and
seemed to think they were bragging about their climbing exploits to me. The
most useful outcomes from using the visual material was that I was able to
further explore the notion of the denial of overt competition in climbing, how
the climbers managed their reputations in the climbing world and their own
body image, as I detail in Chapter 8.

In addition to carrying out semi-structured interviews, in the analysis of the
data, I drew upon a reflexive auto-ethnography via my previous experience as a
rock climber over a number of years. This experience has included traditional
and sport climbing on rock and ice in the UK, Europe and the United States,
where I climbed with both male partners and friends of both sexes. Through
participant observation, I was also able to observe a number of the interviewees
in different sporting situations, which included interacting with them whilst
climbing, in the outdoors and indoors, as well as in social situations. For
instance, I observed participants at parties where large numbers of climbers were
gathered, or in other social settings such as pubs, or climbing and mountaineering events and conferences. In addition, my personal knowledge of some
of the climbers allowed me access to their lives in the private sphere of the home
– where, for instance, I could observe them with female partners, or male, non-
climbing friends. This was important to be able to see how sporting identities are
informed and shaped by men's roles in the domestic arena. It was also useful in
facilitating my being able to 'get at' men's embodied masculine practices, which

an interview itself may not always illuminate, given, as Bourdieu (1977) points out, that much of practice is not carried out consciously.

## Research Issues

In carrying out this research, I have been guided by Benyon's (2002) suggestion, that a conception of how men live their lives and what is going on in their heads, both now and in the past, as well as what guides their presentation of masculinity, is central to the project of theorizing masculinities. How masculinity is performed in 'spectacles' such as sport is, therefore, a key aspect to this innovative research agenda. Benyon also notes the view that the study of contemporary masculinities currently limits our understanding of any changes taking place at the level of male subjectivities. A focus on everyday cultures and sporting masculinities allows men's subjective experience to be central to research investigation, and so, potentially enables our understanding of such changes taking place in relation to masculinities to be more detailed and informed. However, it is important to remember, as noted by Gardiner (2000), that the everyday is not an undifferentiated and homogeneous set of practices, attitudes and cognitive structures. Like him, my goal is '. . . to problematize everyday life, to expose its contradictions and tease out its hidden potentialities, and to raise our understanding of the prosaic to the level of critical knowledge' (Gardiner 2000: 6).

Felski (1999–2000: 353) has argued that men are 'embodied, embedded subjects, who live, for the most part, repetitive, familiar and ordinary lives'. Nonetheless, as this volume argues, we still know relatively little about masculinity in certain contexts, such as at home, at work *and simultaneously* in sporting sites, despite the relatively recent proliferation of theorizing on men and masculinities and this study draws on empirical data to address this absence. To achieve this, I have drawn out differences between men (and between women and men) in how they think about, and practice, extreme sports. How masculinity is 'done' is, as I will emphasize, something that happens differently, across generation and gender. In doing this, a number of sometimes problematic methodological issues have arisen.

As with Holland (2004: 3), feminism has '. . . provided both method and motivation for my work'. Within this broad context, I want to now comment on the notion of 'practice' that informs this study, the difficulty of being able to carry out research on, in this case, masculinity, when the category is often assumed and taken for granted and the issue of my own location in relation to the research in the context of having insider/outsider status.

David Morgan's (1999) conceptualization of family practices has been influential in my endeavour to research empirically and theorize the mundane and extraordinary aspects of everyday life. He sees the family as a constructed quality of human interaction or an active process and so 'not a thing-like object of detached social investigation' (Moregan 1999: 16). Family practices can also be seen as gender practices or age practices for example, making the concept applicable to masculinities. It is his concern with six related themes, which makes this work relevant for my conceptualization of the extreme and the mundane. These are: a sense of the active; interplay between the perspectives of the social actor, the individual whose actions are described and the observer's perspective; a focus on the everyday; the stress on regularities; and a sense of fluidity and an interplay between history and biography. As Silva and Smart (1999) note, Morgan's framework allows us to think of individuals 'doing' family (or masculinity), and not passively residing within a pregiven structure. Thus, according to Silva and Smart, Morgan's thoughts on 'practices' see them not as random, but routine and, importantly, not implying an opposition between structure and agency, though tensions can arise from different and conflicting practices. It is this notion of seeing a dynamic, fluid and changeable relation between structure and agency that my analysis of the empirical data on sporting masculinities draws upon.

Furthermore, researching masculinity, in particular, raises some interesting methodological issues. As I have argued together with Hockey et al. (2007) in relation to the concept of heterosexuality, when comparing it is an identity category to masculinity – as well as to whiteness and able-bodiedness – all these categories achieve and maintain their dominance by virtue of their invisibility and the fact that they are unmarked. The points I raised in relation to the difficulties the researcher might face – when asking people about their everyday, routine heterosexual lives – are also useful when considering how men may, or may not be able, to reflect on their masculinity. It is precisely the taken-for-grantedness of masculinity that can entail a barrier to reflexivity on the part of people living out their lives. How, for instance, can we ask men about how they perceive themselves as conforming to, resisting or failing to live up to dominant expectations of being a man when these questions have, until recently, been addressed mainly by theorists?

Indeed, some of the interviewees in my study of masculinities and extreme sports did struggle to think critically and reflexively about their lives *as men*. Becoming a man was seen as a process coordinated by a succession of events that they had perceived as marking their status as 'masculine'. In learning specifically to be a sporting male, some of the men in the study had been able to control their emotions. For example, in not showing weakness or fear when faced with a dangerous situation, when on a route above the level of difficulty at which they normally climbed or in accepting pain as part of a 'normal' and masculinizing sporting experience. And, in so doing, they found it hard to see such experiences in gendered terms.

However, other participants were able to be open about and critically engage with such processes, which can be seen to constitute 'masculinity'. This was partially due to the extreme nature of many aspects of the rock climbing experience, as extraordinary events such as death of a climbing partner or the need to trust another man, sometimes literally, with their life, entailed that taken-for-granted aspects of masculinity had to be renegotiated or rethought in the aftermath of moments of great sporting intensity or crisis. These aspects of the study are discussed in Chapter 6.

Nevertheless, at times, as with my earlier work with Hockey et al. (2007), it has been a challenge for myself as the researcher to reflect upon, extract and make sense of these patterns whilst also remaining mindful of the details omitted, the lapses, the untold stories, the experiences that people did not – for whatever diverse reasons – want to disclose in an interview.

The last methodological aspect of the study that I want to draw attention to is the insider/outsider status of the researcher, which has been commented on by a number of theorists. Woodward (2006) notes, in relation to ethnographies of sport, that very few male researchers either acknowledge or make known their gender and so their maleness goes unquestioned. She is also interested in issues around the female researcher studying a 'male' sport such as boxing, where ethnographic work has usually been carried out by men in this area, who, she wryly observes, have often 'joined in' and 'who are not surprisingly very proud to include tales of their own sporting endeavours' (Woodward 2006: 6).

In terms of complicating the insider/outsider status of the researcher, she questions whether ethnographies have to be embodied through the same mechanisms of those of the research site. Furthermore, an insider status gained from ethnographic participant observation can be seen to lead to an excess of empathy or subjectivism. Such questions and observations have caused me to reflect on my insider status to my ethnographic study on extreme sports. For instance, my own, embodied climbing knowledge has allowed me to interpret the data, notably around aspects of interviewees' emotional and bodily experiences, in *particular* ways, which may not have been available to the non-climber. However, I would not claim that this necessarily gives me a more authentic or privileged voice as a researcher. Indeed, my insider status has been viewed negatively by a particular section in the climbing community, as it has been argued that this could have caused my analysis to be biased (as suggested on the Web site UKClimbing.com forum, 2005.) (However, this is a claim I could further complicate, given the well established methodological debates around the notion of 'objectivity' itself and situated knowledges (see Stanley 1997 and Stanley and Wise 2008).

In problematizing this dichotomy of the researcher's status further, I would argue that the interconnectedness of my whiteness, gender, class and heterosexual status have had as much purchase on my carrying out the research, in diverse ways and contexts, as has my insider status due to my climbing knowledge and experience. For instance, the fact that I have been a rock climber did not seem to have much, if any, cachet or credibility with many of the climbers, particularly those categorized as elite, given the non-elite standard at which I have been involved in the sport. Moreover, positions are more complicated than an insider/outsider conceptualization often infers in other ways.

For example, as Rinehart and Sydnor (2003) attempt to show, even when they deliberately encouraged a dialogue between academics and activists across a spectrum of extreme sports, the dichotomy between those who seemingly 'act', and those who interpret, was misleading. In their collection, if somewhat to their surprise, 'the athletes-as-authors are eloquent writers, the academics are visceral performers' (Rinehart and Sydnor 2003: 2). Additionally, in relation to my research with some interviewees, my outsider status as a woman when interviewing my male respondents gave me insider access to their emotional lives. Some of them, for example, remarked that they found it easier talking to me because of my gender.

Lastly, in relation to methodologies, Woodward's (2006) point that the personal narratives gleaned from ethnographic practices need to be investigated along with the very public sporting stories that inform media representations of sport, is also relevant to my study of rock climbing. This is not least because of the position that climbing and especially mountaineering has in the public imagination. This is evidenced in the abundance and popularity of the accounts, novels and media representations of sporting bravery and success at all costs, including detailed reference to frostbitten limbs, or accounts of abandoned friends on far away mountains. Such tales, arguably, construct masculinities in as notable ways for the male, armchair mountaineer, as for the embodied climber. Thus, I make reference to such popular sources in this study.

As Edwards (2006) notes, and as I have acknowledged through doing this research, it is important to listen to men. I would also contend that we need to continue to be critically reflective and innovative, in the ways in which we do so. For researching men, as Campbell (2003) contends, can lead to a pushing out of the boundaries of what constitutes feminist methodology itself.

## Terms Used in the Study

I do not, wherever possible, use technical sporting language in this study. Therefore, I did not consider it necessary to include a glossary of climbing terms. In addition, I explain particular sporting terms with which the non-climbing reader may be unfamiliar, as the book progresses. I also include a number of photographs to illustrate some of the central aspects of rock climbing that I discuss here. Moreover, though I refer to particular historical moments in the analysis, I am not concerned with a history of rock climbing or mountaineering per se, though Colin Wells' (2002) book 'A Brief History of British Mountaineering' raises some useful insights in this respect, whilst Abramson and Fletcher (2007) detail some historical shifts in the culture of rock climbing. However, it is pertinent to outline, briefly, some of the main forms that climbing consists of, as I refer to these different activities in the following chapters.

Rock climbing as a sport is very diverse in terms of the styles and activities it can take. Traditional climbing, using ropes, involves placing protection into the rock to allow an ascent to be made. This type of climbing also involves a 'belayer', someone to hold the ropes of the person who is leading the climb (though 'soloing', specifically, means the rock is climbed without the aid of ropes, or other protection or a belayer (see Figure 1). This form of climbing can encompass short or long routes, which can be completed within minutes or days, for example, with big wall climbing. With traditional climbing, either on rock or ice, the fear is that the protection that a climber has placed may not hold (see Figures 2 and 3). Added to this is the possibility of being 20 or 30 feet above the last piece of protection placed, so falling off a route can have serious, even fatal consequences. Mountaineering involves longer routes and is traditionally associated with adventure, risk and danger, with which the public's imagination is increasingly fuelled by global coverage of ascents of the world's highest peaks.

Sport climbing is generally judged to be less hazardous than traditional climbing and, as a consequence, less 'pure' by some in the climbing world (see Figure 4). Sport climbing consists of climbing routes that have been equipped with bolts drilled into the rock. More routes can be climbed in a day with this safer style of climbing. The proliferation of bolted sport climbing, albeit in selected areas, has provoked much debate in the climbing world about its desirability. Some enthusiasts argue that bolting devalues the climbing experience and, as a consequence, sport climbing is sometimes seen as a pale imitation of traditional climbing, the latter seen as the 'real thing'. (See Donnelly 2003 for an analysis of 'adventure' climbing and 'sport' climbing. He sees the debates around these as part of the rich anarchic nature of the sport of climbing.)

Moreover, as I discuss in Chapter 3, although climbing is seen as a 'risk' sport, it is, in some forms, becoming more commercialized than it has been, through increased sponsorship of climbing expeditions, to the appearance of artificial crags, known as climbing walls, in many British cities. Although they were initially conceived of as a training aid for the 'real thing' there is now a whole generation of climbers who have learnt to climb indoors, never having been on a rock face (see Figure 5). This creation of an artificial climbing arena was, subsequently, followed by organized, competition climbing, league tables and, eventually, an international competition climbing circuit (see Dornian (2003) for an argument why indoor competition climbing is the ' best sport in the world' and Lewis (2004), for a very different view of sport climbing and British adventure climbing.) In contrast, the practice of bouldering is a style of climbing a few feet off the ground, without ropes or harnesses and using thick mats as crash pads to break falls (see Figure 6). This form of climbing takes place indoors and outdoors. In practice, many climbers will train inside on walls or use training boards as a way of training to increase strength and stamina (see Figure 7), and will also climb outdoors in a variety of styles. Climbs are also graded according to their level of difficulty, with different grading systems being used in different countries.

Clearly, therefore, rock climbing needs to be recognized in all its different elements: traditional climbing, sport climbing, competition climbing, big wall climbing and soloing, for example, as a diversifying and rapidly changing sport.

**Figure 1.** Soloing: Joe Picalli, The Knock, Burbage Edge. Photographer: Seb Grieve.

**Figure 2.** Traditional climbing: Peter Dalton, Birthday Groove, Curbar Edge. Belayer: Paul Hatton. Photographer: Seb Grieve.

**Figure 3.** Ice climbing: Seb Grieve, Scotland. Photographer unknown.

**Figure 4.** Sport climbing: Neil Bentley, Mecca, Raven's Tor. Photographer: Seb Grieve.

**Figure 5.** Indoor climbing wall: Fast Eddie Robinson, The Foundry, Sheffield, UK. Photographer: Joe Picalli.

**Figure 6.** Bouldering: Rab Carrington, Deliverance Traverse, Stanage. Photographer: Seb Grieve.

**Figure 7.** Training: Mark Busby, The School Room, Sheffield, UK. Photographer: Seb Grieve.

## Conclusion

Finally, although this book has been written with an academic audience primarily in mind, I hope that it will be of interest to the wider climbing community. This is particularly since there is an established tradition, at least for some sections of this community, of being passionately interested in issues of gender, and other inequalities (see, for example, Cook 1994; Lawrence 1994).

In 2005, there was a lengthy discussion on the biggest UK rock climbing online forum of my previous research on men and climbing (Robinson 2002), and which now forms part of this book. Such a response provides a snapshot of a certain section of British, rock climbers' opinions, on the desirability of conducing research on sporting masculinities. Though some of the online climbers welcomed such research, others were more negative, for instance, by questioning the use of small-scale, qualitative research in terms of being able to draw conclusions and, as I have already noted, by querying the validity of data gathered through insider access. However, it was the implicit responses of some of the climbers – to the questioning of the usefulness of looking at masculinity in

itself – which was most interesting. In contrast, and more positively, as one con-
tributor (gender unknown) put it, '. . . why do so many men seem to get very
defensive about gender based research? A project like this is in part, to acknowledge that there has been a lot of work on femininities and women and not as
much on understanding the way men see themselves and construct masculinity,
it is not an attack on masculinity but rather an attempt to open our understanding' (UKClimbing.com 2005). Another, male, forum poster stated, 'I
would suggest that we get on with looking at why climbing does become such a
central part of many climbers' (male and female) identities.'

Choosing to examine rock climbing in the context of masculinity and not, as
might be expected, focusing (as has been the tradition) on the issue of gender
and women climbers, allows hitherto unexamined and even illuminating reflections to surface, particularly for male climbers themselves to consider. The next
chapter lays out the theoretical framework for the study and the implications of
such reflections for masculinity in the context of sport and the everyday.

## CHAPTER 2

# Theorizing Sporting Masculinities

## Introduction

Since the 1980s, masculinity has received considerable attention across a whole range of different research sites, including the home and the experience of fatherhood, educational underachievement, the workplace and personal and sexual relationships. Sport as a site for the interrogation of masculinity has arrived relatively late on the scene. There was some resistance initially, to the acceptance of sport as a field in which masculinities are constructed and rene-gotiated, rather than being a place where masculinity could be just assumed and taken for granted. For example, late twentieth-century sport tended to be mainly represented as reproducing existing gender and other relations of power (McKay et al. 2000).

Initial concerns were with the role of sport as a site for the performance of what has been called 'hegemonic masculinity' (Connell 1995). Sport also offers a very specific context for the interrogation of gender identities because of its public location, in that sporting activities take place largely outside the private sphere of the home. It also carries particular meanings in relation to masculinity. These concern competition, experience of the body and body practices, disci-pline and care of the self, all of which accompany most sporting endeavours and have, in some instances become synonymous with hegemonic masculinity; for example, its association with aggressive competition, physical size and strength, and with particular forms of courage and risk-taking.

However, more recent research has focused upon the problematic of new mas-culinities, which might be forged in contexts more usually associated with tradi-tional, hegemonic masculinity (de Garis 2000). Increasingly, in this endeavour, research on masculinity and sport has been informed by feminist theories in an exploration of the gendered practices and representations of sport (McKay et al. 2000). In place of Connell's (1987) initial description of the dominance and uni-formity of a universal hegemonic masculinity, it has now been seen to be more complex and multifaceted in its operation within different contexts. As de Garis (2000) contends, most research on ideologies of masculinity in sport has been confined to young men in mainstream organized sports. Non-mainstream or marginalized sports have been neglected. But, this is steadily changing and, as noted in the Introduction, there have been an increasing number of works that seek to expand the study of 'new sports' or 'life style' sports. These sports, in general, are also less about competition, status, bravado and supposedly more individualistic, potentially less gendered and more about co-operation.

It is far from clear, though, that all sporting contexts, even those that are not mainstream, present a diversity of masculinities that might be inclusive of social, personal and ethnic differences, as well as not presenting barriers to women's participation. It is the intersection between hegemonic or traditional masculinity, and the challenges of new masculinities in the contexts of non-mainstream sports, especially rock climbing, that fundamentally concern this book.

Chapter 2 will therefore initially explore how a range of extreme, or new sports, have been conceptualized and defined. It will also consider how such extreme sports might allow for the possibility of transformatory masculinities and gender relations. I will then outline and reflect on the theoretical perspectives that I use in this study, including a critical discussion of debates around how useful the notion of a sporting 'subculture' is for sports studies. The chapter will next discuss different theoretical positions on men and masculinities, especially in sporting contexts and include some criticisms of such perspectives. Finally, two central concepts I employ in this analysis of male rock climbers are introduced: 'masculinities in transition' and 'mundane extremities'.

## 'Extreme' Sports

Wheaton (2000a and 2000b, 2004b, 2005, 2007) defines lifestyle or extreme sports as non-aggressive activities though embracing of risk and danger, as usually individualistic in form or attitude and predominantly white, middle-class and Western in composition. However, there are differences between some of these sports in relation to the participants engaging with real danger or life-threatening activities, as opposed to merely 'flirting' with death. Furthermore, Rinehart and Sydnor (2003) posit a view that extreme sports stand in opposition to mainstream sports as they are usually not institutionalized with governing bodies but are, at the same time, also increasingly becoming commercialized. In other words, extreme or alternative sports are 'big business', which I discuss in Chapter 3. In addition, though these sports are usually individualistic, not team sports, team-based versions of such new sports exist, with the examples of Ultimate frisbee (Wheaton 2004b) and adventure racing given in Rinehart and Sydnor's collection.

A number of other key characteristics also define 'lifestyle sports' (Wheaton 2004b). Such activities as snowboarding, windsurfing and Ultimate frisbee are new sports, while others such as surfing have been revitalized with new generations taking up the sport and these sports are characterized by the active, not passive, involvement of participants. The sports are organized around the consumption of new objects such as bikes and boards and involve new technology (for example, in rock climbing with new and improved gear such as climbing boots using sticky rubber to give better grip on the rock, or safer and stronger climbing harnesses or new protection devices). Furthermore, she argues that such new sports call for a commitment in time and/or money and a style of life that builds up around the activity in terms of social identities, attitudes and collective expression. Hence, her characterizing of these sports in terms of 'lifestyle'. As well, ideologies promoting fun, self-actualization and hedonism form around the sport in question. Institutionalization, along with commercialization and regulation, is often denounced and even resisted at times and the sports are usually further characterized by performative, creative and aesthetic factors.

Moreover, Wheaton (2004b) details that such lifestyle sports take place in new or appropriated outdoor spaces, mostly without fixed or limited boundaries. Participants often express nostalgic thoughts for a past rural life, where nature is revered. Macnaghten and Urry (2000) argue that sociology has not dealt systematically with the different social practices which are related to being in, or passing through, nature or the outdoors. However, specifically, in relation to adventure climbing, Lewis (2000) has explored the climbing body in relation to nature and modernity. More recent work has started to think through some of these issues in a gendered context; for example, Wörsching (2007) is concerned with German sporting commodity advertisements and the production of masculinity in the more, or less, masculinist contexts of sport and nature associations.

Lastly, it is through charting differences between more traditional organized sports such as football and rugby with extreme or lifestyle sports, and also between alternative sports themselves, that diverse questions can be asked in respect of alternative sports seeming to offer greater possibilities for resistance and disruption to traditional gendered relationships. This is through, for instance, the promotion of more fluid gender identities and relationships and less emphasis on competition than in traditional, institutionalized and competitive sports, sites where dominant relations between women and men, and men with other men, such as gay men can still be seen. For instance, Midol and Broyer (1995), argue that new sports have the potential for liberating participants from traditional gender roles because of the blurred boundaries they create. Beal (1995) states in relation to the subculture of skateboarding, that: 'sport has also been analysed as a place where dominant values and norms are challenged and where alternative norms and values are created' (Beal 1995: 252 – see also Birrell and Richter 1987).

For my purposes, I am interested particularly with the potential liberatory capacities of a sport such as rock climbing in relation to new and more egalitarian, identities and relations, which I now go on to discuss.

## Transformatory Sporting Masculinities

Schutz's (1973) argument that social reality is constantly reconstructed through the everyday actions of individuals, informs this study of everyday cultures by considering climbers as reflexive actors involved in the creation of diverse, fluid and contradictory identities. The analysis illuminates the ordinary and extraordinary aspects of everyday experience and cultural practices in a climbing culture and, more generally, it reveals the complex and nuanced relationship between sport, society and culture.

In addition, with specific reference to identity, Barker (1999), argues that the 'plasticity' of identity, the self as made up of changeable and multiple identities, is one of the reasons that the concept itself has such political significance. For as identity shifts and changes, it has intimate connections with social and political practices. Barker argues that no single identity is an overarching organizing identity; rather, our identities shift depending on how we are addressed or represented. Wheaton (2004b: 10) further argues that, within new sports: 'Subcultural identities, however, are not static, but are contested and re-made over time.' It is this notion of a shifting identity that my empirical study of male rock climbers begins to explore in Chapter 4 (see also Whitehead 2002; Woodward 2002; Jenkins 2004).

However, Woodward (2006) uses her study of male boxers to disturb this contemporary emphasis on identity as fluid and shifting, as opposed to being fixed and certain.. She argues that male sporting participants' need to secure the self or establish a sense of belonging, illustrate some of the difficulties that result from 'framing identity in a sea of discursive uncertainty' (Woodward 2006: 3). Therefore, the 'powerful draw of such masculinities' reveals the relationship between uncertainty and stability and thus needs to be viewed in the context of the social and psychic, the particular and the universal, as well as agency and constraint.

It has also been suggested that the argument that has been put forward that so-called extreme sports, or lifestyle sports, such as windsurfing, skateboarding, or indeed, as I investigate here, climbing, afford more possibilities for challenging old gender stereotypes, should be problematized (Wheaton 2004b). Newer and individualized sports, in the same way as traditional team sports, can still position women participants as more 'passive' than men in specific sporting contexts and construct discourses in which women are seen as less 'physical' than men, as well as less able, or less competitive, because of their biology. (I explore these issues in Chapters 2, 4, 5 and 8.) Therefore, it is important to note, as Horne et al. (1999) argue, that fashionable new sports are not necessarily classless or genderless. Rinehart and Sydnor (2003) also acknowledge that sexism still exists in media reporting of extreme sports, but, more positively, feel that in such sports categories of difference may be magnified, altered or blurred. As a consequence, they argue political correctness can (positively for them) be thrown out. I examine whether or not extreme sports necessarily challenge traditional gendered relations, specifically in Chapter 5.

The conclusion reached by Wheaton (2000b), that her research demonstrates that windsurfing is not a site for a radical 'new' embodied masculine identification, but that men's relationships with women and other men in this new sport are complex and variable, is borne out in my study. Clearly, rock climbing forms part of the changing discourse of identity and masculinities, and a central question I ask through my empirical research on male rock climbers is whether they challenge traditional/dominant notions of gender roles, identity and power, or merely appear to re-invent them, while in reality reconstructing old ones. Or indeed, is it possible, as Winlow (2001) asks in a study of crime and masculinities, that within the limits of any given culture, an individual can define new patterns of behaviour, which are suggested by (and, I would add, fashioned from) the variations amongst old ways of being? In this respect, Gill (2003) argues that men learn to 'do' different forms of masculinity, resulting in the emergence of more fluid bricolage masculinity (p. 39). Also, which conceptual frameworks can be used to adequately theorize these traditional and emerging, sporting identities?

## Towards a More Inclusive Sporting Theoretical Framework

Gardiner (2000) argues, in relation to developing a critical knowledge of everyday life, that we must go beyond the pragmatic activities of social agents in particular social settings, relating this analytically to wider socio-historical developments: 'Social agents are not "cultural dopes", but nor are their thoughts and actions fully transparent to them' (Gardiner 2000: 7). To allow this wider analysis of sporting social agents, my study is situated in the framework of contemporary, critical sporting studies, informed by sociological and cultural studies perspectives, masculinity studies, as well as feminism and theories of gender relations.

Regarding masculinity in particular, the social significance of sport at both local and global levels has become steadily more apparent since the 1980s, through recent theoretical concern with sporting identities (see for example; Donnelly and Young 1988; Messner and Sabo 1990; Coakley and Donnelly 1999). Despite this interest in masculinities as a field of study and specifically sporting masculinities, it has been argued by Eric Dunning (1999) that sport has been marginalized in attempts to come to grips with the social production of masculinity. He sees this as being related to some theorists' insistence on linking sport with 'hobbies' and 'conceptualizing it as separate from "the everyday world"' (Dunning 1999: 220). More recently, it was argued that the social sciences have still marginalized the relevance of sport to everyday life as well as underestimating its significance in relation to social change (Skellington 2006).

Indeed, at times when carrying out the research for this book, or in giving papers in diverse institutional contexts and locations, I have sometimes experienced a personal sense of frustration. For example, I have found that those theorists who could be defined as broadly being located in the field of sporting studies have

sometimes viewed an emphasis on feminist critiques or on postmodernist concerns with identity and difference as a distraction, or even as superfluous to discussion about sport. This experience confirms Hall's (2002) observation, that the sociology of sport has not yet fully recognized the insights of diverse feminist perspectives. Conversely, I have sometimes experienced a lack of interest in sport when presenting my research on men, gender relations and sport at feminist conferences, or sensed that my sporting concerns have been seen as not so important as other, more traditional sociological concerns such as class, work or the family, at more mainstream sociology events. These experiences have informed my reflections on the theoretical framework used in this volume to think through sporting masculinities. Such a framework, I argue, recognizes the importance of theorizing the experiences of sporting participants across disciplinary boundaries and theoretical positions. In this respect, I am mindful of recent attempts to integrate the insights of sports studies with social theory more generally and to 'encourage the abandonment of sectional division and to embrace theoretical diversity among communities of sports scholars from different disciplinary backgrounds' (Giulianotti 2004: 1). Specifically, I address Wheaton's (2007: 15) argument, that work on sporting subcultures needs to 'borrow from, and integrate with, theorizing in other areas of sport and mainstream sociological work'.

My wider theoretical framework, therefore, is one which incorporates a critical consideration of the literature on men and sport by masculinity theorists, defined either as 'men's studies' or the 'critical study of men and masculinities' (see Hearn and Morgan 1990; Hearn 1998). It is also informed by sporting studies that have emerged in sociological and other contexts, for instance on the attendant aspects of sporting activity such as injury, risk or competition. Fundamental, however, to my thinking about sporting masculinities is the inclusion of wider sociological debates around the body and embodiment, intimacy and the emotions, heterosexuality and gender relations as well as, importantly, the sociology of the everyday. To this end, I explore the everyday lives of rock climbers, for example, where friendships, relationships and work interact with sporting identities. In addition, I incorporate material from the climbing community in the form of online forums, climbing magazines and the work of those who are academics in other fields such as literature (Gifford 2006), in order to demonstrate that there exists rich and varied forms of source material, including those outside of the academic journal article, which can inform sporting studies.

Such a paradigm could be seen as eclectic. Alternatively, I would argue that this way of looking at sporting masculinities in an inclusive framework allows new questions to be asked in different ways about sporting identities, relations and experiences. This can be seen as relevant especially for any theorizing of alternative sports, given that these have been seen as particularly fertile sites for interrogating issues of difference and power relations, for instance (Wheaton 2004b). That is not to say of course, by any means, that I am the first academic to adopt a theoretical framework on sport that crosses disciplinary boundaries or fields of specialism (for one example on masculinities, ethnicity and boxing, see

Woodward 2006). In addition, studies of the everyday lives of sporting participants, which consider sport in relation to the family and work, for example, have
been done (Borden 2001; Lilleaas 2007). But there remains much scope for
research such as I have outlined to be developed, and, in diverse ways. Thus, different approaches to, and perspectives on the study of sport, can be seen to cross
over fruitfully, and allow the analysis of empirical evidence to be more nuanced,
as well as, hopefully, encourage new debate between sports' scholars and others,
in a number of theoretical areas.

## Reflections on the Theoretical Framework

Initially, feminist research foregrounded gender as a crucial determinant of
social relations and has long challenged the claims that men and masculinity are
ungendered. This research also addressed the sporting field as one divided into
men's and women's sports and has concentrated on the historical exclusion of
women from mainstream sports (Hargreaves 1994). Others, such as Creedon
(1994) have examined the core values of the media to illustrate how such values
are gendered when sport is represented and show the role of the media in 'the
way women are oppressed, marginalized or disenfranchised by the current sports
system' (Creedon 1994: 8), although theorists may disagree on the nature of that
oppression and on how to eliminate it. Recently, feminist attention has turned
to thorny issues such the construction of a 'violent femininity' through sports
such as female rugby (Gill 2007), or media coverage of gender-based violence in
sport, as Toffoletti (2007) investigates in the context of the Australian football
league. More generally, feminists have also argued that leisure time is gendered
and that leisure is seen as a kind of capital with women having less time, access
and agency than men in relation to it (Green et al. 1990).

These diverse areas of interest illustrate Hargreaves' (2004) point, that: 'Sport
Feminism is hard to define. In reality, there has been no coherent, cohesive,
authentic sport feminism, but many different manifestations, philosophies or *fem-
inisms* . . .' (Hargreaves 2004: 187). Thus, feminist sports studies can be characterized as having different stages; firstly, a concern with inequality in sport,
secondly, an awareness of feminist theory and its importance for sport studies and
finally, the postmodern age where post structuralist and queer theory are used to
theorize issues of gender and sport (Birrell 2000). To support this view,
Hargreaves (2004: 193) points to the 'resonances' that postmodernism has come
to have, given the complexity of shifting identities and the insecurities of self, in
what can be characterized as modernity. Thus, the work of feminists such as Cole
(1998) is cited, to illustrate a contemporary concern with questions of consumption, lifestyle and aesthetics. Further, the influence of postmodernism in feminist
sports studies is seen to include queer theory's insistence on a critique of normative heterosexuality, (see Seidman 1997 and Eng 2003) and the possibilities of the
pleasures of the body (see Pronger 1998). Gay, lesbian, bisexual and

ranssexual sporting identities have also been placed on the sporting theoretical agenda (Caudwell 1999; Cox and Thompson 2000; Eng 2003 – see also Scraton and Flintoff 2002).

However, Hargreaves also notes critiques of a sporting postmodernist position, for instance from the viewpoint that issues of power and oppression can be negelected. As Scraton and Flintoff (2002) remark, 'We would argue that there are some new and exciting questions raised in post-structuralist accounts of sport but that this does not mean that all the 'old' questions have been answered or that they are no longer significant' (Scraton and Flintoff 2002: 42). Importantly, Hargreaves (2004) also states that sports feminism has neglected issues of sport in the developing world, or has tended to see sport development for women in developing countries as essentially beneficial. Therefore, in her view, sports feminism must not lose its humanism and moral base in a need to theorise inequality and difference. More recently, as King and McDonald (2007) point out, there is such work being carried out on sport which attempts to analyse the production of social inequality within capitalism coupled with a concern about how this is produced through identity categories and relations, for example, Martin and Miller (1999) and Andrews (2002).

In addition, Hargreaves makes a plea that, for sports feminism to progress, it must maintain and further links with mainstream feminism but also, conversely, she states that mainstream feminism itself has neglected issues of sport and female bodies. Thus, in this way, as a sociologist and feminist who could be considered 'mainstream', rather than a sport feminist, my study of extreme sporting masculinities seeks to address this somewhat neglected, though changing, dialogue. I would add that the theorizing of masculinity and gender relations from a feminist perspective, and not just the issue of women in sport, is important to further such debates.

Along with feminist concerns, this study is also informed by what has been termed an interactionist perspective to the study of sport as well as a concern with identity. Horne et al. (1999), in describing an interactionist stance on the socialization into sport of individuals, make parallels between this and a cultural studies approach. This approach is seen to have a conception of sport and leisure subcultures as being able to link a concern with patterns of individual involvement in sport and leisure with wider relations of cultural reproduction, subordination and oppression. Interactionist and cultural studies perspectives are seen to concentrate on the issue of identity and how individuals and groups negotiate their involvement. Interpretative methods are used in these approaches and participation in sport seen as *process*, is central to such studies. Therefore, as I have just implied, a concern with feminism and theories on gender relations in general and sporting relations in particular, underpin this study, as does a post-structuralist emphasis on shifting and fluid identities and a particular understanding of power relations, resistance and difference, which has been especially influential within cultural studies. A central assumption here has been that sport has been seen as a site of cultural struggle and cultural resistance in relation to gender (Hall 1996). In this context, sport is a cultural practice, and one which can be interpreted through a 'circuit of culture' (identity, representation, production, consumption and regulation) (du Gay et al. 1997).

However, as with Hargreave's (2004) discussion of postmodernism, the 'cultural turn' in sociology, has not been without criticism. Martin's (2002) view is that cultural studies has a tendency to focus on micro-politics, at the expense of having a political agenda. Whilst Thorpe (2006), in response to Rojek and Turners's (2000) critique of the 'cultural turn' in sociology, iden-tifies a disturbing lack of any systematic contextualization in sport sociology. She argues that a cultural studies approach is limited by a failure to account for historical change. Further, in contrast, she feels that: 'The systematic and trans-historical tools developed by social historians have the potential to facilitate a more all-encompassing contextualization of cultural phenomena, to examine multiple historical conjunctures, and to help sociologists take time and change more seriously' (Thorpe 2006: 205). However, she does concede that a social history approach to context can sacrifice detail in an attempt to give a general interpretation. And, that this approach can tend towards description but not analysis.

Although I am mindful of these criticisms of the cultural approach, I still consider that my ethnographic analysis of the micro-politics and cultural specificities of the extreme sport of rock climbing has been enabled, by at least some of the insights of cultural studies. Furthermore, I do offer some (limited) historical contextualization of the sport of rock climbing. Additionally, Thorpe herself acknowledges that the 'cultural turn' has indeed produced 'interesting and insightful ethnographic studies' (Thorpe 2006: 209) and cites the examples of Beal (1995, 1996), Anderson, (1999) and Wheaton and Tomlinson (1998) to illustrate this. However, it is important to be both reflexive and critical about the central concepts used in the context of any theoretical framework, as I now go on to demonstrate with a discussion of the concept of subcultures in relation to sport, traditionally associated with a cultural studies perspective.

## Sporting 'Subcultures'

The notion of 'subculture', which is used both implicitly and explicitly in studies on sport, has recently been examined more carefully. This can be seen as important in ensuring a continued reflexivity about the concepts that are employed in theorizing sport, but also because such an examination allows us to consider arguments which would support the use of one conceptual framework over another, or the use of specific terminology over other terms. For example, the anthropologist Dyck (2000) argues that a notion of subcultures in relation to sport can ignore sporting phenomena or relationships and argues instead for ethnographic enquiry into the activities, relationships and meanings of sport. He further argues that ethnographic accounts of sport offer rich evidence of '. . . the myriad ways in which persons, both as individuals and as members of groups, utilize involvement in sport to organize comprehensible lives out of the increasingly fragmented and contradictory elements of contemporary existence' (Dyck 2000: 32).

Other criticisms of the concept of subcultures have ranged from feminist critiques that early subcultural studies ignored or made peripheral women and girls (McRobbie 1994), or failed to include groups due to their age (Holland 2004) and assumed subcultures were internally homogenous, for instance on class terms, or had an emphasis on semiotic and textual approaches at the expense of the material or the use of empirical data (see Muggleton 2000). Thorpe (2006) offers further critique of the concept, in that subcultural theory can be seen to be unconcerned with the dimension of change.

In a study of the musical genre of 'extreme metal', Harris (2007) argues against the usefulness of the notion of subculture, because of its theoretical inadequacies and because 'it is inapplicable to contemporary society' (Harris 2007: 18). As with the later concept of neo-tribe, a postsubcultural term which evolved to discuss phenomena such as dance music, Harris feels the idea of subculture does not acknowledge any possibility that diverse forms of people's interaction (and coexistence) can coexist in a single space. Therefore, with subculture virtually rejected as a concept by him, and no other viable postsubcultural alternatives yet available, he looks to the idea of 'scene' as an alternative to allow him to examine a specific musical practice, such as 'extreme metal', in particular temporal and spatial locations.

Many of my participants referred to the existence of either a historical or contemporary climbing 'scene', where climbers congregate together, over a period of time. However, while some climbers were happy to be part of and contribute to the 'climbing scene' by living, working and/or socializing with other climbers, others rejected wanting to be part of something that some climbers saw as exclusive or 'cliquey'. Even some of the elite climbers, whose livelihoods depended on access to climbing networks and being in the know about who had climbed what route and having their faces seen at climbing events, for example, distanced themselves from aspects of the scene. Therefore, for my purposes, I do acknowledge that 'the climbing scene' is a term used by some climbers to describe their participation in the sport, whilst others distance themselves from such an involvement when it is viewed as elitist or even claustrophobic.

It is also a useful term when describing different climbing activities, or climbing communities, to be able to distinguish between them – for example, in expressions such as the 'bouldering scene', where large boulders are scaled without ropes or aid, or the 'Llanberis scene', which refers to a Welsh community of climbers, particularly in the 1980s, or the 'deep water soloing scene', where, without ropes or clothing, climbers throw themselves off cliffs into the sea. Individuals can belong exclusively to one of these 'scenes', or alternatively they can participate in different 'scenes' where, moreover, their affiliation to them can alter over time.

Within such groupings, particular friendship groups are formed, around for instance climbing ability, a weekly night at the climbing wall, or simply through climbers congregating in a certain pub, or by living in particular neighbourhoods, which consist of large numbers of climbers and mountaineers. Additionally, there are currently, approximately 300 climbing and mountaineering clubs (including student clubs) affiliated to the British Mountaineering Council, which vary in membership and the activities pursued (BMC 2007). Groupings such as the all-female Pinnacle Club and the all-male Wayfarers Club encourage single-sex climbing friendships to flourish, whilst the walking and climbing club 'Red Rope' describes itself as 'socialist'. Furthermore, the idea of 'scene' is appropriate to describe the climbing community in the sense of those who share an interest in diverse events – for example, literature and film festivals such as those organized in the UK at Kendal, in the Lake District, or local programmes of slide shows given by elite climbers and mountaineers. And, a well as a prolific rock climbing and mountaineering magazine and literature 'scene', there is also a virtual community where climbers discuss sporting issues on a number of online forums.

However, specifically regarding the continuing relevance of the idea of sub-cultures, others have argued not for a rejection but for an appreciation of its conceptual history in sporting and other fields. Such a review has entailed a revised agenda for sporting subcultures. This can be seen as valid, not least because many people may consider themselves to be part of a particular subculture, even if some theorists have critiqued the term. In a timely discussion of the concept of subcultures most closely associated with the Birmingham Centre for Contemporary Cultural Studies, Wheaton (2007) argues that using subcultural theories has implications for the study of sporting collectivities, identification and identity politics. This is particularly pertinent for my discussion here of the extreme sport of rock climbing, as it is alternative sports which have been seen to be important sites for subcultural studies (Beal 1999).

As well as acknowledging some of these earlier criticisms of subculture theory that I have briefly outlined, Wheaton also points out that postsubcultural theory, although useful to studies of extreme sports because of an emphasis on difference, resistance and multiple and fluid identities, still continues to exclude issues of race, ethnicity and heterosexuality within its concerns. I would add to that list of absences a consideration of ageing and the life course, which, in this study of male rock climbers, I foreground as essential to theorizing issues such as em-bodiment (see Chapter 8 on the body). Here, I wholeheartedly agree with Wheaton that placing issues of embodiment (and performance and the symbolic) as central to the sporting theoretical agenda around identity, difference and resistance is important. As Wheaton states:

> To understand the meaning and significance of these activities, we need to be attentive to the different ways in which resistance is interpreted, defined, and played out, moving beyond dichotomies of passivity or resistance (Wilson 2002), body discipline or pleasure, freedom or control. (Wheaton 2007: 18)

Feminist critical theories of embodiment are especially useful here (see Woodward 2008), to counteract an absence of the embodied subject in both subcultural theory and, at least until recently, in the theorizing of men and masculinities. (Though such feminist critiques have not necessarily been concerned with sporting bodily practices *per se*.) In Chapter 8, these feminist theories and their critiques of other perspectives on embodiment, such as phenomenological arguments, are addressed in more detail.

Additionally, though Wheaton only fleetingly mentions the importance of the sociology of the emotions to sporting studies, along with risk-taking in sport goes management of emotions such as fear, vulnerability and anxiety. These areas are still undertheorized in sociological critiques more broadly, as well as in sporting studies. (Though work on these areas in relation to sport is emerging, see de Garris 2000 and Lilleaas 2007, for example.) Moreover, though I am not explicitly concerned with the psychic dimensions of masculine identity in this study of male rock climbers, such aspects of masculinity have been usefully explored through psychosocial approaches and those that offer more analysis of the affective dimensions of masculinity (Williams 2001; Whitehead 2002; Woodward 2006). Thus, these emotional dimensions of masculinity will inform the concerns of this book, particularly in Chapter 6 on sporting inner lives, including men's friendships. I also foreground how a consideration of gendered, heterosexual relationships (Chapters 5, 6 and 7) can shed light on the emotional and intimate micropolitics inherent in sporting 'moments' and relations.

Therefore, because of the potentiality of some of the ideas associated with subcultural theory for theorizing extreme sport, I do use aspects of these in my research. Ultimately, however, although Wheaton makes a strong case that the notion of postsubcultural theory should be revised and not rejected, I am not entirely convinced that it is currently, at least, sufficiently developed enough to fully address the criticisms I have outlined. Thus, I also engage with a more eclectic theoretical framework as I have already detailed. This is particularly because I feel that issues of, for example, power in gender relations, are still theorized more explicitly and systematically, elsewhere, such as within (materialist) feminist perspectives.

## Theorizing Men and Masculinities

As I have stated, in relatively recent times, attention has turned to men's participation in sport from a 'critical studies of men and masculinities' perspective, or more broadly from those engaged in masculinity studies. (See, for instance, Sabo and Messner 1994 and McKay et al. 2000.) There is also work being carried out on masculinity that does not fall strictly within this framework but which, nonetheless, has been informed by concepts such as hegemonic masculinity.

More general theoretical insights on how masculinity is constructed and performed have underpinned these sporting studies. For instance, a useful and often cited definition of masculinity which is pertinent to any study of men, masculinities and sport is provided by Connell, who views masculinity as 'simultaneously a place in gender relations, the practices through which men and women engage that place in gender, and the effects of these practices in bodily experience, personality and culture' (Connell 1995: 71).

Moreover, the concept of 'hegemonic masculinities', which Brod defines as how 'particular groups of men inhabit positions of power and wealth and how they legitimate and reproduce the social relationships that generate their dominance' (Brod 1987: 92) has been central to theorizing masculinity since the 1980s and, for my purposes, to sporting studies of men and masculinities in particular. It is also argued that most men do not correspond to the hegemonic model, but that many are complicit in sustaining it. The hegemonic model of masculinity is also seen as heterosexual (see Carrigan et al. 1985).

Feminists Cornwall and Lindisfarne (1994) have used the concept of a hegemonic masculinity effectively. They noted that masculinity varies over time and setting, and also argue that:

Hegemonic versions of masculinity frame relations of inequality. However, hegemonic forms are never totally comprehensive, nor do they ever completely control subordinates. That is, there is always some space for subordinate versions of masculinity – as alternative gendered identities which validate self-worth and encourage resistance. (Cornwall and Lindisfarne 1994: 5)

The concept of change in relation to different groups of men is prevalent in recent literature on masculinity. Connell (1995) further examines the concept of hegemonic masculinity by stressing multiple masculinities and by exploring groups of men undergoing different experiences of change. Some are seen to be wanting to transform gender relations and others are resisting these transformations. So, therefore, a notion of compulsory heterosexuality for men, for example, is seen to reveal both the complexity of changes in masculinity and also the diverse possibilities of real change, in different spheres, including the sporting arena. Specifically, Connell (1997: 233) has also equated sport with masculinity and power, where hegemonic masculinities are embodied through sporting practices and relationships, in particular, 'Sport has come to be the leading definer of masculinity in mass culture.' Further, sporting prowess has been seen to provide a regular and routinized forum for the promotion and expression of learned and generated masculinity (Horne et al. 1999).

However, importantly, this assumption of an automatic relationship between masculinity, power and dominance has been questioned. Messner (1992), in an attempt to problematize the construction of a dominant, hegemonic masculinity in sport, outlines three reasons why sport does not construct a single dominant masculinity. One is the cost of sport to men; the second is men's different experiences of class, race and sexuality in athletic careers; the third is the challenges to sport and heterosexual masculinity posed by the rise of women athletes. He asks if dominant conceptions of sex and gender are challenged in any of these three contexts and argues that individual men in relationships with women can challenge the gender order. Though such relationships are ambivalent, he also found that some men elevate relationships above winning in some sporting activities. Men, he argues, have had to change their attitudes because of women's increasing participation in sport. Some, for instance, have questioned the myth of female frailty. Thus, theorists have argued that some men's behaviour in specific sporting sites can be seen to challenge dominant conceptions of a heterosexual, hegemonic masculinity.

In contrast, however, there has been more limited interrogation of the ways in which whiteness is constructed within the area of sport; however, this is changing, see for example, King et al. (2007). Empirical and theoretical research has also emerged around race and ethnicity, for example Carrington (1998) and Woodward (2006), as well as Abdel-Shehid's (2005) queer theorizing of black masculinities and sport in Canada and McKay and Rowe's (2001) work on the racialized male body. In addition, Erickson (2005) has theorized whiteness specifically in relation to climbing, whilst Bayers (2003) has turned his attention to mountaineering in a historical context of imperialism and white masculine anxieties.

Furthermore, theorists of masculinity have pointed to the silences regarding the masculine body, heterosexuality and how it is experienced as an embodied identity. Miller et al. (2001) have argued that the sporting body most valorized is male, white and heterosexual. Homosociality is seen to be tolerated and actively encouraged, from school sports through to advertisements. Whilst Pronger (2000) claims that reproduction of an orthodox heterosexual masculinity is central to the culture of mainstream men's and boy's sport, discussing homophobia and homoeroticsm in relation to these insights. More recent work (Harris and Clayton 2007) has imaginatively used Connell's concept of hegemonic masculinities to theorize new male sexualities, specifically in relation to sporting masculine identities and metrosexuality, or looked at the gay, male marathoning body (Bridel and Rail 2007) and gay athletes and masculinity (Anderson 2002).

As well as the concept of hegemonic masculinities being central to the study of men and masculinities, along with emerging work on issues such as whiteness and somewhat more established studies on men's sexuality, some masculinity scholars have asserted that studies of men's sports experiences should draw on the theoretical insights developed by feminists on women's sports. With regard to relational analyses, McKay et al. (2000: 6) state that women's experiences are impossible to ignore when studying men and masculinities, citing Messner's call for an 'inclusive feminism'. They also argue that in the same way that male scholars studying men and sport need to take account of feminism, 'so too do women feminists need to address somehow the "man question" in sport and the larger gender order.' Further, they have argued that feminists in the 1980s and 1990s focused on the negative aspects of men playing sport, by highlighting issues such as misogyny, pain and injury, homophobia and violence against women. Feminists also contrasted this with women's sports, where cooperation, rather than competition, was seen to flourish. In this way, the complexities of masculinity, diversity of sporting activities and sporting possibilities for disruption and resistance were ignored or downplayed.

More recently, theorists in a grounded way have started to study differences between men in relation to women sporting participants and gendered relations. But, as McKay et al. (2000) point out, we still need more studies that compare how women and men relate to each other in single-sex sports and in sports where they compete together.

## Critiques of Masculinity Theories

Despite these valuable theoretical developments that I have just outlined in relation to sport in particular, the concepts and perspectives of 'critical men and masculinities' theory have come under scrutiny. Indeed, the concept of hegemonic masculinity has itself been criticized (Robinson 2008). For example, Whitehead (2002: 90) argues that the concept 'achieves what patriarchy fails to achieve: it offers a nuanced account of femininity-male power while staying loyal to the notions of gender and sexual ideology, and male dominance.' Yet, he also contends that, as a concept, hegemonic masculinity is as reductionist a category as patriarchy, its fundamental inconsistency being that while it recognizes difference and resistance, its primary underpinning remains a notion of a fixed male structure. Ultimately, he argues: 'Hegemonic masculinity is a useful shorthand descriptor of dominant masculinities, but its overuse results in obfuscation, in the conflation of fluid masculinities with overarching structure and, ultimately, in "abstract structural dynamics"' (Whitehead 2002: 94).

Seidler (2006) also critiques Connell's notion of hegemonic masculinities for making it difficult to understand the relationship of diverse masculinities within particular cultures, as cultures have been reduced to relationships of power and so we have not been able to theorise the ways in which culture relates to emotional life, for example. He also asserts that hegemonic masculinities 'have sometimes acquired a general theoretical currency that seemed to bear little relationship to the empirical studies they were supposedly meant to illuminate' (Seidler 2006: xxv1). Others, such as Moller (2007), argue that 'while Connell's model of a hierarchy of masculinities offers a powerful tool with which certain practices and images of masculinity can be readily critiqued as undesirable, it lacks any way of appreciating the complex meanings which may be articulated through an image or practice' (Moller 2007: 274). Moreover, especially relevant for my purposes here of investigating the complicated meanings and patternings of sporting masculinities, Moller feels that the concept of hegemonic masculinity does not aid the researcher interested in sporting cultures to understand these attendant complexities. Indeed, as he reveals in his own work on male rugby league supporters, such a focus can reduce our understanding as it does not allow us to comprehend men's vulnerabilities in sporting contexts

Meanwhile, Hearn (2004) calls for a shift from masculinity to men and a focus on 'the hegemony of men'. In this way he seeks to address the double complexity that men are both a social category formed by the gender system as well as being collective and individual agents, and often dominant collective and individual agents, of social practices. However, Connell (2005) argues that the concept of 'hegemonic masculinities' is still essential in theorizing gendered power relations. He also states that although it is time to consider the use of the concept and how it has been used in masculinity studies, whether it is time to reject the category, or re-affirm it, is still very much debated.

Further criticism of the insights of critical theorizing on men and masculinities has emerged on the grounds of race and ethnicity. Gamal Abdel-Shehid (2005) is concerned with exploring how black sporting masculinities have been both constructed and interpreted within critical masculinity studies, which he terms 'Good Boy Feminism'. He exemplifies this stance by the use of Michael Messner's work on sport, which he critiques as being too simplistic in its conflation of sport and patriarchy. Here, Good Boy Feminism's notions of masculinity are seen to incorporate a hierarchical and essentialized notion of maleness. Moreover, black men are presumed to be 'written out of the text of male participation in feminism by virtue of their placement within the "state of nature"' (Abdel-Shehid 2005: 53). He claims that this theoretical framework in question is a heterosexist, as well as racist paradigm, because of an inherent inability to theorize desire and how it works for men in the making and unmaking of masculinity. Men, by virtue, then, of their essential maleness can only be either masculine or emasculated and therefore, Abdel-Shehid sees no theoretical middle ground available.

Such critiques, as I have outlined, raise issues of whether key concepts such as 'hegemonic masculinity' allow masculinities to be theorized in a sufficiently detailed and flexible manner, enabling, for example, issues of difference to be adequately addressed. This is a concern summed up by McKay et al. (2000) who ask if a focus on an oversimplified and universalized conception of hegemonic, sporting masculinities leads to differences of class, race/ethnicity and sexual orientation being ignored.

To be able to start to address some of these, and other issues, around the concept of hegemonic masculinity in relation to sport, I have conceived two new conceptual frameworks for considering any transformations in sporting masculinities and other relations. The first, is the concept of masculinities in transition. The second, is the concept of 'mundane extremities'.

## Masculinities in Transition

As I have argued in Robinson et al. (2007) with evidence gathered from a three-year, ESRC-funded project on masculinities, identity and occupations, theoretical and empirical issues of men and masculinities in relation to space, intimacy, the emotions and the body are now at least starting to be addressed within a variety of disciplines. However, such theorizing starts from assumptions about fluid and multiple masculinities but tends to assume a static framework within which to explore men's experiences. Men are treated as if they inhabit and perform masculinities in one space alone, for example, either the workplace or domestic sphere. Little consideration has been given to how men exist in different spaces, sometimes simultaneously and at various stages of the life course and how they manage transitions between work and home life, between being a colleague, friend, father and partner.

With Hockey and Hall, I was concerned to look at how men's identities might shift across different occupational locations, which were more, or less gendered, in the sites of hairdressing, fire fighting and estate agency. Focusing on men's mobility and experiences, their strategies and performances of 'being' a man, can speak not only about masculinities, but also to gendered, classed and aged relationships across and beyond separate life spheres. Further, in this study (Hall et al. 2007), we began to ask how being a man might involve different kinds of behaviours – or performances – depending on whether an individual was at home or at work. We also asked female partners, relations or friends about how men performed differently, whether at home, or at work. And, although we regarded men's occupational and domestic environments as 'scene[s] of constraint' (Butler 2004: 1), our data on men in different occupations attested to men's individual agency and so demonstrated the liability of masculinity to 'internal contradiction and historical disruption' (Connell 2005: 73). This idea of 'masculinities in transition', or, alternatively, 'mobile masculinities' has been useful for my study of extreme sporting masculinities in looking at how men move from being climbers to fathers, to partners and to workers, and back again over their sporting embodied lives as bodies age, new relationships start and (un)employment ceases. It is, therefore, a useful concept when exploring the ways in which both identities and relations may undergo change.

Such transitions, as I note in Chapter 7 on the family and work, are not necessarily easy nor wanted, and the issue of whether these shifting boundaries mean that new forms of masculinities are drawn and redrawn is considered throughout my study of male rock climbers, in an attempt to give a more complex and nuanced account of masculinities. The voices of the climbing and non-climbing female partners of the men interviewed for the study, are also incorporated, to allow men's individual 'stories' to be scrutinized and placed in different contexts. Further, if men manage their everyday lives through the resources of gendered stereotypes and identities, which they use differently in diverse contexts, how do the extreme situations they encounter through climbing give them different resources to deploy? And, given the neglect still, of age and the life course in theories of masculinity, Spector-Mersel's (2006) idea of 'multiple masculinities', which refers to differences in two contexts – 'across persons' and 'within persons' – is useful to be able to fragment any single and hegemonic idea of masculinity.

## Everyday Sporting Experiences: 'Mundane Extremities'

Dorothy Smith (1987) has argued that the 'everyday' has traditionally been conceived of in terms of men's, and not women's, experiences. In addition, therefore, how can a notion of the everyday be redefined through a sustained critical analysis of men and masculinities? Bennett and Silva (2004: 6) argue that to retrieve the analysis of the everyday, '. . . from the search for the exceptional and ruptural possibilities that has characterised the critique of everyday life' we need to be 'concerned with how social changes come about in and through the ways in which political issues are worked through in the context of the mundane dynamics of everyday life rather than seeking a generalized transcendence of the everyday.' This concern is, indeed, central to my study. However, so too is a consideration of my participants need to, at times, sometimes seek transcendence from the routines of everyday living, through participation in the world of the extraordinary, that is, the extreme world of rock climbing.

The second concept of 'mundane extremities', which I use to explore sporting masculinities in the context of the everyday, has a historical theoretical trajectory. Previously, with Hockey et al. (2002, 2007), in a two year, ESRC-funded cross-generational study of the institution and experience of heterosexuality, we argued that heterosexuality is constituted in those 'key heterosexual moments' such as the acquisition of gender and age-based social status in adolescence. In exploring the significance of such 'moments' we devised a framework that allowed us to conceptualize the relationship between the mundane and the extremes of heterosexual experience. Arguably, we said, it is the power of the mundane that not only keeps heterosexuality 'in place', but also, at times, reveals disruptions to it. We were interested too in how extreme events such as a recollection of 'date rape' or empirical evidence of domestic violence are sutured into more mundane experiences of heterosexuality. Therefore, we argued that the pervasively mundane quality of heterosexual life can shape the way people make sense of extreme events. This means, for example, that memories of extreme events, such as violence against a woman, were likely to be remembered and recalled in some detail by virtue of the fact that they disrupted mundane activities, such as eating. What we found within our data on heterosexuality, then, are examples of participants' reflections on what we eventually conceptualized as 'extreme mundanities'.

To some extent, this framework for investigating heterosexuality was built on work on sporting masculinities that I had conducted earlier and which now forms part of this book. In Robinson (2003), I had initially argued that the extreme was a relatively straightforward concept in relation to extreme sports. Thus, the extreme could be seen in the fact that to be a good or 'extreme' climber, some of the men in this study had dieted obsessively to enable them to reach their idealized weight, even to the extent of weighing their food so that their calorie intake did not go over 1,000 calories a day. Or, alternatively, in terms of the risks taken, the extremes of pain and injury were confirmed in a number of the climbers'accounts.

But, as my empirical work in this area of sporting masculinities progressed I found that an exploration of mundane and extreme experiences in 'extreme sports' reveals the *everyday* nature of the practices that constitute rock climbing in a more problematic way than originally anticipated. In certain contexts, what might be considered 'extreme' behaviour by most people, such as courting injury or evident risk-taking, was viewed as more 'mundane' everyday occurrences by the rock climbers in the study. Conversely, for some of the participants, it was through the mundane practices associated with climbing, such as hours spent freezing on a small ledge on a rock face that close male friendships were formed, and not, as might be expected, necessarily through extreme events such as accidents or daring and spectacular sporting exploits. I go on to discuss these aspects of the data in later chapters.

Central, therefore, to this problematizing of the everyday, the mundane and the extreme, or extraordinary, is the conception of 'mundane extremities'. As I go on to explore, for some of the interviewees, the 'exceptional' activities associated with climbing were very quickly routinized and came to consist of largely standardized climbing practices. This is something that Heywood (2006) has commented on, using Weber's term of a 'disenchanted' world to show how rock climbing, over time, becomes normal, predictable and measured. Thus, what is considered ordinary or extraordinary shifts, according to the location a person has to the sport of climbing as insider or outsider. It also shifts for climbers themselves. A particular example of this would be how climbers' conceptions of the ordinary and extraordinary in relation to their own masculine identities changed as they grew older, in having to reassess where a life hitherto centred around climbing was leading. If climbing as a pursuit was often used to put everyday life in perspective, or to escape from the routine aspects of much of everyday living, the mundane, everyday aspects of life were sometimes adopted by climbers as they aged.

They therefore reinvented the meaning of the previously mundane world of relationships, work and families, over the life course. For example, this was evident when their injured bodies could not let them perform at the standard they had previously achieved, or when a long-term relationship became, perhaps for the first time, a priority. I examine such transitions in Chapter 7 on the family and work, Chapter 8 on the body and Chapter 9, on risk.

## Conclusion

I am, therefore, concerned in this research to explore the 'private realm' of the everyday, in relation to men's public (extreme) sporting performances, as it is this latter aspect which sporting studies, in the main, have focused on. Further, an embodied focus can reveal the gaps and cracks that exist between the public and private spheres: 'What athletes exhibit in games and other competitive events and what spectators watch and celebrate are embodied sports techniques that unite the private realm of everyday body practises with the public world of shared performances' (Dyck 2000: 24).

To further illustrate this public/private dichotomy, Giulianotti (1999: 156) observes in his study of men and football, that masculine identity is complex and multi-faceted: 'Outside football, they adopt other masculine roles as partners, parents, children, workmates and social friends.' Whilst in relation to a more alternative sport, Borden (2001) argues that through graphics, words and ideologies, skateboarders reject the external world, especially paid work and the family. However, how does that rejection inform their relationships and family connections outside of a sporting context?

My research with male climbers prioritizes the investigation of the everyday in a grounded empirical study and allows the charting of men's increasingly shifting and enmeshed relationship to both public and private spheres. It is one thing to state men's identities are multiple, but how do those different identities interact in mundane and in extreme contexts? It is this interaction of public, extreme sporting performances and private, mundane practices, along with the mobility of men across these different spheres, which is explored throughout the book.

# CHAPTER 3

# Problematizing 'Extreme' Sports

## Introduction

Sport is still being theorized in ways that do not always distinguish between traditional sports such as football and rugby and extreme sports such as rock climbing, but some theorists, for example Wheaton (2004b, 2005, 2007) and Rinehart and Sydnor (2003) have clearly made these distinctions, as I noted in the previous chapter. Others have chosen to critique more traditional team sports.

This chapter will explore climbing in relation to traditional, organized team sports and consider differences in how climbers perceive of diverse everyday sporting practices. In so doing, it will further problematize an extreme-traditional sports dichotomy, initially by placing assumptions about this dichotomy in a historical perspective. It will also consider the idea of authenticity in relation to public and personal narratives of rock climbing, the nature of 'obsession' in a specific sporting context and look at whether the ongoing, often decried commercialization of rock climbing affords possibilities of agency for some of the climbers involved. In so doing, I question a sometimes assumed deradicalization of extreme sports in general. Central to the chapter's concerns is an argument that a careful analysis of rock climbers' reflections on the intricacies of their relationship to a risk sport, other extreme sports and traditional, team sports allows for a consideration of whether different masculinities are being formed. Furthermore, it can be seen whether these masculinities are co-existing in extreme sporting scenarios. In addition, I start to analyse the mundane aspects of an extreme sport, by investigating climbers' everyday, sporting practices.

Messner (1987) has explored young men's participation and practices in organized sports and relates this to their own personal sense of failure or success. For the men in his study, most had found sports to be the primary means by which to establish their manhood in the world. Many of these young athletes needed to feel the appreciation of the 'crowd' to think that they are worthy human beings: 'When so much is tied to your performance, the dictum that "you are only as good as your last game" is a powerful judgement' (Messner 1987: 199). He argues that in organized sports the athlete's sense of established identity is insecure and problematic because of the possibility of failure and of success. This is, according to Messner, because success involves the development of a personality that amplifies many of the ambivalent and destructive traits of hegemonic masculinity. Messner further argues that such sporting men are not able to have intimate and lasting friendships with other males and they also see their sporting 'success' as more fundamental to them than interpersonal relationships. (I will discuss men's sporting friendships in Chapter 6.) He also concludes that attempts to make sports more egalitarian are doomed if women and men do not have equality in the home and the public sphere. Similarly, Salisbury and Jackson (1996) have asserted that school sports shape boys in emotional and social ways and also lock many boys into an aggressive and virile culture, through the repetitive process of the masculinization of their bodies. Overall, one's identity is seen to be lost in the process of engaging in organized sports.

Traditional team sports such as football have also been explored in relation to male conformity, amongst other issues. Edley and Wetherell (1995) outline that the identity of 'hard boy' in a study they conducted with secondary school age boys, was organized mainly around school sports, especially rugby. Connell's (2000) argument that team sports define society's versions of hegemonic masculinity adds to this conception of sport as a public demonstration of a representation of a particular kind of masculinity. This is one that is dominant over other, less powerful masculinities, and where masculinities themselves are actively created through the process of team games.

Whitehead (2002) further argues that men's sense of self is validated in places such as the golf house or football ground – in public, not private spheres. Historically, team games, Benyon (2002) demonstrates, are associated with the founding of Victorian capitalism, since the establishment of local clubs playing a part in contributing to a sense of municipal pride. Players on the pitch would be admired for displaying a hard and aggressive masculinity. So, organized team sports have been seen by many theorists concerned with exploring (hegemonic) masculinity as 'an uncomfortable and problematic places for men to be or develop' (Whitehead 2002).

How, then, do extreme sports, with a perceived potential for greater self-expression for men and a less violent and masculinized sporting environment (Salisbury and Jackson 1996), challenge organized sports, which are perceived as allowing hegemonic masculinities to thrive and develop? Is there any truth to this dichotomy as it has been historically conceived and is it as rigid as some theorists have claimed?

## The Lure of the Dichotomy

Salisbury and Jackson (1996), arguing the need for a broadened physical education syllabus for those boys not suited to traditional team sports, contend that alternative sports, as opposed to organized team games, are different from what they see as the humiliating and pressuring climate of, for instance, soccer and rugby. Supposedly, in sports like orienteering, outdoor pursuits, climbing and canoeing, boys can find their own comfortable levels without pressures being brought to bear on them. In these less pressurized activities, they are seen to be able go at their own pace in exploring their bodies and seeing what they are capable of. Although Salisbury and Jackson reveal that schools should and can challenge the dominant culture of an aggressive and heterosexual manliness, through sporting practices, they do not attempt to problematize what count as less pressurized activities. So it is automatically assumed that traditional organized school team sports promote a hegemonic masculinity, whereas alternative sports, such as climbing, are seen unproblematically to allow for alternative masculinities to be formed and nurtured.

It has also been argued that new sports, such as wilderness sports or skateboarding, afford different opportunities of empowerment around demonstrations of skill and strength (Whitson 1990). The presence of women in such sports is also seen to weaken popular associations between sport and masculinity and so broadening the recognized boundaries of traditional masculinities (which I examine in Chapter 5 on gender relations). But, caution is expressed by Whitson because of the place still given to confrontational team games in the sporting hierarchy, so that opportunities for masculinizing practices still remain. Again, it is through such traditional sports that hegemonic masculinity is seen to be reproduced and male hegemony actively pursued. However, this dichotomy, which posits organized sports as straitjacketing men into stereotyped male roles as aggressor and victor, and extreme sports as enabling men to express themselves in new and less traditional ways, is a simplifying polarization.

Conceptualizations that see mainstream sport as *dominant* rather than simply *mainstream* are helpful in allowing new sports and power relations, for example, to be scrutinized (see Wheaton 2007). However, theoretical approaches that have attempted to characterize extreme and traditional sports as being about either cooperation *or* competition respectively are flawed in that they can often ignore variations in how the various sports are played out in practice. Further, this polarization fails to take into account the experiences of specific individuals within both kinds of sports and does not posit the individual male across the life course. This view of men in organized sport fails to consider the myriad reasons men participate, including the joy and pleasure to be had from using the body, for instance, and pushing one's personal limits.

In relation to alternative sports, Wheaton (2000b) differentiates windsurfing as a lifestyle sport, from other more traditional rule bound, competitive and 'masculinized' sports as it is less rule bound, has fewer exclusion policies and is opposed to traditional forms of competition. This, however, was not something that was always fully borne out in the climbers' accounts of their rock climbing activities as this climber, aged 21, testified, when asked if climbers were an '*inclusive bunch*':

I'd say so yeah, in general, yeah. Quite, quite an inclusive bunch, I think, as long as you respect the sort of area and respect you know the obvious stuff like queuing for routes or leaving litter … Like bouldering I think, sort of starting out, I think that can be pretty intimidating, because obviously it is like a pretty sort of masculine environment and everyone, like, climbs with their tops off.

This young climber, in seeing climbing as an inclusive sport, at one level demonstrates Salisbury and Jackson's (1996) perception of alternative sports as more welcoming to all-comers than traditional sports where certain male attributes such as 'manliness' are more highly valued. However, when pressed further, he also speaks of being intimidated in what he terms a 'masculine' environment where climbers have to take off their tops to climb. This may be out of practicality because of the hot weather or, on other occasions, merely for 'the pose'. It is then clearly apparent who has the biggest muscles or broadest shoulders or who is overweight, or not. But it is not just about body self-image but also about perceived levels of ability, which also, he related in the interview, gives some discomfort to him if he is climbing next to others who may be doing harder and potentially more riskier routes than those of which he perceives that he is capable. Furthermore, he goes on to add: 'that probably gave me more motivation to get better', therefore endorsing and not necessarily challenging any competitiveness, something that Salisbury and Jackson (1996) would want to associate with sports such as climbing.

Nonetheless, Salisbury and Jackson were writing about new sports before much of the currently existing empirical work had been carried out. Since then, theorists have resisted the lure of this neat traditional/new sports dichotomy, including Wheaton (2000b) herself. For instance, Beal (1995: 254) when discussing skateboarding as a potential challenge to capitalist ideologies, does allow that 'numerous individual and daily resistances occur in mainstream sport'. Likewise, Fitzclarence and Hickey (2001: 129) avoid the simple dichotomy that team sports such as football confirm automatically 'the "ugly logic" of hegemonic masculinity'. Instead, they ask whether such sports offer the development of alternative ways of being gendered, whilst being careful to avoid a reductionism or hierarchy of traditional/extreme sports that leads to a simple 'yes' or 'no' response to that question. Further, sport is seen to be a paradox in that it inspires and fosters positive traits of hard work, courage, determination, fairness, sacrifice, selflessness, loyalty and respect. But it also encourages selfishness, rule breaking, greed, violence and contempt for others. Conversely, Connell (1987) has argued that the combination of force and skill involved in organized sports such as football, cricket and baseball is also even to be found in individualized sports such as surfing.

The potential of traditional sports to allowing men opportunities to not always have to 'fit' a masculine stereotype is sometimes downplayed in the well documented arguments that see traditional activities as constructing a hard and unfeeling masculinity, However, the tenacity of hegemonic masculinity can also be downplayed in attempts to stress the transformatory possibilities of new sports, including rock climbing. Further, I have argued that it is not possible to understand the dynamics of either extreme or traditional sports in relation to the subtle and sometimes hidden constructions of masculinity in and through sport itself, unless comparisons are made and problematized. For as Hargreaves and McDonald (2004: xl) contend 'The flamboyant world of these new "other" sports are understood only in relation to "established" ones embodying quite different social relations, meanings and values.' To explore some of the issues I have started to raise it is useful to explore, firstly, my extreme sports participants' views on more traditional, organized and team sports.

## Extreme/Traditional Sports: Hierarchies and Divisions

> The topic of in-line skating came up. 'They're all five years behind our style,' said Greg, who would hurl a large chunk of plastic at one startled in liner the following day. 'They think they're better than us,' said another bunkmate, 'they think they're like ...' 'Jocks', said Nick. 'Yeah, jocks!' another said. 'I don't like team sports,' Greg said. 'You have to depend on everyone else. And, if someone screws up, everyone does.' (US sportsmen discussing in-line skating (roller blading), cited in Browne 2004: 152)

Not only do these sportsmen eschew team sports because of having to depend on someone else other than oneself, and so potentially effecting individual success, they are able, by this inference, to insult other extreme sports participants by the most denigrating of comparisons with 'Jocks', those all-American college or high-school football players. Browne (2004: 2) does accept that not all extreme sports participants are against team sports, but asserts that, in general, traditional sports do not 'speak to them'.

A range of views on traditional sports were found in my interviews with the rock climbers, which both support and counteract Browne's view. A climber, aged 50, when asked if he would miss the sport if for some reason he was not able to climb, had managed to combine a passion for climbing with a life long commitment to football: 'I would miss it if I had to give it up now, but if I had to give it up, because I'd, you know, broke me back or whatever, I'd just find, I'd just get on and do something else. I still play football, I've played football all my life.' This pragmatism contrasts with other climbers who were interviewed. Some, such as this climber aged 37, took a classic individualist stance on team sports, indicating that he had 'tried to get into team games, but I wasn't very good at them. I really thrived on more individual sports.'

He supports the anti-team sports ethos to the extent that, in his view, if climbers were to take part in team sports they would not be able to join in with their team mates because of the need to display an individualism not characteristic of a sport like cricket or rugby, for example. For others, such as this man in his fifties, being good at a sport was important in motivating him to climb when he had not had much success with traditional sports such as football. He says:

'You want to excel at something, you want to be good at something, or known at something', but it was only when he

> went to the Outward Bound school … I was sixteen and I was eight, eight stone and erm, you know, I was, I was the best in this group and suddenly you think 'Oh, it's something I'm good at', you know, so, I mean that in itself is a motivation.

Different extreme sports participants are often keen to argue that their particular sport is the most exciting, or dangerous or special. For instance, Farrell (2007: 33) claims that with free diving (the sport of breath-hold diving where some divers can hold their breathe for 9 minutes and dive beyond 200 m): 'No other sport has the potential to take you to the limits of your own mortality so quickly.' Similarly, many of the climbers interviewed were concerned to stress how unique climbing, as a sport, was for them, inadvertently at times creating a hierarchy both between climbing and traditional sports and with other extreme sports. For example, this 60 year old, tries to encapsulate climbings' uniqueness at different levels:

> I've never found, I've never found another sport which gave, which ever gave me anywhere near the same level of personal satisfaction and intellectual erm, because it's about environment as well. It's about wild, wild places. I've never found anything that came vaguely close to climbing,

So the spatial aspect of a particular sport, where it is carried out and experienced by the participants involved is important to consider when assessing how meaningful a sport is to an individual. The emphasis on 'wild, wild places' infers that the sport of climbing can be seen as extreme not only in terms of its risky practices but also in relation to the particular environment it is carried out in, which for some interviewees was obviously part of its attraction. It also helps to explain why more traditional sports do not appeal. However, for others interviewed, for example those who only wanted to climb indoors or spend the majority of their time climbing in this way, an extreme environment is not necessary for their enjoyment of the pursuit of rock climbing.

For another interviewee, a more elite climber, aged in his thirties, climbing was always special when compared to other sports he had tried, even those sports he had enjoyed and *was* very good at:

> I love the kind of adventure side of it. I did like being outdoors and in the mountains, wherever it might be and the challenge of it, and, it just kind of went on from there really. I stopped thinking too much about other sports. But I have had on occasion the odd lapse with climbing. But I think you always come back to it. But there's no doubt I think someone like me, I could have chosen another sport and I think I would have been, you know been able to perform. Should have chosen football, I could have been a millionaire by now [laughter].

Despite having been an all-round athlete, and cross-country runner at county level, he acknowledged that if he had pursued a more mainstream sport, like football, he would possibly be playing at a professional level, and earning much more than he currently did. Therefore, material wealth is clearly less important to him than for some other, more traditional sports participants. Indeed, this lack of importance of the material, or at least its relegation to a secondary place, when the life choices taken had enabled them to climb instead, was at the expense of having well-paid jobs and was seen in a number of the (often) elite climbers' accounts. Some of these men could potentially have had better paid sporting careers if they had been involved in more traditional sports, to the same level and extent as climbing. However, as with this climber, the realities of those decisions were being reviewed as they became older and/or had started a family, when having their own house and being able to afford a mortgage became important (see Chapter 7 on work and the family).

One young climber, in his early twenties, described climbing as 'more magnetic than other sports' that he pursued, but was unable to describe further why this was. Others also created a hierarchy between different kinds of extreme sports, by viewing climbing as one of the most 'extreme' of such sports, but not surprisingly because of the risk and danger attendant with some aspects of climbing. This was evident with a climber, in his twenties, seen by some, at the time, to be one of the best climbers of his generation in the UK, who, when asked if climbing as a sport gave him anything that other sports did not, responded:

Hard one that, because, you know, climbing was the original thing, but now I snowboard. I recently got into skydiving. A few other things ... Fantastic, yes, skydiving, it's absolutely incredible and it's quite easy, but hard to learn. Climbing's different, because, 90 per cent of extreme sports are fast pace, extreme skiing, skydiving, surfing, skating, they're all reaction time, fast. Whereas, climbing isn't. Climbing is a slow drawn-out process and it isn't so much reaction and instinct. It's more like intellect and decision making. So it's a very different, very different thing. And there are comparisons and particularly within the lifestyle side of it, but not so much with the actual practice. So, no, you don't get, you don't get what you get from climbing.

In this way, he creates a division of extreme sports. Climbing is seen to be both cerebral *and* physical, and whilst other extreme or risk sports may compare with the lifestyle associated with the climbing community, including comradeship and shared aims, they differ in the bodily as well as intellectual execution of the sport.

This distinction between sports was also conceptualized in terms of how the sport of climbing was able to engage the interest of participants over time. A climber, aged in his fifties, said: 'I've tried other exhilarating sports like skiing which I enjoy but, nowhere near the same as climbing. Fairly dangerous, very exhilarating, very, very good exercise, but it's a bit monotonous. Never, ever been bored climbing, not in the slightest.' Whilst other climbers used their involvement in other sports, as well as exploiting the diversity of experience that different climbing activities gave them, in an attempt to prevent climbing as an activity from becoming boring and mundane. This accomplished Alpine guide, in his late thirties, reflected:

> I just couldn't rock climb all year round and then go to the (climbing) wall, because I think I would just get bored. And I think that is why I got into winter climbing and skiing. And the best thing about being a mountain guide was that I had to learn to ski and it was ace as it meant I had to go to Chamonix for two winters!

Furthermore, in contrast to other participants, he does not see climbing as a unique activity that offers him something that other sports are not able to give. However, he qualifies that when speaking about friends who are climbers, who have indicated to him that climbing *is* special, and who return to the activity even when they have tried and enjoyed other extreme sports. The argument that climbing is more than a sport, and is about a special kind of lifestyle is borne out here, in his comments that the climbing community, not just the activity, draws people back to the rock climbing 'scene'. As Dant and Wheaton (2007) argue, in their study of windsurfers, it is the shared understanding of the sporting experience that characterizes particular extreme sports, as I explore further in the next chapter on identity. Alternatively, some of my interviewees felt that the thrill-seeking and excitement to be had from sport is the same across a range of activities, others still that the everyday practices of individual sports allow participants to create something specific. The need for the climber quoted above, to prevent what is conceived of as an extreme sport from becoming mundane, is discussed in detail in different chapters, where the idea of 'mundane extremities' is outlined and discussed in relation to the data.

## 'Authentic' Practices

Donnelly (2003: 127) theorizes about the relationship of climbing to mainstream sport: 'The resilience and significance of climbing lies in the fact that it existed for so long as an alternative to mainstream sport, as an unincorporated and self-governing parallel to the dominant sport culture. And climbers have, in recent years, been very conscious of the difference from other sports and have acted to maintain that difference.' Similarly, Browne (2004: 11) discussing in-line skaters states that the 'riders' did not like being lumped together 'with stunt acts and freaks, not to mention skydivers, bungee jumpers or rock climbers'. So groups of extreme sports activists have been keen to differentiate themselves from each other. This can partially be explained by the need some sporting participants have to maintain an authenticity about their particular sport.

Mindful of Woodward's (2006) plea to interrogate both private and public sporting narratives and to further illustrate the comparison of rock climbing with other sports, including extreme ones, I asked interviewees to reflect on the labelling of climbing as an 'extreme sport' in the UK media. For example, extreme sports are being used to sell products such as cars (see *Guardian*, 9 June, 2006), or recruit applicants to the world of estate agency (see *Guardian Jobs*, 2007, p.11) through the construction of extreme sports' participants as 'up for it', risk-takers, both in the mainstream and outdoors press (see Watson 2005). Many of the climbers rejected these labels and confirmed Rinehart and Sydnor's (2003: 12) view that extreme sports athletes are not 'lunatics' or 'daredevils', but 'meticulous performers, giving themselves to some lofty art form'. Thus, by working against such media representations, the rock climbers construct their own version of what are considered authentic sporting practices, in their terms and according to their diverse, everyday experiences.

However, Geoff Powter (2007) a Canadian climber and clinical psychologist complicates this 'insider' perspective on the world on extreme sports. He argues that a number of historical adventurers, including climbers, have indeed crossed over a line between madness and sanity, in displaying pathological and fatal arrogance or narcissism. Furthermore, I would contend that what seemed normal, risk-taking activities to some of the younger climbers especially in this study, when judged by the standards of the outside world, do, in fact, appear foolhardy and needlessly risky. I further discuss the concept of risk, in relation to extreme sports, in the last chapter.

The idea of authenticity was also drawn on by the rock climbers in the study in terms of a distinction made between different types of rock climbing. Some thought that traditional climbing, as opposed to sport climbing, because of the potential risk involved with the former practice, was more 'authentic'. In this way, they confirmed Heywood's (2002) view that traditional, or adventure climbing, could be seen to go against processes of rationalization, such as the commercialization and regulation of the sport. The idea of authenticity even extended to the kind of rock that is climbed, so that those who do routes on gritstone in the north of England, for instance, have a national, or even international reputation, for being 'hard men'. Additionally, whether one climbs outside, in a more 'extreme' environment, or in the safe, more mundane environment of the climbing wall, or sport climbs, can also help to construct a more or less masculine sense of self and public sporting image. Thus, it is through these dichotomies that different kinds of masculinity are constructed and performed. Individual climbers work with these dichotomies (and sometimes against them) to construct a self-image (and reputation) of being a particular kind of climber and so a particular type of man. And, the same man can perform different masculinities across these categories in that a climber can engage with various types of rock and participate in all these climbing practices at different stages of their climbing career, or at different times of the year, or even on different trips.

The issue of authenticity was also present in some of the interviewees' accounts in terms of how climbing was perceived, as opposed to other sports, to be able to bring out a more authentic side to their personalities. For example, this man, aged 42, is able to reflect on how a traditional and team sport such as rugby, allowed and encouraged him to display a macho side to his personality which he found disturbing:

> I played rugby for the county. I'm not very big, but I was really aggressive. I think the first thing I did when I went to college, I must have looked at myself a little bit then, and realized that something like rugby was no good for me, 'cause it made me more aggressive, more competitive. It brought out really nasty sides in me. I hurt people. You find climbing and you don't have to do that.

So climbing allowed him to control his aggressiveness and his competitiveness, both traits that rugby had fostered in him. The question this raises is whether climbing fosters a 'new macho', where, under the guise of individualism in a new sport, old masculine characteristics of competitiveness and aggressiveness can be tempered, or disguised but still be very much present. As I have noted, this can be evidenced in the type of climb done, for example, traditional or sport climbing. Or, alternatively, the issue is also whether extreme sports allow a 'different kind of hard' to surface, where men, through engaging in the everyday practices of an extreme sport, are able to reflect on and change past, 'inauthentic' and sometimes troubling, masculine behaviours.

## Obsession

The mundane and the extreme dichotomy I have referred to could also be seen in terms of the climbers' attitude to the sport, and how important it was in relation to other leisure pursuits, or different aspects of their lives. The current branding (or even fetishizing) of climbing by the media and consumer culture, where climbers are often seen as wild and crazy, can be contrasted and compared with the different kinds of climbers involved in the sport. I initially outlined such different subgroups in Chapter 1. These include the elite and non-elite and also the 'authentic' as opposed to the 'fake' risk-takers, as well as the 'gear freaks' who consume the latest climbing equipment but do not use it and the 'fashion victims' who parade in 'trendy' climbing apparel, but who do not climb. There are also those for whom climbing is a complete lifestyle, even career, and those for whom it is a weekend or less frequent pastime. But such distinctions are both fluid and problematic. For instance, some weekend climbers in the study spoke about climbing with the same passion and fervour, even obsession, that characterized some of the elite climbers' accounts. Thus, in this way, for diverse subgroups of climbers the categories of everyday life were transcended, albeit in different ways. Climbing, therefore, can be viewed as an 'obsession', and this was something that emerged in the climbers' accounts to illustrate these differences, as this man, in his mid thirties, demonstrated:

> Basically, people are obsessives, and the only way they cope with their lives is to focus on something that isn't, well, it doesn't matter if it's not their work, it could be their work, it could be something ... And they'll have something and climbing is no better than any of those. You might as well collect, I might as well collect stamps, d'you know what I mean? It is that sort of thing.

Climbers are often perceived by non-climbing friends and family to be fixated with their sport, as well as there being a public perception of climbers, especially mountaineers, as driven to reach a goal or a summit at all costs. Their obsession is brought into sharp relief and seen as outside of everyday life because climbing is perceived as an activity that is not of the ordinary and is seen as extreme in relation to other, more traditional sports. But this climber thinks such obsession is something for which everybody has a capacity and that allows individuals to cope with everyday life. His comparison of climbing to stamp collecting paints a sharp, even ridiculous parallel of the mundane and the extreme, in his efforts to dispel the image of necessarily focused and driven climbers. There is, to him, nothing inherent in the pursuit of climbing which attracts such individuals. In his view, all people are capable of obsession and different activities are capable of fulfilling such an obsession, if focused on sufficiently.

When asked if he thought whether climbers were, in general, obsessive personality types, or whether he felt he was in any way obsessive about his own climbing, the same climber, replied:

> Right, well, I mean there's two ways of looking at it. I mean for me there's obsessive climbers, who, the only thing they ever will be obsessive about is climbing, probably to the detriment of everything else in their life: wife, you know, family, job, the lot. Or, there'll be some who'll juggle it altogether but they will definitely need ... their thing will be climbing, and it always will be and they'll be trying to do it at the highest level they can. But then I think there's other people who are just, whatever they decide to do, like Tom for example, become quite obsessive, like obsessed about climbing. He's obsessed about golf, driving cars, skateboarding. I think a real climber, the one who really, really loves it more than anything else ... not even bothered with the wife and the family bit.

Two types of 'obsessive' climbers are identified here. One, previously identified, would be obsessive regardless of whatever activity they were pursuing; another, for whom climbing is their only true passion in life, which individuals manage in diverse ways. Not surprisingly, the 'authentic' climber, in his view, is one for whom climbing is everything, even to the point of ignoring relationships and families. Notably, however, this man has made a recent decision not to pursue climbing with the same all-consuming zeal that he did when he was younger. This is because of a new relationship and responsibilities for stepchildren. How an individual manages and negotiates an idealized identity with the realities of growing older and potentially changed expectations of how climbing fits into everyday life, is not without its difficulties, as other climbers agreed. In this way, the interaction between the transcendent activity of climbing and the obsessive nature of some of the participants and their relation to everyday life, shifts over time and is constantly re-worked over a person's life course, which is explored in Chapter 7.

## Extreme Commercialization

As well as changes over the life course at a local level, globalization has also effected both public perception of extreme sports and the opportunities available to extreme sports' participants. Browne (2004: 9) compares extreme and mainstream sports' enthusiasts in the US: 'Their activities were now dubbed "action sports" (or, to others, "extreme sports") … they were now *called* "athletes", and they had "seasons" much like mainstream ball and stick sports.' Furthermore, for those participants he describes who had not taken day jobs (like their friends who had given up on biking or boarding) and had talent, luck and connections, corporate sponsors helped some make a good living. The media hype and participation rates also showed how the sports had been adopted by the mainstream to the extent that participation in team sports had dropped: 'Such statistics were gratifying to hear, but they signified something larger and more important. To the riders, the numbers proved they had been onto something all along; they weren't the freaks, losers, stoners, or slackers so many locals or classmates had thought they were. A ringing cell phone or a new batch of email could bring news of another offer from another major company to endorse anything from food to gear to deodorant' (Browne 2004: 10).

This view of extreme sports enthusiasts as 'athletes' was illustrated by a climber, aged 42, who climbed at a high level:

> A lot of people I don't think ever actually get to that point, because they never really push their limit. I mean, that route I was saying just then at Ravenstor, the 8c, it took me five years to do, you know! 65 days on the route, plus months at the gym. I mean it's obsessive I suppose, but it's a like a sportsman training for the Olympics or something, isn't it?

Five years in training to be able to do a particular climb could be seen as excessive but is not necessarily unusual for elite climbers. So although it could be argued, as Browne (2004) does, that the external and commercial world saw them as athletes, it could also be argued that this was not reducible to a marketing ploy to aggrandise the extreme sports participants for the sake of their public image, and hence profitability. Some of the male climbers interviewed, through their everyday sporting practices, were indeed spending the amount of time and effort that athletes in traditional sports would do to reach a sporting goal. And, for the elite climbers, this identity as an athlete was important to their sense of self and in terms of how the rest of the climbing community, and outside world, saw them. It is this tension between the perceived deradicalization of extreme sports, such as rock climbing, through increased commercialization and the selling of lifestyle sports for mass consumption, and the everyday experiences of sporting men, that I now consider.

Any possibility of liberating and transformatory scripts for sporting participants needs to be seen in the context of the current commercialization and professionalism of a range of extreme sports (see Rinehart and Sydnor 2003 and Wheaton 2004b, 2005). This poses another challenge to a simplified extreme/traditional or organized sports dichotomy, which can assume that alternative sports are less tainted by capitalism and, therefore, grants participants a purity of intention, or superior ethical position that traditional sportsmen, such as overpaid footballers, are seen to no longer possess. Maguire (1999) and Donnelly (2003) outline the worldwide dominance of an international Americanized culture, but also discuss the challenges to such a dominant culture when sport is seen as a field in which ideologies, values and meanings may be contested.

However, Donnelly (2003) argues that the potential for resistance has been exaggerated. He sees rock climbing as a sport as increasingly displaying a professionalism and commercialism in ways that can be seen as having parallels to more mainstream, sporting cultures. He also argues that the consequences of such transitions are not yet fully apparent. Sport climbing, an activity already referred to in this chapter, is used by Donnelly to examine changes in practices and wider society. This type of climbing is seen to disturb the inherent tension between difficulty and risk necessary for climbing to take place and has been linked to organized climbing competitions, which involve different government agencies. These, like the UK government-funded British Mountaineering Council (BMC), can then exert control over participants through accountability or material reward, for example. Though many have now accepted climbing as a sport which can be comprised of different types of activity, including sport climbing, Donnelly (2003: 298) argues this practice 'violates the anarchic and self-regulating nature of the sport.'

Climbing, therefore, can be seen to be in a world of flux, as some climbers strive to become professionals but others, even the same climbers, can be intensely concerned with the ethics of different climbing practices, and can also have a concern for the environment in their manner of practising the sport. The question is: how do climbers themselves make sense of these changes in a sport that traditionally has not been seen as commercial and is in a period of rapid change?

Beal (1995) documents the resistance by some sectors of the sport of skateboarding to such increasing commercialism, stressing people's agency in making social choices and creating alternatives to the dominant culture. But how do we conceive of participants' agency when they embrace at least some aspects of commercialism? Or when a sport such as skateboarding is being considered as

an Olympic sport at the 2012 games in London, and when snowboarding, previously adopted by sporting participants as an alternative to skiing, which was
viewed as a 'safe' sport in its traditional form, is already an official Winter
Olympics sport?

When discussing French 'whiz sports', such as surfing, windsurfing and snowboarding, Midol and Broyer (1995: 208) argue that with these sports 'We are far
from the patriarchal rigidity of control when the attitude is one of "make or
break.' But they also state that although initially, such sports, on becoming official and organized produce innovative forms in opposition to existing ones, later
receive official recognition or are absorbed into the existing traditional organizations. However, this can be taken as evidence of people adapting to a society in
continual transformation, even if such 'elitist groups' can be seen to be uninter-
ested in the 'increasingly marginal masses' (Midol and Broyer 1995: 210).

Meanwhile, Hargreaves and McDonald (2004: xl) ask: 'In what ways has the
media industry specifically, and the culture industries in general, sought to
embrace lifestyle sports?' Wheaton (2004b) also raises the issue of whether such
sports represent superficial, even nihilistic materialistic cultural forms, increasingly appropriated by transnational media corporations to be sold as a package
to passive consumers. She argues that they can be defined as activities worthy of
investigation to tease out the meanings such activities have for their participants,
whether those who are seen as 'hardcore' by themselves and others, who live to
participate and whose identity is linked fundamentally to the chosen sport, and
those who take part in such sports more sporadically. And so in exploring the
climbers' views here, not only can such meanings be 'teased out', but the question of an all-powerful, pernicious and rampant commercialization, as I have
already argued, can itself be queried. The issue raised by Hargreaves and
McDonald (2004) of whether lifestyle sports are a rejoinder to the commercially
exploitative world of more mainstream sport, can also be explored by asking if
and how extreme sports participants work such commercialism to their best
advantage, and, in so doing, whether they are still able to maintain a personal
and sporting ethical stance.

Donnelly (2003) defines what he feels are the two characteristics that have
characterized climbing's history as a sport. Firstly, there is the non-institutional-
ized, self-governing nature of climbing and the hard task of maintaining a
tension balance between difficulty and risk. For the second aspect, he points to
sport climbing, competition climbing, sponsorship and the increasing avail-
ability of climbing industry products from fashionable clothing to equipment
and gear. He therefore argues that climbing is apparently both resisting and
embracing institutionalisation and also maintaining some integrity as a single
activity, through for example, a collective sense of local ethics. Indeed, some
climbers in my study thought the idea that climbing was getting too commercialized, to be overstated

For one climber, in the study, aged in his thirties, who worked for a national climbing organization involved in route setting and indoor climbing

competitions, given that his job depends on keeping people interested in climbing and in attracting new people to climbing as a sport, it is in his interests if it becomes less of a minority pursuit. However, he does not feel that climbing will ever attract enough people for this to be a worry. Further, Wheaton's (2004b) view that lifestyle sports are becoming more appropriated by global media companies aiming to repackage active sports to passive consumers is perhaps not fully applicable to climbing. For rock climbing (as opposed to mountaineering) often makes a very poor, and even boring spectator sport, when watched, for example, on television.

Another climber, aged 44, had a more contradictory response to this perceived commercialisation. When talking about belaying (holding the ropes) of a younger climber who was starting out on his climbing 'career' and who subsequently gained a high public profile and media reputation, he said:

Well, I mean you mentioned Felix earlier, and I've sort of held his rope like early on in his career and all that sort of stuff, and I mean just somebody like that, I just find him amazing you know. I like the fact that he's sponsored, 'cause he said genuinely, he'd probably do it anyway, he just, he likes climbing.

Thus, sponsorship from equipment or clothing manufacturers, as one of the most potent and public symbols of the commercialization of climbing as a sport, is not seen as detracting from the older climber's admiration of the sponsored climber and his achievements, or from his perception of the young climber's own sense of authenticity. Later, in the same interview, he says climbing has 'definitely changed and I don't think the sport's been ruined 'cause you can still go climbing exactly like you used to do'. Whilst he acknowledges climbing has, indeed, been changed through an increased professionalism, he also refuses to see this commercialization of the sport as changing its essential nature. This is a view borne out by Barkham (2006: 9) on the sport of surfing, when he writes; 'Brands, advertising, image, peer pressure, transport and the leisure society may bring people to pick up a board. But the thing that drives so many to return is surfing's intrinsic pleasure.' However, the same climber also holds contradictory opinions on the implications of this growing commercialization of climbing when he considers his own sponsorship in the days when this was not as prevalent as it is now:

You go to some really beautiful places and you do some things that are amazing, you know? And to think that you're there partly with the cameras there, or partly, because, yeah, you know you were getting paid for it. At first, great, you're doing what you wanna do and getting paid. About a few years later, you become a bit bored and it's like everything's planned, and you know you're there partly because you're getting paid, and it does take the romance away from it, doesn't it?

He offers a romanticized version of rock climbing, where categories of financial gain are able to be transcended, despite sponsorship deals with climbers.

Such feelings are contrasted with a view of his own sponsored climbing as progressively becoming boring and mundane. This then results in his partial alienation from the act of climbing. Such a trajectory was a dominant narrative that resonated with the views of a number of middle-aged and older climbers in the study. Even those who had never been sponsored made similar comments about the 'golden days' of climbing before big business took a hold. However, one's position in the life course may also account for the different views held about commercialisation. This young sponsored climber, aged in his twenties, shows himself to be reflexive, even calculating about getting initial sponsorship, by being aware of the wider context in which extreme sports had begun to operate:

> It's kind of always been every climber will know who the famous climbers are, but nobody else will, apart from a few mountaineers. Then extreme sports, where you see visual impact and stuff, it's kind of much more mass market and it's ultimately about selling stuff isn't it? And, it's rather than selling climbing products, it's about, you know, energy drinks or whatever. So, anyway, I recognised that dead early on and I basically I got what I wanted ... I spend like six months or more in the dream locations.

Through his foresight and acumen, the rewards of operating as a climber within the market place for him, are extensive; the chance to climb worldwide being but one of the outcomes of his engagement with sponsors. Far from seeing himself as 'selling out' a romantic notion of climbing as uncommercialized and unsullied by capitalism, he feels that he has demonstrated agency in both his thought and actions. Thus, his experience supports Beal and Wilson's findings (2004), that for the US skaters in their study, commercialization was becoming more accepted and they were less condemning of aspects such as sponsorship as they saw benefits in these changes for the sport and for themselves. Additionally, this older climber, in his forties, when considering his own sponsorship deals, finds virtue in the changes. This is despite his being from a generation, as I have demonstrated, which has been more sceptical:

> I have got paid for climbing, you know, certain parts of the country, money for doing stuff and didn't really ruin anything particularly. For once it was a chance to be rock and roll, wasn't it, and be like Mick Jagger or something, because you used to see the most funny sights. I remember seeing this bloke. I mean he was like, well, I'm overweight now, but he was really overweight and he must have been in his mid-thirties. He was proper mutton dressed as lamb. And he had snakeskin lycra tights on, on this climb, and if he'd have been anywhere else, like walking down the main street, people would have just been laughing, but you felt free to do that sort of thing, you know?

At this time in the 1980s, climbing was both gaining in popularity and, therefore, becoming more mainstream, even if it was not as commercialized as it is today. This allowed some men to experiment with clothes and their identity in a manner which challenged stereotypical views of what men in their mid thirties were supposed to look like. In this way, the opening of the sport up to a wider cross section of people (including women) allowed some men the opportunity to experience different ways of identifying and reconstructing various kinds of masculinity. Climbing was thus a 'safe' space to construct something different through both dress and an identity as a climber.

However, although it can be argued that increasing commercialization encouraged agency, at least for some climbers, through new-found material wealth with sponsorship or an ability to perform masculinity in new, if fashionably dubious, ways, agency in these contexts can be seen to be a complicated business. This climber, aged 37, spoke about trying to remain 'credible' in the face of the expectations of him from his sponsors:

I was very uncomfortable about having gear given to me. That was really alien … I have to wear badges occasionally in photo shoots or like in expeditions, to try and get the logo in, and I feel quite awkward about that. Even the marketing people I work with don't want too much of it either as they just think it looks daft. Because they want authentic shots as if it is happening for real. And climbers that are climbing for real don't have badges all over them. They have a little one like everyone else.

Climbers can still try to affect agency when sponsored so as not to look too overtly commercial. Though sponsors know, in wanting to reach their (climbing) market, that 'cool' sells, so this is then sold and repackaged to enhance product sales of gear or clothing. And by selling 'cool', capitalism also therefore sells authenticity. So, this climber is also complicit in the production of an 'authentic' product, where climbing is seen as still 'out there', even as anti-consumerism. His later comments in the interview also reveal the subtle distinctions in his view between what is, and what is not here acceptable, in adopting certain aspects of commercialism to make a living: '… Scandinavians with their jackets on that they have obviously got when they have been on an expedition to Everest.' He goes on to say that, in spite of a preoccupation with understatement in a British climbing culture, he has managed to overcome his initial embarrassment: 'And now it is almost like a job and my role has changed. Even I would say that I am more comfortable with my role changing.'

Such comments reveal that there are national differences with how sponsorship is perceived within sporting communities. Over time, too, the notion of sponsorship, at least for this climber, has become something with which he is more at ease. This could be construed as a gradual adoption of the values of capitalism and a sell-out to a notion of climbing as anti-materialism. Or alternatively seen as evidence of this climber's ability, as he got older, to take control and deal with the role changes sponsorship entailed, yet still be able to refuse the idea of too many badges, which signified for him, as a British climber, one step too far in accommodating the sponsors. As Thorpe (2006: 221) reveals, in a discussion of female skate, snow and surf boarders, although their 'radical potential' disappeared when boarding became commercialized by the late 1990s, 'commercialization is not solely a co-opting force.' Therefore, sporting identities continue to shift, change and develop in sometimes, unexpected ways, as illustrated by the agency of the climber cited above.

However, how the continually changing and enmeshed narrative of individual identity and mass commercialization plays out is an unfinished story, as exemplified by the sheer scale of recent commercial developments around different extreme sports. For example, in the UK, witness the building of a £20 million 'Venture Xtreme' project for 2011, which consists of the world's first outdoor artificial surfing machine, or a planned £350 million development, which will incorporate an ice wall for climbers and artificial rapids for white-water canoeing (Booth 2008). With this in mind, Wheaton's (2005) call for recognizing the importance of a necessary move beyond cross-cultural comparisons, to an exploration of the impact of global flows on, between and within local subcultures, as well as their medias and industries, is pertinent here.

## Conclusion

This chapter has highlighted both similarities and differences between more organised, traditional and team sports, and newer sports such as rock climbing. Through everyday climbing practices, which lead to climbers defining what is debatably considered an authentic practice or not or, alternatively, an obsessive practice or not, I have started to consider how the extreme sport of rock climbing can be seen as mundane in certain contexts for climbers, at different stages of the life course. In problematizing a notion of climbing as a sport, which is becoming increasingly commercialized through global transitions, I have outlined ways in which climbers might effect agency, albeit in contradictory ways. The chapter also started to investigate the possibility that pursuing the alternative sport of climbing can allow men to reflect on previous masculine behaviours and subjectivities which they found troubling, as with the climber who gave up rugby as a sport because it was too aggressive.

However, adopting an identity as 'a climber' does not necessarily disturb aspects of 'doing' masculinity, when even the rock that climbers choose to climb on, or are geographically forced to climb on, is imbued with a masculine significance of reflecting 'hardness', or not. This is revealed further, with the example of climbing outdoors, where the potential risk of injury is greater than in the secure and weather-proof environment of an urban climbing wall. The former practice is then used by both elite and non-elite climbers to construct a more 'authentic' and masculine self-image or reputation. Even when an individual's sense of masculine identity can be seen as 'mobile' in his engaging with different aspects of the sport, certain climbing practices, for instance, traditional, and thus, 'hard' climbing, can be seen to imbue more status than other, less masculine, practices. It is this shifting and transitional aspect of identity that I turn to in the next chapter.

**CHAPTER 4**

# Men's Sporting Identities

## Introduction

Identity, Woodward (2002) argues, gives us a location in the world and presents a link between us and the society we live in. There is a connection between the subjective positions we inhabit and the social and cultural situations in which we place ourselves. Identity gives us an idea of who we are and how we relate to other individuals. Therefore, this chapter explores the notion of a masculine identity through exploration of a high-risk sport and where identities are investigated through notions of difference and similarity, individual and multiple identities, as well as the relational and collective. Identification is also seen as a dynamic process which allows for the possibility of identity shifts, even if such opportunities are contradictory. Furthermore, as with Jenkins' (2004) study of identity, the focus of this chapter, and indeed the book, is on the mundane, as well as on how the process of identification works for participants in the extreme sport of rock climbing.

If identities are seen as political, that is, negotiated in relation to the power of groups or individuals, then Woodward (2002) asserts that laying claim to an identity creates an 'us and them' situation. MacClancy (1996) argues that sport is a vehicle of identity which provides people with a sense of difference and a way of classifying themselves and others, whether latitudinally or hierarchically, as illustrated via empirical data presented later in this chapter. With regard to the sporting identities demonstrated by the climbers in my study, this concept of 'us' and 'them' can be seen in a number of ways. This was, for example, evident in relation to novices versus experienced climbers, elite climbers as opposed to non-elite, and traditional climbers and indoor or sport climbers. Gender is also a way in which climbers primarily differentiate themselves. This can be seen when men and women climb together and this opposition can create tension and high emotions, for instance, if men perceive women climbers as not 'serious' or hard enough, thus jeopardizing their own climbing success. Or, if their female climbing partners climb harder than they do, either to their dismay, or sometimes delight. These issues are taken further in Chapter 5 where I explore in more detail the gendered sporting relations between the sexes. Moreover, sport can be mobilized to promote recognition of similarity or difference, to foster unity or spark conflict. However, as the anthropologist Dyck (2000) asserts, we need to look under the surface to discover more nuanced and flexible strategies and purposes of sport. This idea of 'looking under the surface' has been useful here, both in interpreting the data, and in problematizing some of the assumptions made by theorists about masculinities and sport.

This chapter, therefore, in the context of investigating any shifts in sporting masculinities, explores issues of collectivity, reputation, status, creation of self and fragmented identities in modernity. Here, I will stress the importance of looking at experiences and relations between participants, both within and between different sub-groups, for instance, the elite participants and others in a single sporting culture. The chapter will engage with these aspects of identity whilst referencing those approaches that see sporting participants as non-passive and able to negotiate their everyday experiences in specific sporting sites.

## Masculine Identities in Flux

Sport means different things to different people. For some it represents the routines of daily work, for others it is cathartic and stress reducing, whereas for others still, it is fun and games. But how it means different things to different people is connected to biological sex, gender and ethnicity. Further, sport is seen to be able to be a vehicle for organizing leisure time and for responding to larger concerns. Thus, Armstrong and Giulianotti (1997) see football clubs as serving their supporters as repositories of gender, class, national, political and regional identities.

To explore these different meanings, Horne et al. (1999) argue that to understand the construction of sporting identities, socialization needs to be seen as a dynamic process and not just a series of constraints imposed on an unsocial and egotistical self. People's choices have a context, but much theorising around sport, they suggest, has seen its participants as passively shaped by their sporting experiences. Horne et al.'s focus on the way people negotiate and reflect on a dialectic of control and power relations is helpful in exploring the climbing interviews in this study. Furthermore, Wheaton's work (2000a, 2000b, 2004a, 2005, 2007), on male windsurfers, is seen to reveal how sport produces and reproduces knowledge, meaning, social practice and power relations at different levels, including the personal, cultural and structural.

Therefore, as well as being a marker of an established social identity, sport remains a way in which new social identities are created. Thus, for MacClancy (1996), sport is not intrinsically associated with particular values or meanings. Indeed, sport is an embodied practice in which its meanings for participants are made, resisted, contested, negotiated and changed *in* the daily rituals of sporting practices. Furthermore, as I noted in Chapter 2, as identities shift and change, they have intimate connections with social and political practices, for instance, in relation to age and gender relations and interaction in everyday situations, which this study of male rock climbers explores. In Chapter 7, for example, changes in age and the life course are seen to affect both the practices of climbing and men's emotional attachment to the sport, including the intensity of that attachment (see also Whitehead, 2002). So I am considering climbers here as reflexive actors involved in the creation of diverse, fluid and contradictory identities as part of everyday life.

However, Gardiner (2000: 8) notes that a concentration on everyday events can 'sidestep sociological roles or structures' and that: '(i)ncreasingly, the "everyday" is evoked in a gestural sense as a bulwark of creativity and resistance, regardless of the question of assymmetries of power, class relations, or increasingly globalized market forces' (Gardiner 2000: 8). This needs to be borne in mind if gendered (sporting) relations are also to be seen as sites of power and dominance in the context of feminist and other criticisms (see Creedon 1994). This point is also important to bear in mind for any critical examination of the fluidity and possibilities of change in hegemonic masculinities, so that any shifts identified in sporting masculinities are seen in the wider context of gendered, and indeed, other power relations such as age or class.

As I argued in Chapter 2, sport is crucial in the maintenance and reproduction of a specifically masculine identity. Dunning (1999) sees sport simultaneously as one of the most significant sites of resistance and challenge to traditional masculinity but also of its production and reproduction. This aspect of identity in relation to rock climbing and its participants will be explored in this chapter and throughout the book, where masculinity is seen to effect men's life choices, including relationships and fathering practices. It can also be seen to both constrain and shape, but also enable, their embodied everyday sporting experiences and relations with others. So for the climbers I interviewed, the way their sense of individual *and* collective identity in the sport of rock climbing changed over time and how potential identity shifts related to their sense of being a man, were central to their subjective accounts of climbing. Furthermore, the climbers in my study demonstrated MacClancy's (1996) view that sport is not merely a reflection on some postulated essence of society but an integral *part* of society. The interviews were, therefore, used by the climbers as a way of reflecting on society, their place in it as individuals as well as their connections to others, whether as climbing partners, friends, fathers and lovers. For example, this climber, aged 42, reflected upon his climbing in relation to his chosen profession:

You know I did a fine art degree … and it is quite creative … so there's also a sense of identity. But I think if anything there was an awkwardness in terms of the transition from always seeing myself as a climber, to then seeing myself as an artist … well, trying to balance the two. Bit kind of Jekyll and Hyde, it's a bit schizophrenic. It shifts from one to the other, you know, but they're not connected … Yeah, there's creativity in climbing, and, you know, I think maybe at the higher level where you might be doing new routes and kind of forging, or new climbs on new crags or new mountains. But I've never been in that kind of league.

Now in early middle age he is able to keep his work and climbing identities separate, unlike other climbers in the study, particularly those who work in the climbing industry. Many of these men chose jobs related to climbing, such as working in an outdoor pursuits shop, or engaging in roped access work (see Chapter 7), to enable them to combine paid work with their chosen sport. Though this man sees his work as an artist and teacher of fine art *and* the sport of climbing as creative pursuits, because of the level he perceives himself to climb at, he does not conceive of his own climbing achievements in creative terms, as opposed to elite climbers who operate at a different level. Further, there has been a tension in the transition from his identifying primarily as a climber to his having other roles. This idea of achieving 'balance' whilst elements of an individual's masculine identity are in transition, or can be viewed as 'mobile', is something I investigate further in Chapter 7. And, if 'balance' is not achieved, how much of this can be put down to men being 'in crisis'?

The idea of a crisis of identity in modernity, where old certainties do not exist and where social, political and economic changes have led to a breakdown in previously stable group membership has been much discussed (Woodward 1997). Identities are also seen to devolve from multiple sources: nationality, ethnicity, social class and community, gender and sexuality, leading to conflict in people's constructions of identity positions and so to contradictory, fragmented identities. But the concept of 'masculinity in crisis' put forward by both academics and the media to explain these shifts, given the global loss of breadwinner and authority figure status for many men, has also been much contested. For example, Whitehead and Barrett (2001) argue that the idea of 'masculinity in crisis' has popular appeal as it seems to provide an 'answer' to the complex changes that have occurred in gender relations. This, however, can be challenged on a number of grounds. For instance, the conception that men no longer inhabit the traditional masculine roles that give them stability and comfort is not borne out in their view. To support this, they cite evidence of the continuation of a 'laddish' culture in Western societies. This can be seen in the large numbers of men still acting in a dominant manner and resorting to violence as a means of self expression: though Whitehead and Barrett (2001: 7) differentiate between the 'hard veneer' of many men and the fragile identity often lying beneath the surface. Furthermore, if men are in emotional or existential crisis then this is certainly nothing new (see also Edwards 2006). Whether men are 'in crisis' both individually and collectively, can, therefore, be explored in a specific sporting context.

## Climbing and Collectivity

Somewhat surprisingly, a number of the climbers when asked why they took up rock climbing, spoke of a sense of collectivity, of 'belonging', as being important to their pursuit of the sport. If identity is relational, and so constructed through relations of difference such as 'us' and 'them', it is also as Jenkins (2004) notes, about a sense of community with other human beings. The notion of a 'sporting community' is one that includes friendship and collectivity through shared experiences and practices but can also foster intense competition and rivalry. In an individualized sport such as climbing, the concept of collectivity would, therefore, not be expected to have as much weight as it would, for say, someone involved in a team game such as football or cricket, where individual players are, in many ways, dependent on the skills of others. The climbing world is also one where performance is judged more on an individual basis. However, though it tends to attract those with a strong sense of individualism, this clearly does not rule out the importance of a collective or community ethos.

Some of the participants defined themselves, when younger, in the context of their school experiences and friendships. In their early life, many of the climbers saw themselves as not belonging, or fitting in to, traditional friendship networks. As a consequence, some of them had no school friends to speak of, but had made lasting friendships in the course of their climbing activities, for instance those made from joining a club, as this man, aged in his forties, demonstrated: 'At school I was always kind of, didn't fit, I didn't fit in the right places, I have no friends really from school. Certainly still have friends from the climbing club.' Another climber and mountaineer, in his fifties, saw climbing as something he was good at, as opposed to other sports, and this gave him standing with his peers: 'I suppose I was, having been a mediocre footballer and cricketer and everything else in my youth, found something that I was actually rather better at than the rest of the lads, (laughter), was quite good.' An older climber, aged sixty, affirmed the collective sense of identity he felt with others who could appreciate the activity of climbing itself, but also the shared love of the geographical locations in which climbing took place: 'So you know there was that, that common bond of enjoyment of it and a deep emotion about beautiful places.'

Other, younger climbers, also stressed the collectivity of climbing, but some expressed such feelings in terms of a spiritual side to the sport which they felt had been gained through friendships made at the crag face, as this man, in his mid-twenties, revealed:

> It doesn't take long to end up with friends all over the world. And that's definitely another, one of the biggest aspects to it, the spirituality side to it, is the friendships that you build with such a completely random selection of people, from all walks of life, from all nations with a common interest.

When discussing the extreme sport of BMX bike riding, Kusz (2003), discusses sports which are characterized by a participation in activities that are individually performed but practised in small groups, as valuing a sense of community. Reflections from these climbers' affirm this viewpoint. Conversely, Bell (2003) argues from a humanistic point of view that risk experiences are only meaningful when they build community. However, the idea that risk sports auto-matically build community was not always borne out in other climbers' reflec-tions. Some did not have a sense of the climbing community as being welcoming, or a secure place to be. When asked how he got into climbing, one climber, aged thirty-eight, revealed that the initial reception he received almost made him retreat from his attempts to enter the sport:

> A few friends about oh, twelve years ago, were climbing and I went down to (names climbing wall) and had, had a go at it, which I would have liked to have continued. But climbers basically, I don't think they're the sort of friendliest people. I think there's something missing in their life and they seem to have an attitude problem. So it put me off for a while.

As already noted in Chapter 3, at climbing walls, activity takes place in an environment that is generally risk free and secure. Indoor climbing routes allow people to hone their skills without facing the dangers that can be attendant with outdoor, traditional climbing. The experience of this climber could be seen to challenge a romanticized model of those automatic collective communities which have assumed to be developed in sports which are risk-taking. This is especially the case at indoor walls, when sporting practices evolve to minimize, or exclude, the very risk-taking it is imagined binds sporting communities together. (A notion of risk is explored further in Chapter 9.)

Collectivity amongst climbers can also be seen in relation to the various and diverse climbing practices that make up the sport. For example, as I have already identified, mountaineers, 'traditional' climbers, sport climbers and boulderers, for instance, may form their own subgroups. In reality, an individual may be involved and identify with more than one group, and sometimes all of these. Indeed, each kind of climbing practice may share some techniques, whilst also requiring some different skills. For instance, technical climbing on slabs of rock, which requires the skills of agility and balance, may be contrasted with more 'thuggy' climbing, which entails climbing steep overhanging rock and necessi-tates a good power-to-weight ratio, with different styles of climbing suiting dif-ferent types of climber. Certain kinds of identity are often formed around a climber being better at one style of climbing than another. For example, it is often the case that 'masculine', 'thuggy', brute strength ways of climbing are more often associated with strong male climbers and others, often, female climbers who are assumed not to have as much strength, will be seen as better suited and more adept at technical climbing, sometimes perceived as 'feminine' in style (an aspect which will be explored in Chapter 8). A climber in his late twenties had constructed an identity associated with attempting steep climbs: 'Certainly, people within friendship groups are recognised as certain styles of climber. So, I was seen as kind of the strong climber, that could, that could get up anything steep.' However, he later tried more technical and 'slabby' climbing, of which he said: 'I wanted to be at the same standard on the slabs as I was on, on the steep stuff and it wasn't really as a pressure from other people, it was, it was a pressure from myself. I can push against myself.'

This potential identity shift was something which he would have to manage in public whilst climbing, in front of friends who had associated him as a particular kind of climber and who climbed in a certain style. However, his main concern was not because of the possibly negative peer reaction to this change but was rather to do with how he managed this identity shift for his own ends; he wanted to be as good at this new style of climbing as he was with the former. Furthermore, though he enjoyed climbing with others and the collectivity from being with a group of like-minded people, the most important aspect of climbing for him, and indeed, for other sports he participated in, was, as he put it, to be able to 'push against myself', which he thought necessary to achieve his goals. In this sense, Jenkins' (2004) ideas are of relevance here, in that using Mead's (1934) distinction between the 'I' (the ongoing moment of unique individuality) and the 'Me' (internalized attitudes of any significant others) he argues for a 'unitary model of selfhood, that unity is a dialectical synthesis of internal and external definitions' (Jenkins 2004: 18–19). He also concludes that reflexivity, seen as central to Mead's conceptualisation, 'involves a conversation with *oneself*' (Jenkins 2004: 41). This man's climbing endeavour illustrates, therefore, how an individual's identity needs to be seen in interrelation with the collective sporting group and can be in tension with it, but also reveals how an individualistic sport such as rock climbing can aid the formation of new identity shifts through such 'conversations'. At one level he is confident enough to leave behind the previous and more secure masculine identity associated with doing strenuous climbs, but still needs to climb at a similar level, to be able to maintain his self-image, when he adopts more 'feminine' sporting practices. In this way, the process of identification is one he actively, if in a rather contradictory manner, manages over time, thus creating a consciously shifting sense of self.

## Climbing Identities and the Creation of Self

On the one hand, theorists writing about sport have characterized sport as more than merely a hobby, pastime or leisure activity (Dunning 1999). On the other, leisure pursuits have been seen as too unstable to produce a lasting identity by others (Roberts 1997). Horne et al. (1999), however, argue that serious leisure appears capable of providing some of the psychological functions of full time employment by structuring time, providing interest and social relationships, giving both social status and personal identity. Additionally, for most people, they assert that the central place of sport is gained through domestic consumption-that is, watching sport as a spectator on television, or in real life.

Being a climber, however, entails not being a 'passive' spectator but being an active participant. Even many of the people who go to watch climbing competitions, which could be seen as a minority spectator sport, will be keen climbers themselves. The men I interviewed tended to support Horne et al.'s perspective: that a meaningful and continuing identity was able to be produced for the participants by an engagement in climbing activities. This could be seen via their responses to questions about whether they envisaged themselves as always wanting to climb and whether or not they still retained an identity as a climber when not climbing:

> I'd climbed for a long time. I'd climbed from being 10 to being about 15 and then I'd given up while I was in that difficult teenage period. So, between 15 and 17, 18, I didn't actually climb, although I sort of regarded myself as a climber, but I didn't have the opportunity to.

Now in mid-life, this man stopped climbing because of a troublesome adolescence, as opposed to others in the study who climbed to help deal with teenage angst. Nevertheless, even when not active he still regarded himself as a climber. Indeed, a number of interviewees spoke about how, if prevented from climbing, for instance through injury, they sometimes constantly imagined working particular routes and doing certain hard or rewarding climbing moves. Others echoed this thought when contemplating the future, as this young, elite climber, in his mid twenties, said:

> I could see myself not climbing for long periods, but I would always consider myself a climber. You know, it's been such a big part of my life for long enough now, that even if I never climbed again … But I could see in the future getting into other things … It might be quite nice to spend, you know, some time doing some other stuff.

He was, therefore, able to imagine himself with multiple sporting identities. However, because of the centrality of his climbing career to his identity, he was also able to imagine a continuous sporting identity, even whilst not climbing or when doing other sports. Thus, a climbing identity did not have to be in the 'here and now' and be physical and embodied, for it to remain meaningful for him. In comparison, another elite climber, in his thirties, when asked if he could ever see himself not climbing, replied: 'Yeah, I can actually, after the last eight months of grimness, I can. You see I don't want to climb easy stuff, I don't like it, it's crap [laughter], because you're not, it's not challenging.' Constant injuries had prevented him from training or reaching the same level of success on difficult climbs that he had achieved in the past. His need to be at the top of his game, and the possibility that he no longer was, was sufficient reason that he could envisage himself giving up the sport. Indeed, within a relatively short period after this interview he had given up and no longer identified as a climber, although he had taken up another extreme sport.

Thus, the climbers spoke about finding their identity through the sport in a number of diverse ways. For some, rock climbing was the most important part of their sense of self. This climber, in his early forties, feels that climbing gives him a sense of his own identity that nothing else can, including other sporting pursuits and his work. He sees this as partly to do with geography, living in a well-known climbing city, which therefore sets him apart from non-climbers. But his identity is also wrapped up with his climbing activities removing him from the ordinariness of everyday life:

> I think it's escapism. I think it is about identity in a sense that I do feel, which I don't find that much in anything else, really. I think there is a sense of how obscure climbing is particularly when you live in [major UK climbing city], but I do think something does kind of set you apart from ordinariness, everydayness.

For other interviewees, though they didn't necessarily reflect on their sporting identity in such an explicit or conscious manner, it was, however, still central to their sense of self. A 59-year-old man revealed that he did not really 'think about being a climber', however, he does distinguishes himself from non-climbers by a display of incredulity in the interview that there are people who live 20 minutes or so from 'wonderful countryside' and are not moved by the sight of such a landscape, or even know the way there: '… you realize that peoples' minds operate on a totally different plane'.

Others in the study more explicitly rejected a notion of a meaningful climbing identity. An internationally known climber, in his early forties, goes on to reflect:

> Climbing isn't important, I mean it just isn't. I mean I love doing it and I don't fancy doing anything else, but, I don't expect anyone else to think it's important, you know, I don't like to talk significant. I don't want to be going to the pub, 'I'm a climber.' There's people I know who do and expect something from it. I mean you know that makes me cringe. I can think of virtually anyone in my street more important than me in what they do with their life and what they've done with it. I mean, I haven't exactly helped humanity by my obsessive search for, like, climbing stardom, have I?

Rejecting a special or privileged identity as a climber, the inference here is that the activity of climbing, especially when taken to its extreme in a bid to gain public recognition or stardom, is not contributing to society in the way the 'ordinary' people do in 'normal' everyday jobs. Here, the everyday is seen to be the realm which is special and not the extraordinary and larger-than-life world of rock climbing, even, or especially when a certain celebrity status, inside or outside of the climbing community, has been achieved by individuals.

Another dimension of the relationship between the extreme, sporting world of climbing and a more mundane, everyday existence was exemplified by this climber, also aged in his forties. Alternatively, for him, rather than climbing to lose his identity, he felt, like others already identified in the study, that if he did not climb he had lost his sense of self:

I just lose my identity. I just lose something which has been quite important to a kind of a sense of purpose to life really. It sounds a bit over the top I know, but it is about a purpose to why you try and keep yourself physically fit or why you might try, and there's something holistic happening in climbing, about a balance. I think it does kind of put lots of things, other things in life in perspective. As well, I think it puts aspects of family life in a different kind of perspective, because you too are a person, you know, I too am a body. There's certain kind of things like a husband and a father and a work colleague, and I think it's too easy to say climbing's selfish. Because, yes, it is, but I don't think it's that different from lots of other things, playing the guitar, or whatever else it might be.

This notion of the necessity of a transcendent climbing identity to put other things in life, like family responsibilities, in context, was shared by a number of the climbers I interviewed who were of different ages. Being a father and a work colleague were different aspects of their identity, but a climbing identity, as well as putting such roles in perspective, also gave a *different* perspective to them. Further, this climber rejects an assumption, held by others I interviewed, that climbing is necessarily a selfish pursuit and one carried out at the expense of being a partner or father or worker. He feels the extraordinary pursuit of climbing informs his other everyday identities in positive ways and so he could not, or would not want to, separate them. As he put it succinctly and with some feeling earlier in the interview: 'I can't not climb'. In this way, it could be argued that it is his choice of a climbing lifestyle, which shapes and gives meaning to his other lived-out identities.

## 'Just a Bit of an Icing on the Cake': Which Identities 'Count'?

In addition to reflecting on their own position in relation to how integral a climbing identity was to their sense of self, participants also spoke about their perceptions of others' sporting identities. In so doing, they raised further questions about who, or what climbing practices could be considered authentic, as I started to consider in Chapter 3.

When asked why he climbs, this climber, in his thirties, expresses the complexity of defining oneself in relation to a sporting identity, when climbing is seen to encapsulate a whole way of living one's life:

I think climbing, along with a lot of other things, is something you end up doing once you get into it, and you just do it because it's there and it's something you've always known. Climbing, to an awful lot of people ends up defining who they are, being a climber. Squash players haven't had to define themselves like this. To me, it's part of your lifestyle and it affects how you do things, what you do, where you live. There's a lot of people not driven by that, but, it's still very important to them.

He acknowledges that people have different and diverse investments in how much a particular sporting identity is part of their notion of self. He also, interestingly, asserts that a climbing identity is different from other sports in that it has implications for decisions made outside of a narrow sporting context – hence some of the climbers choosing to define the sport as a 'lifestyle choice' and not an extreme, or risk sport. As I discussed in the previous chapter, these labels were sometimes seen as too media constructed, which, furthermore, did not capture the impact or influence of the sport over the life course of individuals. For example, later in the interview this man talked about choosing jobs connected with the climbing industry, rather than other professions that may have been open to him. The acquisition of a climbing identity is also seen here as a process, which eventually is all-encompassing, given the regularity with which those sporting practices are engaged with. However, rather than dividing sports participants into those athletes for whom sport involves a complete lifestyle and those for whom sport is less important, the concept of a sporting continuum, where those who do not embrace climbing 'scene' pursuits such as drinking in 'climbers' pubs' in their leisure time, socializing with other climbers, or who do not climb in every available spare minute of leisure time, can still be seen to have a sporting identity which is important to their overall existence.

In considering how different climbers can be in terms of how integral climbing is to their identity, this climber, in his early forties, conceives of a distinction between climbers as 'pretend' and, therefore, inauthentic, or not, in his eyes:

A French woman said 'You can't live, if you live to climb.' I suspect some people that are alive and can go climbing, that's what they do. Whereas, other people, climbing is just a bit of an icing on the cake, it makes life, you know, a bit more bearable or a little pleasure really. But, there's a lot more going on in their lives. But I just wonder whether people on the outside who pretend to be climbers, they want to be seen like that. Like people who are into surfing, hang round with surfboards, look cool, but they want to be like these people who are like cranking up twenty-four waves in Hawaii, you know?

As an elite climber, at some point in his life, he must, to some extent, have 'lived to climb'. But it is through ageing, and now being a climber in early midlife, with a relatively new partner and the equivalent of step-children, that his views on climbing have somewhat changed. He also identifies those for whom climbing is 'just a bit of an icing on the cake', but who may, on the other hand, have 'more going on in their lives' than someone who does 'live to climb'. In this respect, he contradicts the views of some other climbers I interviewed who thought that to be defined as a climber, a person had to be totally dedicated to the sport. Indeed, for a small number of climbers this view persisted even as they got older, with attendant implications for their relationships and attitude to paid work. Some of them, moreover, continued to construct a view of their climbing selves as the 'real me', as opposed to doing this with their other, non-sporting roles. Other interviewees perhaps only climbed at the weekend, but conceived of their activities as certainly more than the icing on the cake. These different notions of how important a climbing identity needs to be, for a climber to be 'successful', or indeed, what defined sporting success, varied not only across the division of elite and non-elite climbers, but also within a category of climbers, here characterised as elite.

The same climber also reflected in the interview on which type of identity in relation to climbing 'counts', and indeed, 'whether they all count', so that from this pluralistic viewpoint, the sport can be seen as a diverse and varied collective of individuals with different identity positions. However, he drew parallels with those who were 'true climbers' and others who were 'buying into a lifestyle … you can dabble in climbing, but, you're not putting in any of the effort.' These are the people, who, for instance, are seen by him to have the right gear, and who go to fashionable climbing locations but who are inauthentic in their pretence at adopting a 'real' climbing lifestyle and identity. This notion – that to be an authentic climber involves hard work and effort, which entails more than striking a pose draped in the latest fashionable outdoor gear – was echoed by other climbers in the study. It was voiced by both the participants who considered themselves 'good' climbers and those who did not, some of whom in both categories had undergone systematic, and, at times, gruelling training programmes. (Though the elite climbers, overall, were more obsessive in this respect. See Chapter 8 where I discuss body practices and training regimes in more depth.)

## Climbing and the Process of Gaining a Reputation

The idea of the authentic or inauthentic climber was something that interviewees also related closely to reputation. A climber's reputation was integral to how they were perceived in the climbing community in either positive or negative terms. Individual climbers sometimes basked in a reputation which was favourable, for example, if they had climbed hard routes and done so ethically. Conversely, individuals sometimes bemoaned a negative reputation, for instance if they were thought to over-emphasize the severity of a given climb, and which they denied doing. Donnelly and Young (1999) discuss identity in relation to how individual identities are potentially confirmed through the creation of an established climbing reputation. They define this in terms of those who choose to join a climbing club, and, they argue, these people tend to split into two groups: rookie or novice climbers who need to establish a reputation for the kinds and severity of climbs they do, and those others who arrive with an already established and documented reputation. This establishing, or proving of already achieved reputations is generally very straightforward, although they point out that there are occasions where 'veteran' climbers catch out newcomers by exposing their exaggerated and so inauthentic claims. (And my interviewees attested to the fact that this can also work the other way, with veteran climbers being 'caught out'!) This can be seen because of poor use of equipment, or if their claims are not supported by their previous climbing history.

The climbers I interviewed were concerned with authenticity in relation to both their own, and others', reputations. And, in contrast to the climbers in Donnelly and Young's research, the climbers I interviewed spoke more about the maintenance of their own reputation, and how their status was seen by their peers in the climbing community, rather than about the reputations of novices or those who did not climb as well as themselves. The concern here was especially with the opinions of their peers who climbed at similar levels to themselves, and this was true of both elite and non-elite climbers. Donnelly and Young, (1999) also point out how reputations, and so identities, once made, need to be constantly remade and that identities respond to both changes in the subculture and outside of it. (I would add that, importantly, this also shifts over the life course of an individual climber.) This climber, in his thirties, confirms Donnelly and Young's view:

> The problem is, you see, I've got a reputation for downgrading things and saying things are easier than they are. And really, in general, that's because everybody thinks it's because I want to be better than everybody else. But it's not, it's completely the other way round. So it means, whatever I can do, if I can do it, well, then, hold on, I can do it, so it can't be hard. So, therefore, I haven't actually done anything hard. The thing is, with me, I am a shit climber who's done some hard things.

He already has a reputation in his local climbing community, and more nationally, for being an incredibly strong climber and for establishing some very difficult boulder problems. However, he is concerned that the climbing community don't take his achievements seriously because of his perceived tendency to downgrade routes. Thus, the pressure of maintaining and managing this public reputation causes him to reflect that his reputation as a 'good climber' is not really deserved. This managing of one's own climbing identity in relation to reputation is an everyday process, and one which was played out for this climber over years, even decades. Later in the interview he talked about how pleased and relieved he was when someone else climbs one of the routes that he previously established and tells him it really *was* a hard climb. Demonstrating that, at least to some extent, he is dependent on other's validation of his achievements and the continual checking of his claims by others in the climbing community. Therefore, he consequently slips between a subjective sense of himself which is both authentic, but also inauthentic, in the context of his own and others' terms.

It was not just the elite climbers to whom the importance of a credible, (public) performance has the most meaning for their identities. A climber, in his late twenties, who would not define himself as elite, also commented on the importance of his sporting achievement so that he can be measured by his peers:

'You want to be better than other people, you want to be seen to be better as well ... if you worry about grades, in some way, then you are competing.' Again, the idea of a sporting continuum is useful as it encapsulates the idea that an unproblematized dichotomy, which places participants into elite and non-elite climbing categories, fails to capture, in a nuanced way, how climbers' conceptualize their own identities, and those of others.

Donnelly and Young (1999), when discussing how individuals acquire an identity as a rock climber, are clear that identity construction and confirmation are central processes in acquiring a sports identity. Construction centres around pre-socialization, information gained before taking part in climbing, recruitment into climbing and the socialization process where an individual receives training in both the skills and lifestyle/culture of a sport: how to dress appropriately, or the use of equipment, for instance. Identity confirmation is where the 'rookie' is accepted, or, alternatively, ostracized by veterans. But some climbers in my study had neither the time nor patience to even think about encouraging new climbers, or those with limited experience. This was particularly true if achieving a reputation in the climbing community for being proficient at difficult climbs was the most important sporting aim. For instance, a climber, aged thirty-five, spoke disparagingly to the point of despising those he identified as having lesser abilities than him, but who would willingly give of their time helping others to climb:

> You always get this student club, the classic example, and you'll get the guy who's actually shit, but will take people out all day, sit on the top of a windy crag being able to give them advice. Whereas me, it's just 'Oh fuck off, I'm going climbing, find your own way.'

But, on the other hand, he says 'Having said that, you need someone. I got taken up through the ranks by people like that.'

His identity comes from his achievements and a reputation gained from not being seen as a person interested in helping others. He feels that these qualities were necessary to ascend what he defines as the sporting 'ladder' of success, and his egotism is clearly apparent here. However, he also speaks of 'Trying to get up the ladder ... It is like this slippery slope and, you know, if you have even a week off ...' The importance of having this success has driven his climbing career to date, and although it has allowed him to acknowledge these contradictions it has also necessitated the choice to uphold the dominant views and practices of at least a certain section of the elite. This ensures that he is not going to slide down the 'slippery slope' and become just an average 'punter' at the crag.

## Sporting Identities and Modernity

The fear of moving back down the slope and the lengths some climbers will go to keep a grip on their reputations and thus their lifestyle choices, can be explained in relation to a crisis of identity, which has been theorized in terms of modernity. Wheaton (2004b), argues that the destabilization of social categories and increased fluidity of social relationships have caused a theoretical interest in fragmented identities. She cites Bauman (1992), who argues that lifestyle has overtaken class as the social relation of production, as well as Maffesoli (1996), who argues that collectivities based around new forms of identification and interests, such as alternative lifestyle and sporting interests, are more fluid than subcultures and so not determined by class background. Along with new consumption patterns and lifestyle choice identities, as well as the importance of lifestyle sports in particular, this indicates a shift to a postmodern culture.

Meanwhile, Borden (2001) argues that loss of identity is an issue for individuals faced with dissolution of past reference points. Skateboarders, he argues, create their own subculture, which is 'a social world in which self-identifying values and appearances confront conventional codes of behaviour' (Borden 2001: 137). They separate themselves from groups like the family, are appropriative of the city, irrational in their organization and ambiguous in constitution, but are also independently creative and exploitative of their marginal or substatus. Skateboarders' cultural identity is, therefore, a way of thinking of, constructing and living that identity in a historical situation. Borden argues that they refuse a binary of childhood and conventional adulthood, and so create a third condition not reducible to those two categories. This identity can also, he argues, be a closed, narrow identity, where skaters have no sense of communion with non-skaters, like any other subculture.

Some of the climbers illustrated these aspects that Borden identifies and, in so doing, revealed that a sporting group is ambiguous in constitution in terms of what participants' priorities actually are. Additionally, the multiple identity positions of a number of the climbers interviewed sometimes led to tension and conflict with both others and themselves. For example, this refusal of a binary of childhood and traditional adulthood meant that they did not always want to put away the 'childish things' of a sporting passion upon being in a settled job or having children of their own, thus leading to relationship or career difficulties. Further, this 'third category' that Borden defines, one that is seen as being between a child and an adult, was not adopted neither readily, nor without difficulty, by all participants.

Many of the climbers could also be seen, like Borden's skaters, to be constructing their own subgroup in terms of separating themselves from other non-climbers. A climber, now in his 60s, still feels that climbing attracts people who do not fit into mainstream culture, but who need an identity that comes from participation in a risk sport 'Yeah, that again is one of the things I like about climbing, personalities, zany people.' This contrasts with a climber, in his early forties, who expressed a view that climbing now attracts different types of people than it did in an earlier era: 'Anoraks. It attracts complete wankers these days to be honest with you. It has really changed, in that it used to attract people who were a bit eccentric, you know, but now, the sort of people it attracts is like, er,

I don't know, bit, bit odd.' As other climbers have already noted, there has been a perceived shift from the kinds of 'authentic' people attracted to climbing primarily as a sporting activity, to those 'inauthentic' climbers, who are categorised by this same man here, as 'poseurs': 'I saw a couple come round the corner, they had climbing gear on as a fashion accessory, so people would recognize they were climbers, so they'd look cool. Whereas before, people would have just thought you were an idiot.' He also stated, initially, that 'You can come from any background really and somehow you find yourself out there climbing. So you meet all sorts of people and there's a bit like a secret club', but later, he said rock climbing 'Isn't like a counter-culture anymore, it's mainstream, isn't it?'

The notion of a 'secret club' highlights the arcane attractions of a distinct sporting subculture and illustrates how extreme sports' participants can have an antipathy to widening the sport out to a broader group of people. This attitude could be interpreted as mean-spirited, or selfish, as Borden (2001) found with his skateboarders. However, alternatively, in the interview with me, this man also displayed a concern with the perceived negative aspects of the commercialization of the sport, such as the cost of equipment, which may deter some from taking up rock climbing. Thus, he revealed contradictory attitudes to different elements of the mainstreaming of climbing, and this included an ambiguous view towards opening up the sport to a wider cross- section of people.

Participants also spoke about being involved in climbing because it compared with other activities which could be seen to be antithetical to conventional norms and values. So for example, a climber, aged thirty-eight, said climbing was 'addictive', giving him an 'adrenaline rush'. Moreover, he thinks that climbing:

> ... would have been good for Keith Richards really. Because, I've been a musician myself, and when you come off tour ... and everything's been buzzing for quite a while and then what else do you do, if that's your lifestyle, if you're really focused?

By conceptualizing climbing in these terms, he perpetuates a stereotype of climbers as mad, bad and dangerous to know. This is something I have already referred to, in Chapter 3, in relation to how rock climbers are conceived of in the popular imagination. However, interestingly, and in contrast, he also sees climbing as a means of escaping aspects of modernity, such as city life, with its associations of normality, stress and constant distractions: 'It's a good thing, because you get distracted a lot in life and even, especially living in a city, you're surrounded by so much, I don't know, so many conventional ideas, so much busyness, so much negativity.' The activity of climbing allows him, on the one hand, to embrace a stereotypical image of the pursuit, but on the other, to simultaneously reject the hustle and bustle of contemporary city life for a rural idyll, which identifying as a rock climber evidently offers him. In this way, caught between a conflicting pastoral and urban existence, his pursuit of a lifestyle sport enabled him to manage a fractured identity position.

## Complicating 'Status' and Sport

The data, therefore, revealed that for the climbers in the study, the creation of subcultural groups and the authenticity of sporting identities were important and inter-weaved issues, in respect of fragmented identities in modernity. Further, for those very committed participants in Wheaton's (2004a) study of male windsurfers, their subcultural status and identity gained from a particular sporting activity was more important than other identities traditionally acquired, through work, for example (see also Maguire 1999).

In previous sections of this chapter, I have started to identify that it was clear from a number of the climbers interviewed that identifying as a climber gave them a sense of status which other aspects of their lives did not, as this man, aged thirty-nine, revealed, 'Something away from making a living, that something's more important. That's, erm, a bit of exclusivity I suppose.' As well as making him feel special and allowing him an identity outside work, his comments also illustrate how geographical location has an impact on how identity is formed and experienced in relation to status: '... maybe that's a Sheffield thing or a higher end of it there. Cardiff climbing club, certainly don't define themselves as climbers.' The active choice of a specific location in which to live and climb also influences the amount of status to be had from the viewpoint of other climbers. One city, as opposed to another, can have more 'buzz', activity and sporting opportunities. As well, such a sense of shared space binds people into a collective identity, even when not physically climbing.

Status, in the interviewees' accounts was also linked to competition and, simultaneously, a sense of collectivity, which was often fostered in all-male groups, as this climber, in his late twenties, demonstrated:

> Certainly, when I was 18, 19 and then in my early 20s, I mean I had quite a strong group of friends and we would be competitive with each other, and I guess we'd be competitive with some outside groups that we knew as well. I think some of that is, I suppose, a desire for respect or status, but you also look for a kind of, er, secure position within that.

The idea of status was also conceptualized in relation to different climbing practices by some participants, as a climber in his fifties showed, when asked what being a mountaineer specifically meant to him, as opposed to other climbing identities:

> It's (mountaineering) one complete thing. It's not just a steep bit of ice, steep bit of rock, it's the whole thing. Probably the worst activity I did, the thing that least turns you on, is bouldering. That to me is just, er, it's too hard for me and I don't do it, probably different from a lot of the younger lads I'm working with now. I'll prefer to go for, er, a jog round, nip up the hill and back. But I think it's almost gonna go full circle. I think there's very few people now doing very hard natural

climbing. If they want the very hard technical stuff, they're gonna be going on the sports routes, the boulder routes.

As an 'old school' mountaineer – bearded, 'rugged' and experienced through travel to dangerous climbing locations, which, in some contexts, gives him a certain cachet – he reveals in his comments that the climbing world, like any other, is subject to cycles in terms of which aspects of a particular sport are popular, or not, at any given time. However, he also establishes his own hierarchy, by inferring that there are now fewer climbers wanting to do the 'hard' and 'natural' routes that traditional climbing entails, with the greater risks attached to this style of climbing than sport climbing or bouldering. Thus, climbers create their own sense of identity in the face of prevailing trends and fashions in a sport, seen in his comment that things are eventually 'gonna go full circle'. But he also establishes his superiority over, other, younger, climbers with his reply to being asked if these choices to climb differently mattered 'they want to do half a mountaineering job, then … [laughter]'. This was said in a joking manner but, at the same time, he established mountaineering as the benchmark by which other types of climbing are to be judged.

In comparison, other climbers were not overly concerned with a need for climbing to be able to give them a 'special' or exclusive identity and did not seem to desire any status that climbing was able to give them. This 50-year-old climber reflected: 'Yeah, I suppose for me climbing's, er, sort of a lifestyle rather than … it's about a way of looking at the world as well as a way of being in the world, you know?' Moreover, this stance chimes in accordance with his anti-materialistic views: 'I don't like having things. It's a whole ethical stance to the world. I don't want things that other people haven't got. I don't want to be in anyway, erm, what's the word? Not superior, but …' In this way, his views accord with a number of the climbers interviewed whose identity was construed as signifying an anti-materialism. Though for some, this stance changed when a career became important, or when they had children.

Therefore, the relationship between climbing and status are complex, when viewed across the life course, as viewed from the perspective of this climber in his sixties:

It's really in some ways quite selfish though, especially when you're young and very focused on what you want to do. I continued to climb because I like the outdoors. I like mountains and it's a friendship network. So, I was not like people who were simply in it because of the status of being able to climb very hard. And a lot of those, when they weren't able to do it at the highest levels, dropped out and did other things. For me, there was always a, a, much wider context.

Climbing is seen here as a selfish, and self-absorbing activity, when one is very young. Implicit in his viewpoint, as he got older, however, was that climbing became to be appreciated for different reasons. He did not climb at particularly hard levels compared to some of the elite climbers in the study, therefore, the status to be gained through climbing routes recognized as difficult was not achievable but neither was it seen as desirable. For him, a different kind of alternative status is gained. This was seen by his dismissal of those who were 'simply in it' for the more traditional kind of status, or of those climbers, according to him, who were not able to appreciate their surroundings, or who valued friendship networks less than their reputation in the climbing community. This complicates a picture of elite climbers being seen to possess a higher status in the climbing world, whilst novices are climbers with lesser reputations who look on those more experienced, or reputedly better climbers, in awe, or even jealousy. And, of course, elite climbers can possess a deep love of the outdoors and non-elite climbers can be seen to have a fierce need to achieve, as I have discussed.

## Conclusion

This all suggests that extreme sporting identities are complex across age, ability and status. With the latter category, the data in this study can be used to illuminate Wheaton's (2007) question, of whether the clearly maintained boundaries and identities present in sport are redrawn through contests over status. These (masculine) boundaries and identities have been seen in this chapter to be shifting, due to the diverse investments climbers had in accruing status, and other aspects of identity, from their participating in an extreme sport. What is more, the data presented here can be used to challenge an assumption (Wheaton 2007), that sports participants such as climbers, windsurfers and skaters have a more shared or secure sense of status and identity, one which is seen to cut across perceived internal differences. This could be seen in expressions of anxiety over sporting performance and any subsequent, potential loss of reputation, that lead one climber to abandon climbing for another sport.

Furthermore, identity needs to be looked at not just in relation to rock climbing in the more conventional terms of reputation, competition and achievement, which have often been the concerns of those researching men and sport, but also in the context of the different values placed by participants on attendant everyday activities. This can be the importance given to friendship networks or even the view to be had from the top of a cliff. In this way, masculine identity can be seen to be fluid, as well as cross-cutting, across subgroups, for instance, the elite and non-elite, but also across the life course.

The 'conversations', that Jenkins (2004) identified which take place between Mead's 'I' and the 'We' in an effort to forge a unitary account of selfhood, entail that there is a constantly shifting internal (and external) dialectic. This can be seen between the individual and the rock climbing community, as well as, as I have started to identify, a wider circle of partners, families and workmates. For a more complex view of any perceived shifts in masculine sporting identities, such a dialogue needs placing in the midst of these mundane, everyday relationships. Furthermore, these extreme sporting men can seen to be in flux, as they negotiate identities across different practices within an extreme sport, as the climber who had switched to a more 'feminine' style of climbing revealed. However, this, I would argue, is not necessarily evidence of a 'crisis', given his continued, and traditionally masculine, need to achieve. Further, the traditional 'slab' climbing, adopted by this man can also be a dangerous style of climbing, due to not always being able to place adequate protection. The next chapter looks further at potential movement in masculine sporting identities, through the issue of diverse, gendered, climbing relations.

# CHAPTER 5

# 'Belay Bunnies': Sport, Gender Relations and Masculinities

## Introduction

I stated, in Chapter 1, that rock climbing is one of the fastest growing extreme sports in the UK and that women's participation in the sport is growing. Ryan (2005a), in an article published on a UK climbing forum, documents an earlier period in climbing's history in the 1970s and early 1980s: 'Mixed teams at the crag were rare and if a woman was at the crag she was more often than not being "taken" climbing by her boyfriend' (Ryan 2005a: 2). Things, he argues, have now changed: 'Girls who climb, if you haven't noticed, are on the ascendant. They are participating in the climbing world as never before, at the crags, down the gym, appearing in the magazines in greater numbers. Many of them performance wise, are up there playing in the first division, and an increasing number have joined the top boys in the premier league' (Ryan 2005a: 2).

As I indicated in Chapter 2, there has been research done on women in sport from a number of perspectives which can inform an investigation into their participation in rock climbing, as well as on sporting gendered relations. Feminists, in particular, have theorised women's exclusion from mainstream sport and the prejudice they face from men in diverse sporting contexts in a number of ways, emphasising power relationships in the process. More specifically, for my purposes, research has been done on the disadvantages faced by women involved in mountain leadership training or the outdoor world (Sharp 2001; Kiewa 2001) and on the importance of women's early childhood experiences of outdoor activity and having an interested partner to allow them to take up such activities later. Others, such as Green et al. (1990), however, are clear that the family and work obligations of women effect their involvement in leisure activities. Sexuality has also been identified as an issue in that it is hard to develop a public identity as a lesbian (or gay man) in sport (Kivel and Kleiber 2000). There are, however, debates on whether women are disadvantaged in comparison to men or not in sport. Fillion (1996) for instance, argues that women are not naturally more non-competitive than men.

As I explore in detail in the chapter, there has also been research on gender relations in different extreme sports. However, this research has not, in the main, been concerned with gender relations in climbing per se (Appleby and Fisher 2005), although some research has been done (for instance, see Young 1997; Da Silva 1992; Kiewa 2001; Robinson 2004). This chapter will draw on some of this research and starts from an assumption that that sport represents and creates social relations, including those of gender (Hall 1990). In addition, gendered identities are seen as simultaneously relational and oppositional and that to further understand masculinity, we need to consider femininity, and understand gender as well as gender relations. The chapter is, therefore, centrally concerned with the potential transformation of gender relations in the context of British rock climbing and the relationship of this to any significant disruptions of the everyday practices of masculinities. To do this, I will initially discuss how the concept of gender has been understood in relation to sport. After outlining debates surrounding any potential shifts in gender relations in terms of how they are 'played out' in different extreme sports, I will then, through the data, look at the gender politics of mixed-sex climbing. Further, to put such everyday practices in a broader context, I will also outline the wider, social context of inequality within which gendered climbing relations occur, especially in relation to how discourses of gender and sport are constructed in the media. Finally, in terms of (heterosexual) social relations, the experiences of the female participants in this study (as climbers in their own right or non-climbing partners of men, i.e. wives or girlfriends of male interviewees) will be explored, as well as a consideration of women who climb with other women.

## Gendering Sport

As Horne et al. (1999) state, sport fundamentally demarcates gender. Gender itself has been conceptualized in relation to women and men's participation in a number of different sporting sites. Ferrante (1994) argues that gender appears to be a natural organizing principle as it is encoded into the philosophical under-pinnings of cultural symbols of specific sports. Moreover, Laberge and Albert (1999) argue that in relation to sport there is a dualistic understanding of gender:

> Promoting a degendering process among men in sport would have to be effected via a cultural understanding of the cultural supremacy of men's sports and of the forms of practice associate with hegemonic masculinity, while enhancing the status of women's sports and bodily practices associated with femininity. (1999: 259)

There is the more general issue of whether we want to abolish gender altogether or reconstitute it in new bases (Connell,1987), which is relevant when considering sport and gender relations. Could the construction of androgynous roles in new sports be a possibility, or, alternatively, should we celebrate traditionally feminine characteristics? Plate (2007) takes this line of thought further and challenges views that rock climbing as a sport is necessarily masculine and a sport in which femininity and athleticism are seen as contradictory. She uses

Koivula's (2001) work on 'masculine' sports, which are traditionally characterized as involving risk, strength and aggression, and 'feminine' sports characterized as using balance, grace and non-aggression, to ask about rock climbing in
particular: 'What can be inferred from men using traditionally feminine characteristics such as grace and balance to show strength and courage, while women
utilise their femininity to engage in 'risky' masculine behaviours?' (Plate
2007: 3).

Whether women's participation in sport, especially sports typically construed
as masculine, upholds or transforms gender stereotypes has been debated in
relation to a number of sports. For instance, Benson (1997: 150) challenges
feminist views that see women body builders as necessarily being transgressive
of gender roles, as they exemplify 'parodic excess', of stereotypical feminine
characteristics, such as 'big hair'. Likewise, Mennesson (2000) argues that
female boxers simultaneously challenge the gender order by participating in a
traditionally male sport, but also, at the same time, help to reinforce the status
quo by upholding traditional kinds of femininity. More positively, Young (1997)
has argued that women who climb or play ice hockey or practise martial arts, for
example, are actually creating new meanings in their chosen sport for themselves
and at the same time are reconstructing what could traditionally be termed
female-appropriate behaviour. This issue of whether women are producing different meanings, and moreover, in the process challenging both the construction
of traditional femininity *and* masculinity, is explored in the next two sections,
which include an analysis of the data on men's views on climbing with women.

## New Sports and Gender

Work has been done on gender relations in traditional sport. For example,
Messner (1992) found that male athletes needed women as nurturers and carers
to function. But, more recently, studies have looked at newer, less traditional
sporting environments to examine men's attitudes to women participants. Beal
(1999), for example, found that of the forty-one skateboarders interviewed, only
four were women and other women associated with the sport were defined as
(in-active) 'skate betties'. This stands in interesting comparison to Wheaton's
(2000b) 'windsurf widows', women who did not participate in the sport but
stayed at home or what this study identifies as climbing 'belay bunnies', women
who don't usually climb but who hold the ropes of their male partners to ensure
that they can climb safely.

In later work, female skaters interviewed by Beal and Weidman (2003) said
they were not taken as seriously by males and felt patronized or protected. They
also felt that they had to be better than the men or become 'one of the guys'.
Male skaters tended to see them as less physically capable, and even if not inten-
tionally discriminating, they were unintentionally. Meanwhile, Beal and Wilson
(2004) found that female skaters also used their participation in the sport to

differentiate themselves from traditional femininity. Male participants however, needed to separate themselves from females by not taking part in sports such as in-line skating, where girls could not be distinguished from boys as the skill level was the same for both sexes.

However, it would be wrong to say that men's views towards women extreme sporting participants are homogeneous. Windsurfing has been investigated by Wheaton (2004a) as a 'male heterosexual arena', through men's attitudes to both female participants and those labelled 'beach babes'. Her findings however, revealed diverse viewpoints to women windsurfers, ranging from respect and acceptance to negativity. Wheaton uses the concept of an 'ambivalent masculinity' in her study of windsurfing, where she argues that women and 'other' men were less excluded than in traditional, institutionalized sports cultures. As Beal and Wilson (2004) found, in relation to skateboarding, she also saw a difference between older and younger extreme sporting participants. For instance, 'laddishness' as an identity, characterized by heterosexual prowess, was performed by younger participants who were keenly aware of their status within the windsurfing community and they tended to see women as passive, or even as sexual objects. The younger windsurfers' girlfriends tended to be 'girlies', that is, non-windsurfers or less able windsurfers than their boyfriends. Older men, on the other hand, had a wider range of work and family-based identities to draw upon.

Borden (2001) also identified contradictions in gender relations in relation to skateboarding. He found that though skaters are mostly young men in their teens and twenties, with 'broadly accommodating dispositions towards skaters of different classes and ethnicity' (Borden 2001: 263), here too, gender relations are not straightforward, with female skateboarders being discouraged by convention, including sexist objectification. Older skateboarders were also seen to face prejudice, whereas homophobic attitudes and a homosocial masculinity were created in a skateboarding environment. Borden sees gender relations as complicated, in that though there are rare positive promotions of female 'skaters', the views of male 'skaters' about women range from acceptance to the view women that should not be participating (Borden 2001: 144).

Alternatively, Midol and Broyer (1995) argue that patriarchal gender relations can be challenged by men in 'whiz sports', by their dropping their defences. But, in general, when discussing non-traditional sport as an arena in which to fight gender oppression and contest gender relations, most theorists agree with Kay and Laberge (2004), who suggest that this promise does not always hold true at the level of practice in specific sports.

With a growing number of female rock climbers and some of these women achieving success in climbing hard routes that most men could not climb, men's attitudes to increased female participation in a range of new sports needs further analysis. This is especially true of sports where women are increasingly performing at high levels. Consequently, as I have argued, in considering sporting gender relations we need to include the experiences and views of different sporting subgroups, for instance the elite as well as the more casual participant, taking into account transitions over time from one group to another, to be able to fully make sense of whether, and how, such sporting relationships are shifting. My data revealed that in these contexts, gendered climbing relations are complex and multi-faceted, especially when viewed over the life course.

## Gendered Climbing Relationships

In the interviews I conducted, a significant aspect of identity for interviewees was gender difference and how it was perceived, in terms of male climbers comparing themselves to female climbers. In this respect, there were diverse responses to women climbing, which substantiated the findings from those studies on gender relations in extreme sports to which I have previously referred. For instance, in Kiewa's (2001) research with Australian climbers, she found that both sexes have generalized and stereotyped assumptions, in that women are seen to be focused on climbing relationships, whilst men are seen to concentrate more on the activity itself. In reality, however, individual climbers were seen to support, or indeed resist, such assumptions.

Speaking about his relationship with a girlfriend with whom he climbed, a male climber I interviewed, in his forties, said:

> I suppose, looking back on my behaviour, sometimes it was terrible [laughter], absolutely diabolical. You know, what used to annoy me with Ruth is the inconsistency. Ruth was never like a climber as such. You know, you get these people who climb, their identity is a climber.

In this way, he supports Kiwea's conclusion that women are perceived not to be as focused on the activity of climbing as men are. However, Kiewa also found that the more relaxed attitude that some women had towards climbing, did not necessarily mean that they thought climbing to be unimportant.

Overall, Kiewa (2001) argues that, although there were variations in how individual female and male climbers conformed to gender expectations, in practice, there was little deviation from gendered *expectations* as such. For instance, in her study one male climber felt he could be more open and forceful in his opinions when climbing with men rather than women, with whom, he said, you had to '*step round things*' (Kiewa 2001: 9). Plate (2007), however, takes issue with Kiewa's conclusions, arguing that the realities of gendered climbing are more complex than she makes out. For Plate, therefore, Kiewa's view, that men and women are focussed on different aspects of the climbing activity, assumes men will possess 'masculine' and women 'feminine' characteristics, accordingly. This then simplifies gender relations (as well as, I would add, reinforcing hegemonic masculine behaviour) and posits a binary approach to the concept of gender itself. Also, Plate argues, climbing relationships, as well as the activity of climbing, should not necessarily be thought of as mutually exclusive elements of the sporting experience, as Kiewa implies.

In fact, the climbers interviewed in my study revealed diverse, and sometimes contradictory attitudes to being asked what they thought of the increasing numbers of women climbers, thus illustrating the importance of Plate's argument; that we must be careful not to polarise the experiences of climbers of both sexes or, further, work with a dichotomous conception of gender. Some men were clearly positive regarding what they thought about women entering the sport and, what was more, women climbing well was something to be welcomed. One man, a climbing guide, in his thirties, reflected on this issue: 'I have climbed with a woman as an equal on two expeditions. She is ace, you know. Don't really have a problem with it. I think climbing is so much better now with climbing walls and women getting into it.' As well as seeing it as 'ace' that more women are entering the climbing world, it is the fact this woman can be seen as his equal, and not as a threat, that is the most telling issue here. It is relatively easy for men to proclaim in a generalized fashion that they are pleased that more women are now rock climbing but it is not until men are challenged in relation to their own sporting achievements, as this male climber revealed, that we can begin to see how things are changing with regard to gendered sporting relations and in the formation of masculinity.

Whilst, some of the older, male climbers in my study were also pleased to see the emergence of greater numbers of female climbers in the sport and were enthusiastic about their increased proficiency. One ex-climber, in his sixties, spoke of how, in the past, women climbers only existed to impress, or perform for. However, these days, he said, they are 'just fantastic'. He cites an example of one woman who '... strips off and gets into whatever. Boy, you should see her climb. And, you know, it's just amazing, 'cos she's my age.' Such views support Wheaton's (2000b, 2004a) work on male windsurfers, which found that older participants were more thoughtful, and accepting of women participants, than younger ones. In general, the younger climbers interviewed revealed contradictory views to female climbers, though were perhaps, overall, more accepting of female rock climbers than the young elite windsurfers in Wheaton's study. For instance, one young, elite climber in his twenties agreed that 'Basically, there's no two ways about it, it's a hugely male-dominated sport.' However, in contrast to his earlier view, he later stated (only semi-humorously) that women:

> ... never have to get dirty now, it's not a pre-requisite anymore. You can easily go to the climbing wall or you can go to a nice cliff with a well maintained path at the bottom of it, so that's good. And bouldering, chicks dig bouldering [laughter]. You don't even have to put a harness on, you don't even have to leave the path.

Even when men do approve of more women entering the sport, such acceptance can be double edged. On one level his attitude is positive but on another he maintains that one of the reasons women have started climbing in greater numbers is because of the diversity of climbing practices the sport now affords. New sporting practices such as bouldering, where, as I have said, large boulders are scaled without the need for ropes or the placing of gear, ensure that women do not have to 'get dirty'. He also posits an idea that women may well prefer to climb indoors, rather than outdoors, where it is more risky. Thus, he also upholds gender stereotypes, which have positioned women as not liking the 'rough and tumble' and the risk involved, in extreme sporting activities. The diversification of climbing as a sport, therefore, affords greater numbers of women more opportunities to get involved and, at the same time, more men appear to welcome this, if in contradictory ways. However, this does not in itself ensure that the way men conceive of this development necessarily challenges traditional conceptions of how gender is constructed.

This failure to challenge gender stereotypes could be seen in the views of one male climber, aged 38 years, who describes different types of women who feel they have to compete with men 'trying to be one of the lads', and also speaks of the 'pathetic woman I've gone out walking with and she's been in tears all the time'. Indeed, the women he actively wants to climb with have 'just mucked in, they're part of the crowd, they're very supportive'. When asked if he ever climbs with women who are better than him, he replied, 'If it was some big head woman climber, I wouldn't climb with them anyway.' He goes on to say, 'I don't think I've climbed as good with females who've climbed as good as me, and that's not because they're climbing better than me, I don't find that a problem.' Unable to reflect on his own perceptions, of what, in his view, makes a woman acceptable for him to climb with, this non-elite climber is unable to offer an explanation as to why he does not climb with women who are better than him, perhaps unsurprisingly given that he obviously feels threatened by competent female climbers.

A number of climbers made it clear that they did not generally climb with women but attempted to explain this in terms of not wanting to climb with anyone, including other men, who climbed at a lower standard. For instance, when asked if he mostly climbed with women or men, one elite male climber, aged 39 years, replied, 'There's more men climbers that want to climb with me, and there's more male climbers. Probably at the level I climb at, I just don't know that many female climbers.' Other studies bear these findings out. For example, Kiewa (2001) found that one male climber reported that many of his friends did not climb with women, thinking it would hold them back. Another of her interviewees said that he would climb with women, but that these experiences were seen more as social events. This has the effect of making it hard for women to gain credibility as serious climbers. However, women themselves could uphold these attitudes by only climbing with men when they wanted to climb seriously; one woman in Kiewa's study asserted that men are more reliable as climbing partners.

Additionally, some of my participants' stereotypical views on climbing with women changed over time. For instance, this climber in his thirties, always prioritised his own sporting performance above climbing with women, or men, who climbed at lesser levels than he did: 'I wouldn't, I just refuse to go out with girls, because for me, my time was precious and the last thing I would do with anybody, girls, boys, was go pandering to them.' Yet, the terms he uses are unintentionally revelatory, with 'girls' and 'boys' and 'pandering', suggesting a very patronizing approach. However, this picture is transformed when he speaks about climbing with an elite, female climber:

... we went on an [ice] climbing trip together and we were both absolutely rubbish. I'd been once. She'd never been. We borrowed all the stuff, we had no idea what we were doing and where we were going, and I was just; 'Don't, we might as well just soldier on', and she was bursting into tears. But, after like a year later, it was completely the other way round. I was just like; 'Oh, get me out of here. I don't like this. Get me to the top.'

Thus, over a period of time, and as this female climber became more competent, so moving further into an elite group category, he was forced to reassess his previous attitude towards her abilities, which initially had been one of annoyance that she had displayed her emotions on a climb so openly. It was only when he was placed in a position where he was tested by a woman, who, in this instance, was climbing better than he was, that he felt able to reveal his fear and feelings of vulnerability. Such data throw light on debates around the emotions, intimacy and trust. Lynn Jamieson (2002) argues that intimacy should be thought of as a set of practices and that it is through these that the way men are 'doing intimacy' differently can best be perceived. Meanwhile, Williams (2001) wonders if gendered emotional stereotypes are breaking down around a pluralization of masculinities. In this context, men's views on and relationships with women climbers can reveal much about changing patterns of male, intimate and emotional relations (see Chapter 6 for a fuller discussion of men's experiences of intimacy, fear, vulnerability and friendships).

Therefore, the attitudes I found in a number of the views of the male participants are supported by Wheaton's findings that the elite male windsurfers were intolerant of men with lesser ability and of women. However, she simultaneously found that, 'I witnessed the elite men encouraging and assisting the elite women, acknowledging and admiring their skill and courage. Hostility and sexist attitudes coexisted with support and encouragement towards elite women windsurfers' (Wheaton 2004a: 148). In this way, in diverse extreme sports, women entering the elite levels can require men to alter their behaviour towards them. As I have shown, this can mean that men become more accepting of women's achievements and capabilities than before, particularly when they can be seen to equal men's sporting performances, enabling traditional, masculine behaviour and practices to be challenged. Creedon's (1994) assertion that women are challenging and changing the 'masculine' world of sports is, therefore, borne out in a range of risk sports.

Further, Whitson (1990) in discussing new sports, argues that '... the demonstrable achievements of women in such sports, indeed the presence of women in sport, have helped to weaken the popular association between sport and masculinity' (Whitson 1990: 28). However, the ambiguous attitudes shown towards women climbers, even the elite, by some men, challenges an image of women who climb at high levels being accepted into a climbing culture, regardless of gender (see Appleby and Fisher 2005). In my study, elite females could be de-valued by their exploits being perceived as 'manly' and so uncharacteristically 'unfeminine' for a woman. Conversely, women could also be denigrated for displaying behaviour typified as 'feminine', as the former example of the elite female climber who was judged adversely for bursting into tears, reveals. Such diverse and sometimes contradictory meanings given by men to women who participate in the sport of rock climbing, can also be seen to be constructed in and through wider cultural discourses, which I now go on to explore through discussion of how the media represents gender relations in sport.

## Sporting Media

At the symbolic and discursive level, how are gender relations in different sporting contexts being played out? Kane and Greendorfer (1994) theorize that an increased presence of female athletes in the media does not so much represent a fundamental social change – rather it illustrates how these 'feminized' images represent an attempt to reinforce traditional and stereotypical images of female sexuality and femininity. This, in turn, trivializes their athletic achievements and, further, constructs female athleticism as of less importance than males. Over a decade later, does women's involvement as participants in new and extreme sports challenge such media constructions?

In a study of sporting adverts, Beal and Weidman (2003) found that such images highlighted core values of risk-taking, individualism and traditional masculinity. Contrastingly, Beal and Wilson (2004) concluded that female skateboarders have found some avenues open to them, for example, the use of the mainstream press to publicize their exploits. Though they argue that this strategy reinforces their marginalized status in the skateboarding world as there is little or no representation in specialist magazines.

On a similar note of changing imagery, Booth (2004) concludes that, despite an influx of women into the sport of surfing in the late 1990s, and also the appearance of high profile female role models who can be seen to encompass more aggressive riding styles for women, these changes go hand in hand with younger female surfers constructing a sexual image to engage sponsors. Seen as counterproductive and detracting from their athleticism, Booth argues that 'Whilst these conditions imply sweeping cultural change, closer analysis reveals little firm evidence of a new gender order in surfing' (2004: 101). Moreover, surfing magazines directed at women give out contradictory messages around, for instance, adverts portraying only one type of idealized female body.

Ryan (2005b) cites an advertiser's defence of the use of 'fit' women climbers in an advertising campaign for climbing apparel: 'In our opinion the outdoor industry seems to be stuck in some crazy second wave feminist politically correct time warp. No one wants to acknowledge that women climbing today are fit, attractive and for the most part very comfortable with the power of their sexuality' (Ryan 2005b: 2). As a counter argument to this position, Ryan argues that the adverts represent a 'self destructive consumerism' and that the acceptance of such advertisements is mostly by male and female climbers under 25, who have grown up with sexualized images of women.

Also discussing rock climbing, Loomis (2005) cites the mountaineer Kath Pyke's view, that the mainstream climbing media portray sexist media images so women with beautiful bodies who sports climb grab media space, unlike women mountaineers who are not glamorous enough and cannot even sometimes be identified *as* women, if photographed, for instance, after a long and demanding trip. More positively, Pyke also argues that the emergence in the US of publications such as *She Sends*, a climbing magazine for women, and *Chicks with Picks*, a women's ice-climbing meeting, can help to portray an array of female climbing role models for women. However, because they are not mainstream these innovations can be seen to reach too few women climbers, preaching, as it were, to the already converted.

These dominant cultural discourses can be seen to provide a wider social context for how everyday sporting gender relations are enacted in practice, affecting women's self-image and sporting relations with men. They can also inform how men perceive them in everyday sporting situations. Rinehart (2005), therefore, concludes from an analysis of media images of women in new sports that brand advertisers posit themselves in the market place as 'outlaws', opposed to mainstream culture. They achieve this at the expense of objectifying women and negatively influencing those involved in such sports, especially, young male adolescents. However, such an analysis fails to account for the diversity of views held by men towards women in the world of extreme sports. It also does not allow for the agency of sporting participants, nor changes in views across the life course.

Moreover, gendered climbing relationships, in particular, can be seen further and in sharp relief, in an examination of sporting heterosexual relationships where (life) partners also climb together, or when women choose specifically to climb with other women. These aspects of rock climbing also serve to illustrate the importance of the wider, everyday social relations that inform a specific sporting site but are often invisible in those accounts of sporting relationships, which only stress the discursive.

## Heterosexual Contexts for Climbing Relationships

I forgot to tell you that this was our first married climb and it was to be our first married row on a route for Gill and me. It would have been easy to get nostalgic about this climb, pretend it was some honeymoon experience, but the truth must be told. It was only a few moves off the ground when our 16-year-long whirlwind romance came under threat. It was a row of the 'You call this a Diff?' kind. In my enthusiasm for this route I'd neglected to convey the actual guidebook grade. A little lichen can threaten even a marriage of convenience. Perhaps Gill would get access to my pension earlier than I anticipated. My life expectancy was certainly being shortened by the silent tension that followed the withering question. Here I was Getting It Wrong Again, just as I had as an unmarried man. (Gifford 2004: 68)

A number of theorists have commented on the importance of the gendered dynamics in a climbing, heterosexual relationship. For example, Appleby and Fisher (2005), in an account of their study of eight high-performing female rock climbers in the US, document that all but one of the climbers interviewed were introduced to the sport by men, usually their boyfriends. Further, they found that the women accredited their climbing competencies to their male partners, concluding that men initially acted as gatekeepers to the sport for the women involved and then as coaches on whom the women's sporting success was often dependent. The women also worked hard to prove themselves as competent climbers in their own right. Only then could they be seen as separate from their male partner in the eyes of the climbing community.

This is in contrast to the vast majority of my male participants, aged from their early twenties to their seventies and who had diverse skill levels and achievements in relation to the sport. These men entered climbing in a number of ways, for instance, through parents who were involved in some way in outdoor pursuits, through organizations such as the scouts or university climbing clubs, or through older male friends who were already active in rock climbing.

However, to support Appleby and Fisher, many of the women I interviewed stated that, like me, they started to climb by being taken by a man with whom they were also involved in a relationship. And, a number of the male climbers in my study talked about going climbing with girlfriends or wives. This male climber, aged in his thirties, felt he would be 'very protective' if he climbed with someone with whom he was in a relationship and so therefore stated 'I don't think I perhaps want a female who climbs.' He also infers that some women gain a reflected glory from climbing with a male climber who is better than they are and, by implication, infers that this does not come from their own climbing achievements or efforts, when he says 'I noticed, with a lot of sort of relationships, really it's, you know, the woman wanting to say "This is my sort of 'star' I'm climbing with."'

An alternative view is put forward by Kiewa (2001), who found that one of the woman climbers that she interviewed felt a pressure to be more vulnerable and so more feminine when she started a relationship with a male climber. However, Dilley (2002) found in her study of female rock climbers in the UK that where women had mainly climbed with men with whom they were in a relationship at the time, these women experienced different climbing dynamics.

Such differences could be attributed to whether the relationship outside the climbing partnership was a positive one. If so, the climbing relationship was generally harmonious and productive. Where it was not positive, the climbing relationship experienced aspects such as threats to personal safety, a general lack of support and doubting of the woman's ability. Dilley concludes that the diversity of women's experiences show that heterosexual relationships are not monolithic, and, do not necessarily support a hetero-normative discourse (see Hockey et al. 2007 for a broader discussion of the diversity of heterosexual relationships). Her work also serves to illustrate the importance that I have remarked on, of considering how climbing relationships interact with the wider social relationships of the participants and how such an expansion of the sporting focus allows new questions to be asked.

I have already identified that men can be over-protective to the women that they climb with. In addition, one female climber in my study, aged 58, reflected that, 'In a lot of couples I know, the man will get very impatient and not want to climb with his wife or girlfriend, because she's a bit slower and she doesn't do routes as hard as him.' The interviewee's climbing relationship with her male partner, and their relationship in general, was very fulfilling for them both. He had even given up the sport for a period when she was ill and they could no longer climb together. In contrast, the question of why women (and, indeed, men) continue to climb with each other, when the relationship may be frustrating or fraught, is an interesting one. However, some of the male interviewees, when reflecting on climbing with a woman they were in a relationship with, had neither an impatient nor protective attitude, given the obvious competency of the women involved. Thus, they revealed positive shifts in attitude to women climbers.

It is through an exploration of men's attitudes to women who climb that the question of if, how and to what extent, gender relations are pluralizing in positive and more inclusive ways can start to be explored through a consideration of extreme sporting activities. As I have noted, women's entry into this sport disrupts those practices and has the potential to challenge traditional gendered ways of behaving. However, some women choose not to climb with men in the main, or even at all, and make an active choice to climb with other women.

In her study, Plate (2007) uses data to show that many of the women she interviewed find a deep satisfaction in the activity of climbing with other women. Thus, she suggests that for her female interviewees, climbing with women allowed them to focus more on the activity of climbing and not necessarily purely on climbing relationships. However, this choice does not always mean that they escape men's interference. The US climber, Tiffany Skogstrom's experience (cited in Ryan 2005c) is that there is still sexism against women in the climbing community and that this can be seen in the everyday practices of the sport. For instance, when men give women instructions on how to climb when they were neither needed, nor requested. This was substantiated by one climber

I interviewed, aged 32, who spoke about her experiences when climbing with a female friend, 'We were OK at climbing. We were doing the VSs (relatively easy climbs) and just getting on with it quietly. This bloke kept making comments and, being very, very, patronizing about it.'

Other female participants had similar experiences when out climbing with other women in that some men could not stop themselves proffering unwanted advice or assuming women could not be going to lead on difficult climbs. As Ryan (2005c) notes, such sexism can be overt, subtle, done deliberately and through ignorance. He also argues that there is substantial evidence to show that women's climbs are downgraded when climbed by men. Further, similar accusations have been voiced much earlier in the climbing community (see, for example, Lawrence 1994). Moreover, Dilley (2002) also found that women in her study felt that men were threatened by their climbing ability and that women were constructed as incompetent climbers through a number of variables such as: the 'belay bunny' syndrome, the lack of female role models, the low expectations of female climbers themselves, the presence of controlling male partners and their low expectations of women's skill and physical ability, as well as the lack of opportunities for women to improve.

However, not all the women I interviewed substantiated Dilley's findings. One woman climber in her thirties now felt confident enough in her own abilities to offer assistance: 'I've gone up to men loads of times and said "Oh, I saw somebody do it last week and they just did that and that really helped", you know, help them out.' This example does signify that some changes are occurring with regard to traditional gender practices at the everyday level, particularly when some men, at least, are willing to accept such advice. Furthermore, even Dilley (2002) can conclude that, overall, her women participants thought that the rock climbing world now accepted women *as* climbers, at least more so than in the past.

At one level, for a woman to choose to climb with other women is a personal decision, often based on past experiences of climbing with men. In addition, the choice can be based on personal politics or sexuality, as shown by one woman interviewee who identified as a lesbian and who had made a conscious decision to climb only with women. There are, however, wider implications for such decisions at a time when climbing is diversifying and becoming more commercialized (as I outlined in Chapter 3). For instance, Loomis (2005), in an article on the past, present and future of women's mountaineering, argues that sometimes female mountaineers prefer being in all-women mountaineering teams, partly because this can offer good sponsorship opportunities.

Meanwhile, Ryan (2005a) asks if women climbers should be in a separate category from men or have their own competitions, female climbing magazines and women only climbing courses. Or, alternatively, should they compete on the same terms as men, as the top women climbers continue to do. He also notes that some women don't like women-only climbing events or feeling 'empowered' and don't want to be defined as a female climber – just as *a* climber. This is a view endorsed in an earlier era by Annie Smith Peck, one of the first women to make a career out of high altitude climbs. In her comments to the *New York Times* in 1911, she said: 'A woman who has done good work in the scholastic world doesn't like to be called a good woman scholar. Call her a good scholar and let it go at that. I have climbed 1,500 feet higher than any man in the United States. Don't call me a woman climber' (cited in Loomis 2005: 8). Therefore, gender is not necessarily a charged, or even relevant issue for some female climbers, neither, necessarily, is climbing with men, or indeed, heterosexuality per se in sporting contexts. And, when women climb with other women, how gender is 'performed' can still be imbued with tension or even rendered paradoxical, as I now discuss.

For example, the reaction of a woman climber in my study, in her late twenties, to being brought flowers by her female friend and climbing partner instead of having the piece of protective gear replaced for the one that had been left behind whilst out climbing, and which would have been the traditional and usual action to take, is interesting in relation to stereotypical gender roles. She says, 'And I was like 'What!' [laughter] "You spent twenty quid on some flowers?" But, anyway, we stormed out to the crag next morning and I got this piece of gear out.' The offer of flowers was taken as an insult by the interviewee, who took pride in her own climbing skills and abilities. What might be seen as normally gender-appropriate behaviour takes on new meaning in a sport such as climbing, where gender meanings are not only contested between the sexes but amongst women climbers themselves.

Nor can it be assumed that it is male climbers who will always be the harshest judges of women involved in the climbing scene, as earlier data in the chapter suggested. This was evident in the interchange between myself, a male climber and his girlfriend/climbing partner, both in their twenties, when discussing women who accompany their boyfriends to the crag but who don't climb themselves. He said:

> I've been in Pembroke, August Bank Holiday, a lot of fashionable-looking people, a lot of very good climbers as well. But a lot of them have got girlfriends who don't climb, who just sit around the top of the crag. I suppose at least they're being sociable and sitting around chatting with each other.

But it is his girlfriend who is most dismissive of the women, adopting what might normally be seen as a traditional, male response: 'There's cafés for that sort of thing, or they can walk, they don't have to sit.'

In addition, the everyday relations that climbers have with non-climbing friends and partners can also illustrate the complexities of sporting, heterosexual relationships in other contexts not connected with sport. The non-climbing partner of an elite male climber, in her late thirties, contests a version of the climbing scene as necessarily being a more inclusive one, just because more women are involved in the sport. When asked about male climbers' attitudes to female climbers, she replied:

It's very hard to pinpoint, but there is a macho-ness to it. You know, the surfing mentality macho-ness is very much: 'We're boys and girls don't surf, and if they do, they don't do it very well', kind of thing. The climbing men, I don't feel are like that. They're quite accepting of women who climb. But there's still an attitude towards them. I think particularly when they have a family, or relationships, for the climbing's kind of up here and the relationship's down there.

Her view, borne out by my own experiences of having male partners that climb, is that for some men, climbing as a sport dictates how much time they spend with their families and partners and indeed, what their priorities in life are, regarding for example, childcare and domestic work. She also adds that some male climbers: 'See men in their kind of gang as weak, if they defer to their relationship.' However, she and her partner negotiate his climbing participation and so he does not conform to this image of men that she draws, despite his risking being seen as 'weak' by other male climbers, if he prioritizes their relationship. Thus, even if many men may be more publicly accepting of women in new sports such as climbing, in the private sphere, gendered stereotypes and expectations can still persist and transformations may not be as evident as in the sporting site itself. Additionally, she further makes complex a notion of changing gender relations when asked about her own acceptance, or otherwise, as a non-climber with the female climbers in her partner's sporting circle. She states: 'It was really quite vicious to begin with, and I hadn't really experienced anything like that before … an almost vitriolic sort of "What do you think you're doing, coming into this when you clearly have no interest?"' The fact that the female climbers she refers to are generally an elite group is of relevance here. In an earlier example given in this chapter the sporting performance of an elite female climber caused a male climber to reconsider his previously discriminatory and gendered attitudes. Here, the unwelcoming attitude of these women contrasts with the argument that sees the feminization of new sports as automatically leading to a positive shift in challenging gender identities and roles. Her perception of the reactions of elite, female climbers to her, the non-climbing partner of an elite climbing male complicates notions that women entering and being successful in a sport necessarily entails that all women will benefit from the breaking down of sporting gender stereotypes. As Whitson (1990: 29) argues regarding extreme sports, '… changes in gender, as well as relations are likely to require painful readjustments for many of us'.

## Conclusion

It could be argued, that at the core of exposing gender relations in different sporting contexts, with a view to transforming unequal, exclusionary and stereotyping practices and gender performances, is the notion of gender itself. Using the concept of hegemonic masculine practices, is, however, problematic in investigating gendered sporting practices. This is not least because, as Whitehead

(2002: 94) asserts, it conflates patriarchy with hegemonic masculinity and so results in a 'lost subject' (applicable to both women and men), subsuming them 'under a blanket, often bland, descriptor of male dominance, with little accord given to the exercise of resistance.' I would also contend that the concept is not sufficiently flexible to be able to account for the complexity of transitions in gender relations. For example, one sporting subgroup, that of elite men (and women) climbers, can display aspects of hegemonic behaviour in one context but not in another. Eschewing any simplistic notions of equality within newer, extreme and more individualized sports such as rock climbing also entails potentially confronting uncomfortable assumptions about gender, with respect to *both* sexes. And, an examination of gendered sporting relations can also reveal femininity, as well as masculinity, as complex and in flux.

Additionally, a theoretical and empirical focus needs to be directed not just to the contradictory experiences of the sporting participants themselves but to the wider relationships that make up their everyday lives as friends, parents, partners and lovers. In this way, we can gain a fuller picture of conformity, but also resistance to stereotypical gender identities, relations and performances. Here, again, the concept of hegemonic masculinity is not fully able to account for transitions in sporting participants' lives, as they move from public to private sphere, and back again. Further more, the complex, power dynamics which exist between women and men in sporting sites *and* in the domestic sphere, as well as their interrelation, are rendered invisible.

In Chapter 8, on sporting bodies, I return to gender issues specifically in relation to gendered physicalities. However, in the next chapter, I analyse some of the issues I have started to raise here – those of intimacy, emotions and friendship between male climbers, areas that are still relatively undertheorized in both sporting and masculinity studies.

# CHAPTER 6

# Sporting Inner Lives: Emotions, Intimacies and Friendship

No words are exchanged, there is no feeling of triumph, exaltation, conquest – all those wearisome imperial abstracts that the uninitiated imagine to be the province of the mountaineer. Instead, they have to contend with the climbers' usual summit reaction: "The mind was still too wound up to allow such feelings to enter ... the greatest moment of our climbing careers, and there was only a kind of numbness."

Perrin, *The Villain: The Life of Don Whillans*, discussing Don Whillans and Dougal Haston's climb of the South face of Annapurna

## Introduction

What exactly do we know about men's sporting intimate, inner lives? Indeed, how do men conceive of their own, emotional sporting moments? As I have previously argued with Hockey et al. (2007), popular and gendered assumptions about 'men's emotional inarticulacy' (Rutherford 1992; Lupton 1998) can be seen to be reflected in the lack of sociological attention given to the emotional dimensions of men's experiences of heterosexuality. In Chapter 4, it was identified that, in general terms, masculinity has been seen recently as 'troubled': men have lost their traditional occupational identities and, therefore, a 'breadwinner' role within households (Connell 1995). Seidler (1989, 1992) has stressed that men have had to deal with the consequences of their emotional alienation from themselves. He has also noted their painful struggle for a suitable 'emotional language'. The emotionally inarticulate male may now be asked to take more emotional responsibility for himself and others but, despite this, there are authors who have felt that, 'Men's deafening silence about their own sexuality as opposed to the objects of their desire continues' (Middleton 1992). Indeed, elsewhere, (Robinson 1996), I have argued that men can emphasize the 'male wounded psyche' at the expense of analysing male power and privilege.

Furthermore, whilst authors such as Williams (2001) have pointed to research that has seen men as relatively unemotional and incapable of making intersubjective connections, Hearn (1993), in contrast, has argued that sites such as the male-dominated workplace are emotionalized through the controlling of other people's emotions – and the emotion of controlling 'emotional labour'. Alternatively, in Robinson et al. (2007) I argue that many forms of masculinity can now, at one level, be seen to constitute emotional expressiveness. Witness, for example, the public tears of sportsmen or the raw anger of campaigners such as the UK organization, Fathers 4 Justice. In terms of 'undoing' gender, then, should this be seen as a chosen form of feminization or, as Boscagli (1992) argues, evidence of men's power and a symptom of anxiety in a time of crisis?

Such analysis has led a number of theorists, including Connell (2000; 2005), to argue that a consideration of emotional relations in the context of masculinity, are fundamentally new directions in theory and research. This mirrors the recent interest in emotion in social theory more generally and the insights of feminism in connecting heterosexuality to men's position of social dominance. With Hockey and Meah (2007) I concluded that we still vitally need empirical evidence in detailing the changes (or even lack of them), in relation to the supposedly natural, intimate and hidden character of gendered, heterosexual relationships. Specifically here, in the context of sporting masculinities, what does empirical evidence reveal about the everyday practices of men engaged in an extreme sporting activity where emotions such as fear and trust are necessarily, at times, managed and controlled? Further, how are issues of intimacy dealt with in male climbing friendships? What then does this reveal about how their emotions are handled in mundane contexts, for instance in terms of their everyday heterosexual relationships and, indeed, over the life course?

In this chapter I will discuss whether, in an extreme sporting context, men are able to manage and display emotions such as trust, fear and vulnerability in ways that they may not feel able to do in everyday life, through, for example, keeping control in sporting situations. I will also consider through an analysis of climbing literature, if men's capability for expressing emotion should be seen in a historical context to assess whether men are now able to privately, and publicly, reflect on their emotional and intimate selves. Through my data on male sporting friendships, I will examine how men 'do' friendship in extreme and intimate sporting contexts, arguing that we cannot examine these relations without taking into account men's position in the life course, and their wider roles in the family or in relationships, for instance. In addition, the issue of trust will be explored in terms of how extreme and mundane sporting contexts reflect and shape intimate relationships in different ways.

All these questions around sporting masculinities raise the question of how we might go about conducting an analysis of material relating to emotional experience and the ways in which individuals might reflect upon that experience, in particular here, men. As Ingraham (1999: 12) suggests, we can explore the ways in which both sexes make sense of their emotional experience, and how these relate to the 'continual state of crisis and contradiction' of heterosexuality as historical and material conditions shift and change. This can be achieved, for example, by examining cultural manifestations such as film or popular culture.

She also goes on to say that creating an illusory model of heterosexuality that draws on the romantic 'heterosexual imaginary' prevents us from seeing how institutionalized heterosexuality works to organize gender, whilst at the same time preserving racial, class and sexual hierarchies. Could we then also talk of a 'masculine imaginary' that similarly operates to sustain, organise and promote masculine practices, but also serves to keep masculine power intact? If so, what happens to that masculine imaginary when it is challenged, for example in relation to rock climbing, when large numbers of women come into the sport as discussed in Chapter 5? What also happens to such an imaginary masculinity when men are forced to reveal fear and vulnerability, halfway up an almost sheer rock face and the only way out is up?

Though empirical data for men in such situations is sparse there are, nonetheless, convincing arguments to suggest that it is by actively participating in diverse narratives or scripts that women and men develop a sense of who they are and what their relationships should be like (Jackson 1999). Rapport (1997) has argued for a need to acknowledge that not only do individuals author their own lives but also that they engage in the continuous rewriting of new or amended narratives, in the process reflexively reformulating their own intimate (and so for my purposes) sporting environments. These narratives can be seen in popular, cultural manifestations of rock climbing and mountaineering, such as climbing biographies, climbers' prose accounts of their sporting exploits and the proliferation of extreme sports' magazines, as well as in the data I now go on to analyse.

## Feeling the Fear: Taking Control

The world of rock climbing can be used to illustrate these different views on men's emotions and also to identify if there are any changes that might be seen to be occurring in how men conceive of and subsequently perform those emotions. At one level, as recognized in Chapter 5, this specific sporting site can be seen as one that is becoming more feminized through women's increasing participation (and, conversely, where women are sometimes perceived as being more masculine). Additionally, the pursuit of the activity usually requires the controlling of emotions, in a kind of sporting emotional project with which climbers engage if they want to climb to the best of their ability, or gain the most they can from the experience. Rock climbing is also interesting to examine in this context because of the gamut of emotions climbers may experience in a short space of time. For instance, a number of climbers spoke about experiencing emotions ranging from being gripped by fear, to laughter, to relief and sheer peace or happiness. And, these emotions can be experienced on a single route. However, even when soloing (that is climbing unaided and without a partner) climbers are involved in relationships with a number of people. This ranges from their climbing partner or partners, to non-climbing partners who may be present, or at home. It is also pertinent to keep in mind Dant and Wheaton's (2007: 12) point about new sports, that 'The experience of whiz and flow, the buzz and excitement can be appreciated both internally, as emotions are stimulated by physical sensation, and externally, within a social context in which such experiences are shared.' Thus, experiencing pain or fear in a sporting activity can provoke, for instance, a chemical reaction, which can then produce an intense emotional and social response. The question of displaying the emotions of fear or vulnerability, in particular, can be usefully explored through the climbers' own accounts of their climbing practices and experiences.

At one level, as has been argued (Harris 2005: 159), people play sports such as football partially because of the need to manage socially respected needs and tensions. These are seen to be generated through our need to be emotional and spontaneous and because of a perceived need for constrained social behaviour. This figurationalist explanation of sport and its emotional ramifications, may be better placed to explain a 'safe' sport such as football, where the potentiality of death is not a real possibility (see Dunning 1999 for discussion of this perspective). In this account, sport is seen to have a civilizing effect by allowing participants' emotions, which can never be totally banished, to be controlled and managed. But where real danger *or* risk is a distinctive possibility, such theories may have more limited purchase. Furthermore, many sporting studies, with some exceptions (see Smith 2000, for example), do not consider men's changing emotional investment and participation in sports as they age and go through the different stages of the life course. Men's very different emotional reasons for their involvement in the same sport, and, the diverse emotional satisfactions to be gained from such participation, have not yet been fully investigated through a consideration of various sporting contexts. My climbing data reveals men's very different emotional connections to the activity of rock climbing. For example, a man, in his early forties, spoke about taking up climbing as a way of channelling his emotions and previously violent tendencies. In this sense, sport allows him to engage and in a public manner, with internal, psychic issues. Another climber, in his thirties, reports the satisfaction to be gained from his ability to control his fears:

> Lead climbing, it sort of puts you in a position where you've got to try and be in control of your emotions, or your fear basically. If you are able to do that, climbing gives you a … [pause] It's not a high or a rush I wouldn't say, I think those two words are probably quite inappropriate, but it gives you an immense feeling of satisfaction, if you are able to do that.

Both these climbers can be seen to be using the activity of climbing in traditionally masculine ways: to 'master' and control fear in an instrumental fashion, or, to manage socially unacceptable and unruly emotions. Seidler (1991) posits that men learn to leave their emotional histories behind them and, therefore, run the risk of being unwittingly controlled by that history with which many men have not yet come to terms. Men strive for control, as these climbers do here, but such satisfaction is always only partial and short lived. Nonetheless, Seidler (1998) and Williams (2001) describe men's increasing propensity to take responsibility for, and, I would add, reflect publicly on their emotional lives, as the climbers in this study have done. Such control can also be undertaken in a sporting environment for other reasons. For instance, Woodward's (2004, 2006) work on boxing practices illustrates elements of male boxers' self-control of feelings as well as the body, by their actively taking control, sometimes as a way of resisting racist taunts and harassment.

Moreover, Whitehead (2002) argues that we need to move beyond a dualism that sees emotion, or its acceptance at least, as exclusively a female preserve and men as being emotionally incompetent or even repressed. This is not least because such a view stereotypes women as being associated with irrationality and emotion, not reason and rationality. However, we also need to go beyond a consideration of men and emotion that has emerged, in large part, from the literature defined as 'pro-feminist' men's accounts of the repressed male psyche (see Robinson 1996 for a discussion of this tendency and the implications of men taking such a position for feminism and gendered relationships). As Whitehead (2002: 177) notes, 'Despite the overwhelming evidence of many men's emotional blockages, it would be both simplistic and misleading to assume that all men are either lacking the emotional depths apparently available to women or are overly emotional when it comes to aggressive and violent expression. In short, as Hearn (1993) puts it, we should not presume men to be either too much in control or too much out of control of themselves.' Hearn's view is useful in exploring men's complex relationship to the issue of sporting control, emotional or otherwise. The comments of a climber, aged in his fifties, reveal a distinction between control of others and of oneself, when asked about whether an element of control was inherent to climbing:

> I don't think in terms of controlling anything myself. I don't like to push my will on people, or, even on myself, but I am a person that likes doing things with my body. But whether it's a control thing, I don't know. I mean that's, that's putting a pair of conceptual spectacles on and looking at it from a particular point of view. I don't look at things like that. It's nothing about control for me, it's about being there, it's about enjoying yourself.

He described himself as 'a child of the 60s', a self-philosophy he interprets as about eschewing control of others and also, at least initially in the interview, of himself. Later, somewhat contradictorily, he says that as he got older, 'I mean I do control myself, but only sometimes.' He, therefore, problematizes the notion of control, choosing to stress the sporting activity in terms of enjoyment, yet still having to exercise self-control when the everyday practices of climbing necessitated it at times.

Another, older climber in his sixties, when asked if he had seen male climbers show any emotion, for instance, by expressing fear or through crying, proceeded to describe a situation of potential danger he had once found himself in. He related his ability to express fear on the climb and, simultaneously, his feelings of being, if only momentarily, out of control, having to depend on his 'second' who was holding the ropes to save him from injury. But he also felt it important to quickly retain an element of control so that his judgement was not needlessly impaired at a risky moment. Whitehead (2002) argues that to trust, one must let go of fear and the desire to control, but here, to the contrary, emotional control does not have to be about maintaining an image of macho masculinity, but can be seen as something important to the climbing task at hand and the desire to avoid danger and possibly injury or death. Neither does keeping control pre-clude displaying emotion in front of other men, as this man attested to.

In de Garis's (2000) study of male boxing, learning not to be aggressive was a sign of 'being a man' for one of the older boxers. De Garis argues that, in this way, he constructed a mature masculinity where vulnerability was seen as an asset. In contrast, a 71-year-old climber in my study, when asked if he ever dis-played explicit emotion such as fear, replied that in 'his day' there were only few and far instances of men openly doing so whilst climbing. He also agreed with his wife, also in her seventies, and who had accompanied him on many climbing trips, when she characterized young climbers by saying, 'The attitudes have all changed. They will come out with swear words, but I can't ever remember seeing it. They leave mess on the rocks and they're queuing up to do a climb.' Such a contemporary display of emotion, illustrated by the reference to swearing, is viewed negatively. This is also seen as part of a trend for younger climbers to lose control in other, diverse ways. For example, as part of a general tendency to lose control of the climbing environment or the lack of control younger climbers might have over their own participation in the sport, simply through the sheer numbers entering it. Indeed, these different perceptions of how losing control is construed need to be placed in these contexts of broader social changes in the sport of climbing, as well as in relation to diverse models of emotion which men of different generations may be expected to adhere to. Such generational shifts in terms of how men conceive of and can express emotion, through losing control, are complex. Thus, for example, the 50-year-old man who described himself as 'a child of the 60s' was perhaps the most reflexive on emotional matters, however, the older man, in his sixties, had been able to openly lose control in front of another man, despite it not being the 'done thing' to do so.

Meanwhile, Seidler (1992: 2) argues that men are preoccupied with sustaining control of themselves to avoid feeling vulnerable through a loss of self control, and, furthermore 'ward off threats to our male identity that come with our vul-nerability.' And so, to control this vulnerability, men 'often move into activities' (Seidler 1992: 2). But in comparison, a number of the climbers' accounts revealed that these men moved into the sport, at times, to avoid controlling others, if not themselves. In addition, by taking part in the pursuit of rock climbing, some of these men did not avoid feelings of vulnerability. Moreover, this consideration of male emotions, and control of these, can also shed light on the dynamics of gendered relations and how they are implicated at an everyday level in constructing masculinities. As one female climber, in her early thirties demonstrated, it can, therefore, be women who, if unwittingly, uphold a stereotype of the 'always in control' male:

> I mean David and I were friends for a long time before we got into climbing, but he has always been into the outdoors. I think that is something I found really attractive about him. And the fact that when we're climbing together and David's leading, he's always really in control. I guess I do rely on that a bit too.

Though she also told me that, 'I think it's also a trust. You really are exposed in that climbing situation. I think that's a real kind of attraction.' Thus, this independent woman who has a career and wide friendship network, is drawn to her partner partly because of the trust that occurs in a risk activity although her need for this can coexist, and seemingly unproblematically here, with more traditional gender roles, illustrated in the continued reliance on his being in control, something that she finds '*attractive*'.

For men too, control and trust are often inter-related as this male climber, in his thirties, relates:

> I just find it almost a constant fight to like, stay in control. At the start of the year, the way I used to get over it was to go and do three or four scary routes. Because once you get over the fear, then you can relax a bit and start getting into it, trust yourself. But you need to go and scare yourself, you need to go out and remember, that sort of halfway house between, 'Oh shit, I'm going to die', and, 'No, I'm not, I'm going to get to the top.'

Whitehead (2002) has suggested that some discourses and narratives of masculinity allow greater trust between men. This is demonstrated by the climber's management of fear and vulnerability. Such displays of emotion will usually take place in front of a climbing partner, often, another male. In effect, the management of fear is only possible because of the trust these climbers place in their climbing partners. Vulnerability can be shown in an extreme situation and the fear involved, depending on how it is managed and performed, seen as acceptable. However, it is the public management of such emotions that often concerns these climbers. Therefore, to show such feelings on a low-grade climb, or a climb seen as well within one's limits, can be met with derision and thus a perceived sense of failure to keep composure. It is not just that trust, or the lack of it, is a key factor in facilitating *or* disrupting the possibilities of climbing success and wellbeing for the climbers I interviewed, but so too is the fact that men can manage intimacy by engaging in conventional masculine practices and so avoid it (see also Kerfoot 2001). My data reveal that we need to think in a more complex and inter-related way regarding how the issues of emotional control, trust and displays of vulnerability interact; that is, across the generations and in relation to how the same man can display control in one context, but not in another. Furthermore, it is apparent that heterosexual desire can be constructed, at least partly, through male control and this in turn can effect how men manage their feelings. I return to the issue of trust later in the chapter, where it is discussed in relation to the inter-subjectivity of male sporting friendships.

## Emotional Legacies

Another source that can be looked at to assess masculinities, assumptions about emotions and intimacy, and any shifts which might be occurring in relation to these aspects of men's sporting and everyday experiences, is a diversity of climbing literature. This includes, as I have already noted, climbing and mountaineering publications, such as monthly magazines, climbing biographies and autobiographies and poetry and prose writing. The British academic, poet and climber, Terry Gifford (2006) in discussing changes in the genre of climbing literature, details a historical shift from the so called 'Rock and Ice' age. This era was defined by a new generation of the postwar working class, exemplified by climbers such as Joe Brown and Don Whillans and those involved with the Rock and Ice Club, which Gifford (2006) argues 'created an image of men who said little, wrote nothing (certainly not poetry), but acted eloquently'. Though he is primarily concerned with how such an influence came to bear on the ways in which emotions might be expressed in the genre of climbing literature, he is also interested in the implications this has for the practices of rock climbing in general. He cites the British climber Norman Elliott, who sums up the Rock and Ice 'myth', regarding the damage done by this to British climbing culture: 'Their racism, sexism, cynicism and satire cut us off from the whole area of emotional expression of the sport' (Gifford 2006: 159).

A recent biography by Perrin (2005) of the aforementioned Don Whillans, someone who has been seen to be an iconic sporting hero, but also a moody and violent 'villain', draws a picture of the UK climbing community particularly in the years 1950–75. In a critique of Perrin's book, Stainforth writes: 'What emerges, ultimately, is a rather sad, even tragic picture of a psychologically complicated man – a self-ruined archangel, in Perrin's wonderful phrase – who was "temperamental , bellicose, quick to take offence", and whose public persona of witty superstar concealed a simmering cauldron of "rancour, ego, resentment, (and) aggression"' (Stainforth 2005: 1). Indeed, Whillans was denied the Queen's birthday honours because of an incident with police. It might be assumed that in the twenty-first century, male climbers are now more capable of publicly and legitimately showing emotion and not aggressively, as some of my data suggest. However, Gifford, in discussing the reluctance of the editors of British climbing publications to publish poetry based on climbing experiences, asserts that, 'The persisting horror for climbing editors is an embarrassing outpouring of emotion indulged, celebrated, explored by poetry. Here is the sad paradox concerning climbers, who might regard themselves as an uninhibited, adventurous, wild-at-heart lot, being inhibited by poetry's threat of an open, uncontrolled display of emotion' (Gifford 2006: 159). In fact, my data do show that climbers of different ages are prepared to display vulnerability and admit fear, as well as claiming an intimacy with male climbing friends not always found in other non-climbing friendships. However, to acknowledge that in public and for this intimacy to translate outside of a climbing context is sometimes still taboo, as I go on to discuss in the next section.

Gifford continues, however, to acknowledge that British prose writing has been influenced in recent times by 'more emotionally expressive US models' such as Roskelley (1991) or the work of American, pioneering female mountaineer Arlene Blum (1980, 2005) whom he sees as transcending a macho, repressed writing style (I discuss Blum further in Chapter 9 in relation to gender and risk). An example of a British climber and mountaineer who has reflected self-consciously on his climbing exploits, and in prose form is Paul Pritchard. In his book, The Totem Pole (1999), he discusses why he was taking too many risks with his climbing. One accident he blames on being 'screwed up' by a girl who, he thought, if unconsciously at the time, might notice if he hurt himself. Another and more devastating accident was caused after he was trying to escape high seas, where he dislodged a block which struck him on the head, nearly killing him in the process. Instead, he survived after a long recovery. He speculates that this incident occurred, '... because I felt trapped. I had it all, or that's what the majority of my friends figured – big house with a beautiful garden, nice car, as many holidays as I would care to take. Happy at home with Celia. Basically I was very comfortable. I was taking too many risks and I didn't know why' (Pritchard 1999: 57). Such open and public self-reflection on his life and intimate relationship is a long way from Gifford's depiction of the expressionless, inhibited and emotionless male climber from the Rock and Ice era.

## Sporting Friendships

Earlier in this chapter, I began to discuss Williams' (2001) question of if, and in what ways, gendered emotional stereotypes might be breaking down around a pluralization of masculinities, for instance in terms of men taking emotional responsibility. Changing patterns of intimacy and emotional relations have also been explored in the previous chapter on gender relations. For instance, I discussed one male climber's experience who, in climbing with a woman who was better than himself, could admit his fear and feelings of vulnerability. Also, in that chapter, the question of if, how and to what extent masculinities are pluralizing in positive and more democratic ways was explored through a consideration of different extreme sporting activities in which women are increasing in presence and competence. Ordinarily, and in mundane ways within the extreme, men's emotions are made explicit and are 'handled' within the practices that constitute these. As I have shown, women's entry into this sport disrupts those practices and renders both the mundane and the extreme problematic. Another interesting aspect of my interviews concerns the light thrown by men on 'doing intimacy' in the extreme sport of rock climbing and the further insight this affords on emotions and trust in the context of sporting friendships.

Using a feminist perspective of Gidden's (1992) notion of the pure relationship, Jamieson (1998) has argued in her own empirical study of gendered relationships, that though some change is occurring in this respect, the 'doing' of intimacy is not the central organizing axis in women and men's private lives. Another argument is put forward by Kerfoot (1999) who, in arguing that men can't 'let go' in relationships, also argues men cannot connect with others, whilst Whitehead writes, 'Ways of being a man and exhibiting masculinity intrude into men's experiences and displays of intimacy, potentially rendering it synthetic, strategic or to be avoided' (Whitehead 2002: 173). Men, from this perspective, are seen to manage rather than fully experience emotional situations, which can be extended to the question of their relationships and friendships with other men. Additionally, as Whitehead notes, a number of writers on masculinity have argued that men both fear and avoid the unscripted response and uncontrollable situation: 'In seeking to control the uncertainty that might be generated by emotional intimacy, many men – consciously or otherwise – reach for conventional practices and behaviours of stereotypical masculinity. Here, masculinity becomes a means of rendering social relations manageable, not a means for disclosing intimacies' (Whitehead 2002: 174).

Using a feminized model of what emotionality is, or should be about, Whitehead (2002) explores these issues around men, masculinities, intimacy and the emotions through focusing on a problematization of the public/private divide, particularly in relation to work in comparison to home life. He concludes that feelings of love and anxiety are not easily abandoned as men move between home and work. Similarly, intimate relations are not produced solely in the private world. However, he notes this public/private dualism has not been that much explored in relation to areas such as leisure. It is my argument that a focus on male friendships in the context of an extreme sport can expand on the limited theorizing of the emotions and intimacy that has been done in a sociological sense. Consequently, this adds to, and sometimes critiques those studies already carried out on men and friendships in diverse sporting sites, often done from a masculinity studies perspective. Indeed, as de Garris (2000) argues, the study of ageing has been absent from such accounts.

My interviewees' accounts of their climbing friendships support Messner's (2001) view, that the claim that men in sporting situations bond without any intimacy is not substantiated. Further, men's subjective sense of self can be seen to be wrapped up in their climbing friendships, and, therefore, the possibility of change to their subjectivities through a connection to others must be seen as a possibility. In addition, the idea that men are emotionally inarticulate is not borne out by my interviewees either. For example, a large number of the climbers spoke of having most, and sometimes all of their friendships, within climbing circles. Even when out with well-known climbers or those much more accomplished than themselves, they considered that true friendships have been forged out of shared, extreme sporting experiences

Davidson et al. (2003) point out that a number of theorists have argued that women and men 'do' friendships differently. They also draw upon Webster (1995) so that, for men, identity is seen to precede intimacy, whereas for women these aspects are coincidental. Moreover, Miller (1983) has asserted that most men are disappointed in their male friendships which are defined by men as being 'thin' or insincere. Further, Davidson et al. (2003: 174) use qualitative data to conclude that 'men, throughout their life course, may have had reduced opportunity to pursue intimate relationships.' They also argue that over the life course, men's friendships are generally forged and maintained in the workplace. Whilst, outside of work, friendships are made through social clubs, sports and other leisure situations, which are characterized by: 'side-by-side sociability, focusing on activity and often on competitive pursuits' (Davidson et al. 2003: 182).

However, in my study, one climber in his forties, when asked if he took up the sport because it offered opportunities to compete or the chance of encountering danger or risk, replied, 'It wasn't, no. It was mainly the friendship and the, you know, being part of a group.' This attitude is contrary to ideas that sport is a place where hegemonic masculinities are constructed and performed through a celebration of danger, risk and competition. It also opposes a view that extreme sports, in particular, can be seen to represent an exemplary masculinity where men are in control and supremely confident, sovereign over themselves and superior because of this (Kusz 2004). For this man, having gone through a troubled adolescence and now entering early middle age, the primary attraction was the camaraderie and friendship network that climbing afforded. However, as Kusz also notes, this is often a *white* masculinity. Furthermore, in contrast, Davidson et al.'s (2003) conclusion that older men attach much importance to individual autonomy and independence, as well as holding ambivalent attitudes to features of the 'female script', such as a need for intimacy and social engagement, could also be borne out in other climbers' accounts of their friendships. This could be seen in the comments of an ex-climber, now 61, who had suffered a brain haemorrhage and who spoke with some regret about the subsequent loss of sporting friendships:

> There were probably two or three people who I saw increasingly less of, and I see almost nothing of now, because the only point of contact was climbing. I mean, there are others that I see a lot of, but there was more to the relationship than climbing.

As I have already noted, Wheeton's (2000b, 2004a) study of different groups of men within the sport of windsurfing, found that men's relationships in a sporting culture varied because of age and socio-economic background and thus, in relation to status. The 'laddish' culture at the core of this community was rejected by some of the participants, especially the professional, middle class and more educated men. For many of the men though, camaraderie and social-izing were a major part of the windsurfing experience. Further, the non-elite men in her study were, overall, less competitive and more supportive of each other than the elite participants. Though Wheaton also acknowledges that even at the subculture's core, the elite men displayed aspects of behaviour which had parallels with the non-elite. In comparison, this climber, in his thirties, would not classify himself as an elite climber, although he climbs with some of the best climbers of his generation:

> Some of them are really good at motivating me, well, one or two individuals, even though they're obviously infinitely better than me. They're friends and you're just out there enjoying yourself climbing, and sometimes I climb a lot better because of that ... you know, there is some ego, esteem and that kind of thing.

This account of climbing with the elite, which fostered his friendship *and* motivated him to climb better, reveals that non-elite climbers can also have a need to achieve and perform well. But, more than this, the example again com-plicates Wheaton's picture of the different subgroups in an extreme sport. For it is only through looking at interactions *between* different subgroups when these groups cross over, as well as relationships within them, that a more complex picture of male friendship emerges.

The same non-elite climber further demonstrates this complexity, when describing a dangerous climbing situation he was in with an elite climber:

> He was just as shit scared as me. But, it was not that I was like, 'Oh great, Jake's scared.' It was, 'Oh, Jake's scared like I am.' People all suffer from the same frail-ties, and sometimes you don't see that ... When you actually know a lot of the people involved quite well, and over a long time, you know their frailties, so there's less of the sort of admiring and hero worship.

In fact, this recognition of shared frailties cements their friendship because the elite climber's fear is not construed negatively here but rather in terms that make the difference in their climbing abilities (and any competition which could ensue from this) of *secondary* importance to their intimate friendship. Further, any notion of awe that might derive from climbing with a 'celebrity' is eschewed, because of their long term friendship and the intimate knowledge gained through this. In this sense, climbing can be seen to be a different sport from more organized and traditional sports, such as football. It would be inconceiv-able for, say, a Sunday League football player to find himself on the same pitch as Beckham or Ronaldinho, and rarely would those different kinds of footballers even find themselves in the same social situation. As one climber said generally about 'famous' climbers, 'You're going to come across them at the same kind of venues. The social event thing is, it's a small sport, you know.' Thus, these everyday experiences which are outside of the sporting context *per se*, inform the friendships that are formed at the rock face between elite climbers and the non-elite. These shared spaces entail that, potentially, different groups of climbers can be more intimately inter-active and inclusive. In this way, ability is only one measure of how sporting sub-groups form. However, that is not to say that sub-groups will not form in any case on ability grounds but there is certainly more opportunity for friendships *across* groups to develop in climbing circles, than with some other sports.

## 'Extreme' Trust?

Whitehead (2002), discusses trust in terms of such transformatory conditions as individualization in Western societies. He argues that where old orders are seen to be breaking, new trust systems will then emerge, and he asks, 'In short, what part will gender play in facilitating or disrupting trust and, thus, ontological security and wider social mechanisms?' (Whitehead 2002: 171). Moreover, his assertion that trust will have no small part to play in facilitating or disrupting any negotiations between gendered groups and individuals can usefully be explored in relation to male climbing friendships. How does, for instance, the environment of rock climbing allow men to show their trust in other men? How are their friendships effected by the need to both display trust in a climbing partner and to be oneself a trusted 'belayer' or 'second'? Can friendships formed through intense and sometimes extraordinary situations, be seen to challenge traditional and masculine ways of 'doing' friendships and gender relations, more generally?

I have already established the fact that a number of theorists have argued that men don't 'do' friendships in the same way that women do. However, as Whitehead (2002) argues with the idea of men not being able to be as intimate with others or show emotions such as vulnerability, we must be careful not to confuse the ideology with reality. (Or, indeed, fail to problematize the ideology itself as gendered.) How, then, does the sport of climbing afford men a space to reveal sides to their character they may not be comfortable doing in more 'ordinary' situations of everyday life? One man, aged 28, spoke about his experiences of trusting other male climbers:

> I think you're quite right about that safety element and the fact that, you know, 'You looked after me' plays an element as well. And, there's a lot of bonding that goes on. It doesn't necessarily need to be a particularly hard climb, but I mean, if the weather changes, if you're on a long route and you get soaking wet through … I think those kinds of experiences always help kind of cement friendships.

The climb undertaken does not have to be especially difficult, or even risky, for a close and intimate friendship to develop, as this data shows. Everyday experiences, such as getting soaked by rain, can help foster a good friendship. Thus, a conception of traditional male friendship that may be seen to be formed and bolstered through elements of competition or bravado, does not explain this climbers' account of his intimate relationships with other men.

However, some of the climbers also appear to see 'real' intimacy occurring in other and 'more extreme' sporting contexts, such as mountaineering, where trust is assumed to be greater because of the perceived risk involved. For instance, one climber, in his thirties, commented that:

> ... if you're doing a big route in the Lakes, you need a partner more. And you want someone you can climb reliably with, and you know absolutely you can trust and you know their strengths. Whereas, when you're climbing round here you just need someone to hold your rope, and the routes are not long and you don't have to be able to navigate down by torch.

In this instance, authenticity of trust is measured by the extremity of the situation in which the climbers are involved. It also reveals that trust is perceived and negotiated in different ways, depending on whether the climbing experience is rated extreme, or more mundane.

Similarly, a climber in his twenties, found it very important to talk at length to convey the complexity of his feelings about his male climbing friendships. At different stages of the interview he also revealed that friendships can be fostered through the mundane *and* extreme aspects of the sporting experience. Initially, he said:

> Oh, God, yes, trust is absolutely crucial. I've got lots of good mates that aren't climbers as well, but, I'm not as close to them as my climbing mates emotionally. Maybe that's because, you know, when you climb with somebody you do spend time on ledges together, or driving to the crag, or driving up to wherever you're going.

In his account of long term climbing friendships, he sees trust as a 'crucial' element, but what is interesting is the way he chooses to talk about and illustrate this. This is not through accounts of nights spent freezing on mountain tops, or tales of 'derring-do' that dominate popular and media accounts of climbing partnerships, as in the book (Simpson 1988) and film (2003) of *Touching the Void* but through the mundane activities of sitting on a ledge, perhaps waiting for others to finish their climbs, for instance. It is in and through these ordinary and usually undocumented moments of mundane activities in climbers' accounts, that occur over a period of time, sometimes even years, that he feels able to talk about relationships with other men. Later in the interview, he continued:

> ... we talk far more about how we are and what's going on in our relationships than I ever do with any of my other mates, like I say, that I go down to the pub with ... My mates that are not climbers, definitely are not actually very good at talking normally about their emotions.

Thus, he contradicts Messner's (2001) notion of men's covert intimacy, which is seen as a 'doing' intimacy and is not achieved through talking. But when pressed on this, and asked if intimacy was sometimes attained through the extreme, and not the mundane situations he had previously described, he said:

> If you put yourself into dangerous situations in any walk of life, with people, you tend to see sides of them that you perhaps wouldn't again if you just went down to the pub, or, certainly that you don't see in a working environment. So, if you are on a hard route and you manage to climb it, or even if you don't and you abseil off and all's safe and good, when you get back, you've had a really strong, shared experience.

Therefore, being in a situation of potential danger where trust has been a major factor in creating and sustaining a climbing relationship, entailed that characteristics not usually seen in 'every day' life had surfaced. It is also a trust that has meaning because it evolves over time and. in contrast to his earlier comments, when trust was seen in terms of shared mundane experiences, it is the extraordinary context of climbing which allows this to flourish. This is further given meaning by his emphasis on, and contrast to, the everyday world of work. In one sense, this evidence does not support Whitehead's (2002) assertion that friendships can appear less demanding than relationships. The same climber's friendships are partnerships which have taken hard work and effort to sustain, so that these men are able to be comfortable in a situation where absolute trust is a necessity, 'I think it's also important that [they hold you]. Let's face it, if they drop you or whatever, I mean you fall off. So, you've got to know somebody well and, I think you get that when you climb with them.' Instead, Pahl (2000) and Whitehead's (2002) suggestion, that it is friendship, not coupledom, which will come to provide the most constancy for people's relationships, has some purchase for these male sporting relations. Conversely, as I revealed in Chapter 5, men's close climbing friendships do indeed have the capacity to cause tension and resentment in heterosexual couple relationships. Thus, in this context, the evidence supports Whitehead's argument, that

> Whether based around straight, gay, white or black identities, men's friendships with other men can be seen to be crucially important in sustaining masculine subjectivities and men's sense of identity as men. In addition, recognizing this does not take us very far from the earlier point made by Seidler that men's same-sex friendships very rarely provide the possibilities for social transformations between women and men. (Whitehead 2002: 158–9)

Moreover, the views of the female partner of the previous climber cited complicate the picture he drew of his male climbing friendships even further:

> I was thinking when you were asking about that male bonding. It's really clear to me that when he goes away, he doesn't feel if he hasn't climbed with one of these

close friends, that he's not got back in touch with them. Whereas, I feel that I need to have one to one time with a close friend, and we really need to talk ... There is a difference there, where, I think with my girlfriends this could be in other situations.

She feels that he does not necessarily need to have the 'one to one time' that she considers important with her close friends to be able to maintain the relationships. In addition, and unlike her male partner, her close, female friendships develop and are sustained in diverse situations outside of a climbing context. So whilst it may be that it is potentially through the mundane activities associated with rock climbing, and not necessarily the 'extreme' elements of the sport that foster male friendships and intimate relations, her view is that such male closeness does not flourish in everyday life, for instance, at work. In this sense, her comments can be seen as a gendering of what actually constitutes intimacy for both sexes.

## Conclusion

From the evidence I have presented in this chapter, it is clear that in the context of rock climbing, men's displays of emotion, characterized by the interviewees' willingness to display their feelings and to allow themselves to be 'out of control', as well as their capacity to trust other men and to form sporting friendships, is apparent. In this sense, the data revealed that, far from men not being able to 'do intimacy' as some theorists of men and masculinities have argued, many of these climbers feel that their closest and most intimate times with other men are forged at the rock face. This may be in extreme situations, as the climbers who spoke about friends who had died in climbing accidents demonstrated, through a capacity to reveal how much the loss of friendship had meant to them. However, the climbers in the study also revealed that it is through the mundane, ordinary situations attendant with the everyday practices of rock climbing, that deep and lasting friendships may also be fostered. Although, for some men this did not translate into other friendships – with male work colleagues, for example. Women's voices are pertinent here, when they speak of men 'doing' friendships differently from the perceived stereotype of men's superficial attempts at intimacy but also tell of men not being able to always move this intimacy over into the mundane and everyday world. What is more, the friendships that men form through the practices of this extreme sport are usually white and, though certainly not exclusively, are often also middle class in constitution, as well as predominantly heterosexual.

Further, if we look at sources outside of sociological discourses, for instance in climbing literature, we find that male climbers still, in the main, have difficulty in expressing emotion in the public sphere. Perhaps because, as Gifford (2006) has argued, it is too much associated with being 'out of control'. There is evidence though, of men starting to be able to reflect publicly on their climbing experiences, through the prose of climbers and mountaineers such as Simpson (1996), Cave, (2005) and Pritchard (1999), the latter case having been discussed in this chapter. However, that is not to say that earlier generations have not been openly reflexive about their sporting, emotional experiences (see Craig 1988). In addition, for elite climbers, it is usually through an extreme incident, such as a near-fatal climbing accident, or another life-changing experience, which both allows them to do this and to receive public recognition and endorsement from the climbing community. These extraordinary feats are something that Heywood (2006) has described as part of the resistance in the sport of climbing to any risk of conventionality, or responsibility. However, my data has shown that these tendencies can coexist with the more mundane world of everyday practices. The next chapter develops in more depth some of the issues raised here, where it has been demonstrated that any individual 'sporting project' cannot be divorced from how men manage the everyday worlds of relationships and work, over the life course.

**CHAPTER 7**

# The Sporting Balance: Family, Relationships and Work

## Introduction

Haywood and Mac an Ghaill (2003) argue that studies of masculinity and class might be fruitful if they moved away from privileging workplace practices as defining men to the broader cultural practices that men take up. A parallel point can be made about sporting masculinities, where I have already argued that a theoretical and empirical focus needs to be directed not just to the contradictory experiences of the sporting participants themselves, but to the wider relationships that make up their everyday lives as workers, parents, partners and lovers. By seeing the 'bigger picture' we are able to have a more fine-grained analysis of how people embody, perform and feel about gendered relations and identities. Additionally, any deviation from or adherence to, traditional gendered roles and identities, can then be re-assessed. As I noted in Chapter 2, the idea of 'transition' is a concept in this endeavour.

In Robinson et al. (2007), I implicitly argued that studies of the identity category 'masculinity' account for its performance in both private and public spheres. However, men's transition between them has been neglected. Whether conceptual or empirical, a division between sport, for instance and 'everyday life' represented by work, relationships and the family, is reproduced in much sports studies literature, which continues to imagine them as 'separate spheres'. How they combine remains an issue about which we know little, from the perspectives of men, or, indeed the women, who are connected to men's lives in different ways. By investigating the experience of men of different ages, we can ask whether masculinities and femininities are now less centrally defined by difference. For example, in Chapter 5, my data was used to ask whether the sporting lives of women and men might be converging – and here, I address what scope men of different ages might have for reframing traditional or hegemonic masculinity. These issues are of use in exploring sporting masculinities across the life course.

Identity, as argued in Chapter 4, was understood as processual, always under negotiation, never 'finished' and the outcome of ongoing performance (Jenkins 2004). What I have been considering through my exploration of different kinds of climbers, based on skill level and age, for example, are different performances of masculine identities, a concept that is now well established in theoretical work on masculinity. What interested me in Robinson et al. (2007), however, was the notion that the practice or 'doing' of masculinity (Morgan 1992) might vary not just between men, but within the same man as his social context changes. I asked how social context – the workplace and the home – operates to give particular form to the identity category 'masculinity' and how individuals moving between contexts manage their identities. Further, while I accepted the view that there is indeed a plurality of gendered identities, how they actually come into being is less well understood. Masculinity, therefore, because of this transition, or mobility, between spheres, was located at an unstable place. Consequently, we can see how masculinity might become subject to doubt, reinvention or reinforcement as men's relationships with home, family and work undergo change.

Therefore, in this chapter, I am centrally concerned with finding out how male climbers of different ages and sporting abilities understood any transitions they were experiencing – for instance, as they become older and work and/or relationships become more central to their lives. I will explore if, and how, events such as impending or actual fatherhood reveal the extent to which their strategies for managing such changes represented any reformulations of their masculinity. I will also consider the degree to which men discover themselves shifting between potentially contradictory forms of masculinity, as they move out of the sporting world of rock climbing and into a domestic, or work environment. If a male climbers' contextual sense of who he is (and who he is not), serves to illuminate further the issue of masculine identification as being seen as processual and essentially incomplete, then the interviews with female partners of male rock climbers can reveal the ways in which other people identify and categorize men, revealing contradictions between male accounts of identification and how their performances in different spheres may be interpreted differently by someone else. By comparing men's performances of masculinity as they move across and between, sport, work and the public spheres as well as private domestic spaces, it is then these shifts of emphasis that can provide a nuanced, situated account of the processes of masculine identification. In this chapter, some of the practices through which traditional, socially and emotionally distanced masculinities may be either reproduced or reappraised, are made visible through the male climbers' accounts in my study and the voices from other sources, including mountaineers and adventurers.

It is true to say that the public sphere has traditionally been seen as more essential to masculine identification. Collinson and Hearn (1996), for example, describe how particular workplace cultures have an appeal to those masculine values of aggression, individualism and competition. Therefore, paid work, politics and leisure are often seen as integral to the practice of masculinity. As I noted in the previous chapter, in reality, however, the separation of public and domestic spheres is blurred, as emotions and work practices produce slippage between them. Whitehead (2002) has problematized the notion of a distinct public/private divide, arguing that it is not compartmentalized at the level of the emotions: 'feelings of anger, frustration, love, anxiety and passion are not easily switched off as we physically move from home to work and vice versa' (Whitehead 2002: 117). The rethinking of this dichotomy in different and largely unexplored ways is central to my project here on sporting masculinities. So, too, is a consideration of male negotiation of identity across the life course. Calasanti (2003) explores how intersections between age and gender relations shape 'manhood' over a person's life and in old age. He also argues that studies on ageing have ignored manhood, whereas theories of men and masculinities could be seen to have mainly omitted a life course view, especially in relation to older men. Here, the climbers' various relationships to others – at home and in a sporting context, for example – reveal that gender identity negotiations both develop and are complex, across the life course. In this way, a historical dimension is brought into the analysis, through an acknowledgement that the older rock climbers discussed in the study, are not only older, but have also lived through different historical times (see Hareven 2000).

Lastly, as discussed in Chapter 2, when I started this project, I had initially conceived of rock climbing as an extraordinary activity in the context of the everyday, with the extreme being seen as part of the extraordinary. Rock climbing was a pursuit, undertaken I thought, to escape the ordinary through engaging in risky and extreme sporting activities. Indeed, some climbers' testimonies about the reasons they climb do uphold this dichotomy. However, subsequently, through my interviews and data analysis, I have come to problematize this approach and the assumptions underpinning it, seeing it as only part of the picture for these climbers' sporting trajectories, indeed, rejecting the implied binary.

The concept of 'mundane extremities' emphasizes the utility of looking at the everyday practices of men in specific sporting environments, to investigate what the extreme reveals about both shifting masculinities across the life course, as well as the reconceptualization of the boundaries of the mundane and the extreme. Many of the men I interviewed either stated, or implied, that wanting to escape the mundane by doing something extreme had to be continually worked at, with the result that relationships and family responsibilities were seen as necessities when they got older and could not climb as hard or as often. Engaging with the more mundane aspects of life, represented by paid work, for example, their position in relation to the extreme needed to be reinvented. This was done, for instance, by climbing ever harder routes, or climbers engaging in more and more potentially risky activities such as big wall climbing abroad (see Chapter 9 on risk). Further, the extreme continually shaded into the mundane.

So, if climbing as a pursuit is often taken up to put the rest of the world in perspective, or to escape the ordinariness of much of everyday living, the mundane and the extreme shifted considerably through the life course for some of these male climbers. Such transitions were not always desired or easy, for example, when getting older did not allow them to climb at the level they had been used to. The embracing of the ordinary was seen as a necessity, not necessarily a welcome choice or act of agency as I explore later in this chapter. Conversely, other men embraced the routines of a family or steady relationship or job, and characterized as obsessive the wholesale pursuit of the sport, into middle age. Thus, the everyday was reinvigorated by a reflexive reconceptualizing of the world of the extraordinary and how it effected the mundane. Thus, Chaney's (2002) view, that we need to be aware of the boundaries between everyday life and the extraordinary and how they are negotiated, is of use here for a more complex understanding of how the extreme and the mundane are inextricably bound together.

## The Wider Picture: Relationships and Family

For the men in my study, as they got older, being in more settled heterosexual relationships, and/or having children were turning points for how they related to the sport of climbing. For example, in terms of climbing continuing or not continuing to be a focus for their lives, or the amount of time they either wanted to give or were able to give the sport. Their reflections as partners, or fathers, cast light on gendered relations in general. Indeed, climbers sometimes expected others to lose their interest in sport because of impending parenthood, for instance, as this female climber in her early thirties demonstrates, when talking about climbing friends, 'Gary and Sophie, for instance, mates of ours, are both pure focused on climbing. But, they're not anymore, 'cause they're just about to have a kid. That's gonna be fascinating, 'cause Gary's, like, an obsessional climber.'

For others, as with this mountaineer, aged 55, it was the importance of his bread winner position as a mountain guide, that was a major feature in any decision made about how often to climb:

> I mean, I couldn't have done that full-time instruction without the long Alpine season, 12–14 weeks, and you make your money, to be brutal about it. So I couldn't, we couldn't have survived as a family, not enough money to start with, without that fourteen weeks. So, when the kids were very young, my wife would come with me. Of course, as the kids got older, I couldn't then as it was just so darn expensive to take them all.

Economic necessity entailed that the geographical distance between this man and his family caused an emotional distance, which was more acute as his children got older. Another climber, aged 50, when asked how he balanced climbing with family responsibilities, revealed the ebb and flow of tension in relationships and at different stages of the life course:

> I think there was a tension developing when I was younger, when I was still climbing and mountaineering and I'd just got married. That was because, I s'pose, my wife wanted more time with me and I was still committed to a lot of things.

But now, my kids have grown up, my wife has a fairly independent lifestyle of her own and so it's not, it's not an issue, really.

However, he contradicts himself, when he later said: 'Some people ask me, are you ever gonna' go out in the mountains again ... just not got the time and the opportunity and the money. I've got three kids. I don't go away now. I mean I used to go away for three and four months at a time.' Initially, he stated that there was no longer any tension in his relationship, but then implies, that in reality, he regrets the fact that he cannot go mountaineering because of his continuing family responsibilities. Thus, he maintains an illusion for himself of freedom and agency, in regard to decisions made over any sporting investment. However, the balance between his climbing pursuits and his family life are more complicated than he acknowledges. This balancing act could be seen in a number of the climbers' accounts in a need to manage their home life with continuing climbing aspirations. Perhaps the illusion of having the freedom to pursue climbing activities was necessary, for some men, to be able to take on the roles of responsible father and partner. In contrast to this, some of the interviewees also referred in derogatory terms to the spectacle of the middle-aged climber, who continued to have nothing in his life *but* climbing. When this 44-year-old man, an elite and well-known climber in his youth, was asked about whether his attitude towards climbing had changed, as he had aged, he reflected:

I mean in some ways I do find it quite puzzling. Some people who are quite, like old, seem to be so into climbing. It does seem almost like they haven't grown up. I wouldn't think that if they were crazy about climbing and they did other things ... I'm glad I'm not just obsessed with climbing anymore.

As well as feeling that climbing could not 'fulfil everything', as he got older, he also commented on those climbers for whom the sport was 'everything'. Especially those who are: '... still trying to be Peter Pan. When you're still thinking about doing this route at the weekend, and you're like 40 odd, and it's more interesting to you than your wife and kids, or your job, or whatever. I think it's a bit weird.'

If the ageing, 'Peter Pan' figure was constructed as an object of pity by some, there was also an ambiguity expressed by those who no longer climbed, or at least not at the level that they used to. The same middle-aged man made comments throughout the interview about his weight gain and lack of former fitness. Despite his now being a successful business man, he admits to still wanting the excitement which climbing had given him: 'When you get older, you need a bit of it, everybody needs a bit of that kind of thing in their life, don't they?' And, as an older climber, who was less fit and body conscious than in his youth, and who had exchanged the extreme thrills of climbing for running his own business, he looked back nostalgically on youthful climbing exploits. Moreover, another middle-aged climber spoke of his 'halcyon days' of climbing well, days out at the crags and the 'craic' of being with his mates who shared a similar lifestyle and philosophy. He did not talk about the mundane aspects of work and his family with the same enthusiasm as he did for climbing. He did, however, perceive a need to be a responsible partner and father, as his body aged and his past climbing glories had faded (see Chapter 8 for further discussion of climbing bodies). These shifts need to be placed in a context of changing gendered relations in general. For example, this can be seen in the expectations on men to be a new type of father figure, as well as the increased likelihood of women contributing to the family wage, which entails new responsibilities for men in the home. Further, the notion of an obsession with climbing was acceptable for this man when in his youth, but was seen as something that needed to be tempered with age. For those who remain consumed with climbing when they have a family, this was something that was only possible with the support of others, often female partners who took more share of child care and domestic work than their male climbing partner.

## Sporting Negotiations

Some of the climbers spoke in depth about whether and how climbing affected their relationships with their partners and how they were then negotiated for the duration of their climbing career. Such reflections were revealing of gender relations. In addition, they also brought out differences between the generations in terms of the acceptance shown, for instance, of climbers being away from home on trips, or being so occupied by the pursuit that it defined, and sometimes limited, those relationships. One female participant, in her thirties, when asked if she thought that excessive climbing had ever caused relationships to end, reflected on her own partnership: 'That was always a worry of Rod's, early on in our relationship, that it would be climbing that would split us up. Because he'd seen it in other relationships, though, I think a lot of men aren't aware of that, or the impact that it has.' Certainly, this young climber, aged 22, declared confidently, 'I've just got a girlfriend and she doesn't climb at all but, erm, I don't think that's affected my climbing whatsoever.' His concern, therefore, was more about whether his relationship effected his climbing, rather than whether the pursuit of climbing had an impact on the relationship! Other climbers, with more experience of relationships, had reflected in greater depth on this issue. This was sometimes from bitter experience and sometimes from a reflexive self-knowledge, as this man, in his twenties, revealed:

> I mean, fundamentally, climbing is a very selfish thing, you know, like it's you and your journey. But, within a relationship that's about understanding each other's values and how they want to spend time, but also giving up some of it. But I've never really had a serious relationship before, largely because I haven't been willing to sacrifice for it, and that's been the deal. Fine, nobody gets hurt. But, recently I've met somebody who I get on with really well. She climbs, but she's

also a surfer, so like you say, strong, independent. So, you totally get to do your own thing, but sometimes you do things together as well.

He has sufficient self-awareness to recognize the selfishness inherent in seriously pursuing climbing, or, for that matter, any sport when the individual concerned is both skilled and ambitious, as he is. Thus, he does not fit the stereotype of the unreflexive climber who is not aware of the effect that adopting a climbing lifestyle can have on a relationship – for instance, by choosing to spend holiday periods on climbing trips with male friends, or only reluctantly giving up their climbing activities to be with the family. In this way, decisions taken about an extreme pursuit had consequences for men's (and women's) roles in the private sphere. Another climber, aged 39, spoke of his relationship with his partner in terms of a 'trade off' in that previously, he had, 'put climbing first and everything else would come second, including my relationship. That's probably jeopardised relationships in the past. Whereas, as I got older, I realised I wanted a serious relationship, so realised that I would have to compromise the climbing.' However, he felt that, 'I've definitely gained more than I've lost.' Therefore, he saw the compromises he had made to be worth it. Others reached a satisfactory compromise only after protracted and sometimes painful discussion, over time.

With this elite climber, in his early forties, it was not until the start of early middle age that he realised climbing was not fulfilling all his needs, and he considered changing his habits: 'I needed to sort of stop having climbing as the motivating reason for being alive. I don't want it controlling me too much ... but I just wasn't really getting the thing out of it that I wanted anymore, you know?' For him, failed relationships were acceptable in his youth (indeed, climbing could be seen as *the* successful relationship) because he 'always had climbing to fall back on' when the 'mundane' aspects of life were not working out. His comments also revealed a particular conceptualization of heterosexuality in that it is only when he 'ended up falling in love, that provided a new catalyst, like a fresh start'. On becoming part of an established couple, he felt the need to reassess his involvement in sporting pursuits. Rather than rejecting climbing altogether though, when his participation proved problematic with the onset of a new, and serious relationship, he has worked through it to a kind of 'balance'. This was something achieved however, when his female partner also engaged in a process of self-awareness, 'She's learnt from me that she needs to find something for herself, rather than just worrying about children.' Thus, over the life course, the activity of climbing only continued to make sense for him when his everyday, 'mundane' relationship was in harmony with his (extreme) sporting, masculine self. Furthermore, it is only through an understanding of gender relations in the everyday, which include arguments and self-searching between couples, as well as the needs and psychic development of non-climbing partners, that we can start to fully comprehend sporting masculinities across the life course. Focusing on male climbers' shifting positions to the mundane world of partners and relationships, and their continuous and changing interaction with the extraordinary world of climbing, allows us to see how a climber's life trajectory is sometimes one of struggle and renegotiation with those close to him.

Exploring how these interactions are carried out across the generations can also allow a reconceptualization of the worlds of the mundane and the extreme. For instance, the mountaineer father, aged in his fifties, of a son, in his early twenties, who also climbs, expressed amusement at his son's girlfriend's attitude to his climbing:

> I mean, I sort of, er, smile rather unkindly, but my lad can't do anything without almost getting permission. He always, sort of, fights against that. He says, 'I want to go off and be with me mates, in the pub.' And I say, 'Well, why, why don't you?' 'Oh, I'll get grief.' I go, 'Oh, right.' Older, wiser, you see all these things.

Yet the father has also had to renegotiate his relationship with his own wife. Previously, because of having to go on climbing expeditions, he spent little time at home. However, he and his wife now take separate holidays out of choice, not necessity. In this, he illustrates Smith's (2000) work on British non-elite road runners. He argues that they often approach middle age with more independent teenage children and also find themselves having to negotiate a more egalitarian relationship with their partner, who has, perhaps, emerged from the burdens of child care and wants more leisure time for herself. It is also possible to read the young woman's refusal to accept his son's going out without her 'permission' as more typical of a current generation of women who are not as used to putting men's needs and pursuit of leisure, before their own.

In contrast, evidence from older women and men interviewees, in their seventies, reveals a more complex picture. A male climber, aged 73, spoke about his wife's attitude to his long climbing career:

> She's always been wonderful really. She's never, ever stopped me from doing what I want to do. I went to the Dolomites climbing for three weeks. My friend would have given his eye teeth to go, but his wife put her foot down. There was, you know, a lot of friction for probably six months.

It might be assumed that his wife was of a generation of women that put their husband's interests and pursuits, above her own. However, when questioned about her attitude towards her husband's climbing, she said, 'I'm always of the opinion, I don't own him and if that's what he wants to do, it doesn't matter.'

Further, in spite of the worry when he is absent, she feels his going away on climbing trips has added to their relationship. However, whether he would have been so understanding if it was her leaving him behind does not, of course, arise as an issue, given the inherent assumption that she would look after the home and family whilst he was away. Another older climber, aged 59, was more thoughtful on the implications for partners and families left behind when male partners went on trips: 'I have had doubts about climbing. I think anybody whose climbed as long as I have and lost friends in the mountains, you've actually seen the cost and the pain and misery that it's brought to people, families and friends.' However, he later spoke about his own selfishness in wanting to climb, when he said, 'I think you have to be sometimes, if you want to live your dreams.'

Whether leaving behind family responsibilities or relationships for longer periods, on a mountaineering expedition for instance, or for more sporadic amounts of time with a weekend of climbing, both can be viewed as either irresponsible, or acceptable, if an individual is pursuing dreams. These themes have recently been discussed in the literature on other extreme pursuits. The writer, Jonathan Raban, who set out to write about a voyage to Alaska, charted his marriage breakup instead. Writing about his relationship with his young daughter when leaving for the trip, he says:

> She squirmed behind me on the top stair and pressed her face into the small of my back. 'I kiss you', she said, measuring each word, 'because I love you. But I won't mind when you're not there. I'll be glad'. She was talking like a grown up, her words at war with her face. I'd always known that it would come, of course, but never thought it could come so early – this milestone moment when parent and child first find themselves speaking to each other through protective masks. 'Julia, I have to go. It's my work – it's what I do so we can all live here in this house. I'll be thinking of you everyday, and I'll be home soon I promise. (Raban 1999: 1)

This response to his daughter's 'protective mask' could be seen as justification for his desire to travel to far flung places, so that his position as male breadwinner in the family, and, therefore, the one responsible for putting a roof over his family's head, is seen to legitimize his leaving. However, Raban's reflection on the consequences of his leaving his family behind does reveal anguish over his actions. The men in my study could be seen to justify their climbing decisions in similar ways to Raban, but they also cited other reasons. For example, that female partners did not 'own them', or, couched in terms of a romantic individualism, that they were 'pursuing their dreams', and, that climbing as a sport was seen to be 'good for you', as well as for the balance of any relationship. Mick Fowler, who is a 'deskbound' taxman and also one of the world's most successful mountaineers, admitted in a published interview (Cooper 2005), that it is a tricky balance between family and climbing holidays. His female partner, in the same interview, said, 'It's never easy when Mick goes away, knowing all too well the dangers and remoteness he faces in the Himalaya … But having been there myself, I understand why he needs to fulfil his urges in the mountains' (Cooper 2005: 2). However, some partnerships centred around climbing are not so balanced, as Maria Coffey's work (2003, 2004) establishes.

Coffey (2004), reflecting on her relationship with the mountaineer Joe Tasker, who disappeared whilst climbing Everest, writes:

The mountains were his biggest passion, and I had to fit in where and when I could. He claimed that he made no demands on me, and therefore, by default, I could ask little of him – no commitment, no promises, and precious little shared time. I suppose that in the long run it was more honest than making plans for babies, a house and growing old together, but it left me feeling hopelessly insecure. (Coffey 2004: 142)

In comparison, many of the women she details in her book who were left behind by their mountaineering partners, are strong and resourceful. Her opinion is that a new breed of mountaineer may be emerging, one that is more aware of a need to balance family commitments with travelling, and whose existence can be seen to challenge the view that men who don't exercise caution in the mountains, are heroic. However, she relates the views of a female partner of a climber, thus: '... all the climbers, they pursued a passion which was above their responsibility and love for their family, and which took precedence' (Coffey 2004: 141). And, in so doing, Coffey reveals that for women placed in this situation, some have no choice but to accept the relegation of the mundane world of family and partnerships to a lesser and more ignoble sphere, in contrast to the extreme pursuit of climbing with its attendant, life-threatening adventures.

Evidence, however, of Coffey's new breed of mountaineer, is to be found in the account of an internationally famous climber Adam Todhunter, in the US-based *Rock and Ice* magazine in 1998. He describes how the thought of impending parenthood made him choose to end his climbing career:

As I clung to an overhang, and imagined the baby, then small enough to fit in my closed palm, I felt painfully exposed ... I suspected, with the confirmation of this life in utero, my personal exemption from disaster had expired. My luck was up, and the angels had diverted their attentions to the child. 'Get down', said a voice. 'Get down.' There is danger here and it does not serve.

In my study, a number of the interviewees did go on long trips, when, for example, their work as mountain guides required this. However, for many of the female partners interviewed the tension came not so much from the occasional long climbing trip abroad made without them but, in fact, was borne out of the niggles and built-up frustrations caused by the frequency and longevity of the absences of men pursuing a climbing lifestyle. It was the mundane issues of contention – the lost weekends, the enthusiasm shown by partners for climbing and not family pursuits, for instance – that rankled.

How far then do such shifts in male subjectivities contest Whitehead's view (2002) that self-recognition for men as subjects continues to come from work, the pub, the football ground, the golf club, management meeting, salesroom, or office, and not the family and home? Certainly, some climbers continued to derive their primary sense of self from climbing, and this did sometimes cause conflict, if it was seen as desirable that instead, they spend more time with partners or on childcare, for example. Alternatively, as Simon Yates, a British mountaineer illustrates in reviewing his chosen climbing lifestyle: 'For many years, I had never made much effort when it came to getting girlfriends, perhaps because I was so preoccupied with climbing and forever on the move. Not surprisingly, my relationships were infrequent and usually brief' (Yates 2002: 126). Yet, some men I interviewed underwent a sea change at different points in the life course – for instance, when a child was about to be born, or when they no longer climbed at the standard they used to. Or, further, when they looked back and reflected on a climbing career after undergoing life's more 'mundane' experiences. How then can such shifts in men's subjectivities and, sometimes their behaviour, be explained?

## Life Course Transitions: The Work–Sporting Balance

With Hockey (forthcoming), in relation to my work on masculinities in transition across the life course, I draw upon Brannen and Nilsen (2002), to allow the problematization of arguments that the modern, standardized life course has been superseded by a postmodern heterogeneity of individualized 'planning projects' (Beck-Gernsheim, cited in Brannen and Nilsen 2002: 515). Instead, I argue, young people in our study of men in different occupations were caught between these two approaches to planning their futures. Further, I note in this context how fluid processes of classification and transition between phases often seem to characterize the contemporary Western life course (Hockey and James 2003). The shifting economic and social conditions of late modernity have, arguably, eroded 'traditional' social systems, bringing scope for individual choice and innovation (see Giddens 1991). Though, alongside these changes, there exists standardization and chronologization persisting within people's perceptions of their lives, for example, in the numerical marking of age and the quantitative monitoring of bodily processes. For, as Vincent (1995: 54) has argued:

> In industrial society in the last part of the twentieth century, age is becoming more important in relation to people's experience. It is becoming a criterion that more people use to interpret and understand their experience of society and to structure their own consciousness and actions.

The wider context within which this development has taken place does, however, need to be acknowledged. Thus, Beck (1992) highlights contemporary trends of individualization that offer scope for creativity and experimentation for transforming family structures, education and employment experiences. This entails the question of how collective identities might relate to new opportunities for personal choice and reflexivity which enable individuals to create 'do-it-yourself' biographies, rather than simply pursuing life trajectories governed by gender, ethnicity, family and class. If life becomes the outcome of personal decision making (Beck 1994, 1999) these processes of individualization also need to be seen within a context of proliferating risks that may be faced in isolation (Beck 2006). In some ways, such views can help explain different climbers' relationships before they had children, or established a long-term partnership. Furthermore, for these sporting men, the ideas also illuminate a problematic transition from youth to adulthood, in that some of the climbers had contradictory feelings about engaging with 'adult goals': establishing a career, 'settling down' in a long-term relationship or having children. Moreover, as I discussed in the previous section, it was often the female partner of the male climber who 'allowed' him to continue climb, as long as it fitted with her ideas of what was acceptable. One woman, in her early thirties, said, 'I like it that's it's part of his life. I like having a small part in that. I think because he's not obsessed by it, he's not sort of going out every night. I think that I would find that frustrating if I wasn't so into it. But, because he's not like that, I don't really have a problem with it.' In this way, women often managed both their partner's involvement in climbing and, in terms of the life course, the sometimes uneasy transitions these sporting men faced when becoming fathers, or, establishing more settled relationships. However, this 'managing' was not always straightforward, as one woman illustrated when speaking about her partner's wish to climb:

> Since other people have gone away, got work, it's more difficult to find people for him to climb with ... But if you had him, Paul [her partner's climbing friend] there climbing, or offering to climb with you five days a week, I think it'd be very hard to turn round and say 'No, I don't want to climb five days a week' [laughter].

As I have demonstrated, this potential or actual loss of sporting autonomy, which some men face as they undergo life course transitions, was greeted in diverse ways by the male participants. These views ranged from those who embraced the mundane world of family, to others who had rather reluctantly accepted the need to modify their extreme climbing activities to be able to engage with the mundane on terms that satisfied their female partners. Others still, refused the mundane altogether, as exemplified by the 'Peter Pan' figure identified earlier in the chapter. These different stances were negotiated with female partners, sometimes over an extended period of time. Feeling the need to exercise personal agency within standardized chronologies, the climbers' individual life trajectories are evidence of the coexistence of the persistence of modernity's regulated life course alongside late modernity's trend towards individualization. These life-course transitions come into sharp relief when data are examined that deal with the climbers' employment choices.

Borden (2001), in his discussion of skateboarders and the urban environment, argues that young skateboarders reject both society as a whole and the normative patterns of the family, particularly 'the work-leisure, workplace-home sociospatial routines of the traditional nuclear family' (Borden 2001: 151). This is illustrated, he finds, in advertisements that offer a binary opposition between skating and having a job as a wage slave. One such advert he details carries the tagline: 'Fuck work before it fucks you' (Borden 2001: 165). (A similar slogan was adopted by some climbers in the 1990s, which exhorted them to 'climb now, work later'.) What is more, Borden's skateboarders also reject the family in a way that characterizes a general condition of youth subcultures, which is seen by him as a 'revolt against the fathers' (Borden 2001: 165). The primary concern of skateboarders, he asserts, is to not be like the traditional family and especially not to be the conventional son, and so by extension, the conventional father. He documents skaters who, on becoming parents, find themselves to be disillusioned and unhappy with the mundane activities of family life such as schooling and other aspects of a conventional parenthood. As I identified in Chapter 4, in rejecting this model of adulthood, skaters therefore reject a binary choice of childhood and conventional adulthood, creating in its place a way of being which is not strictly either of these categories. Some skaters therefore, reach adulthood but meanwhile refuse some of the conventional ways by which adulthood is defined, for instance, employment. There were also similarities with my study and Wheaton's (2000b and 2004a) recognition, that age and life experiences were key variables in terms of how the windsurfers she interviewed competed with and related to each other, as well as providing a context for how they conceptualized and made sense of their own sporting achievements. Regarding sporting identities and relations, a focus on age and the life course can, therefore, illuminate the world of paid work as well as heterosexual relationships in the private sphere of the family that I have previously discussed in this chapter.

An awareness of historical change, as well as social and life course changes provides a context in which to examine the participants' relationship to, and views on, paid work. For instance, some of the older climbers I spoke to conceptualized a 'golden age' in 1980s Britain, where many climbers were on state benefits, and honed their climbing talents, sometimes to world-class standard. As one 42 year old, said

> Got another job and then jacked that in completely to go climbing, and then there was the big economic crash and I spent years on the dole, avoiding work really. Basically, except in terms of the money, I was a professional sports person.

Or, as another succinctly put it, 'Well, thank god for Mrs Thatcher. She doesn't know what she did for British climbing and I'm sure would be horrified to find out.' Areas in the UK such as Sheffield in South Yorkshire and Llanberis in North Wales were well known locations where those who climbed at a range of grades formed close communities, sometimes over many years. These times were often viewed by a number of interviewees as a period in which they had little or no responsibilities in terms of paid work, family ties or relationships. Such an era was also sometimes mourned in its passing by participants, because of wider changes in society, often defined by climbing becoming more commercialized in a material world, and because of their own sense of ageing (see Chapter 3 on the implications of commercialization for climbing). Many had taken jobs that had connections to the climbing world, precisely to enable them to continue to climb as they grew older. A 39-year-old climber reflected, 'I have my job because I want to be involved in climbing.' Another man, in his thirties, after talking about getting older, the passing of 'the golden age' of climbing for him and new found responsibilities of paid work said:

> One day you enjoy the fact that you're dead scared. Then the next day you enjoy the fact that you are really strong. And the next day you enjoy the fact that you're just having some banter at the crags with people. And it's different when you're sixteen as to what it feels like now. Now, sometimes, it just feels like the only time I can shut off completely from the world.

In this way, he illustrates how the sport symbolized both his youth and how it allows him to deal with the everyday realities of being employed.

This shift within the climbing community, for many ageing climbers at least, from the laid-back anti-materialism of the 1980s to a concern with mortgages and gainful, regular, paid employment in the 1990s and beyond, can also partially be explained in terms of the ageing process and life course trajectories of individual climbers, as I have previously discussed in this chapter. Indeed, when asked about why he had eventually taken a steady, relatively well paid job, this climber, in his thirties, contemplates whether it is age or the nature of the job itself that has enabled him to regard employment differently:

> I don't know if it's become more important through getting older or anything, but just the way my job has developed over the last eight, nine years. There is a certain street, well, not street cred, respectability ... so my reputation and what I'm doing internationally. Therefore, I'm getting better known because of what I'm doing now, because of my job.

Additionally, many, if not most, participants combine climbing as a pursuit with employment, opting to climb outdoors or train indoors at climbing walls at the weekends, or in the evening after work. One such climber, the aforementioned Mick Fowler, has received media attention due to his high profile as a serious climber, coupled with his job as a tax inspector. For instance, in a recent interview, when asked why he had not considered being sponsored, which would mean he could give up his job, he stated: 'That thought has occurred at times over the years but I prefer to keep climbing as my hobby and retain my enthusiasm to it' (Soutar 2005: 19). Others in my study (often, although not always the elite climbers), as already noted, chose work associated with the climbing industry – for instance, working in an outdoor pursuits shop, at an indoor climbing wall, or an adventure sports centre. A number of interviewees had worked in the roped access industry, especially when younger, in their twenties or early thirties. This latter work is relatively well paid, compared to other jobs associated with climbing or outdoor sports in general. Roped access involves working on ships, oil rigs, cleaning windows of large buildings and other work on large structures where climbers using ropes have a practical, and economic advantage, over the use of cumbersome and expensive scaffolding. One man, in his early forties, who still worked in the industry, had a very negative view of this occupation. He clearly defined the work as a job, rather than an extension of climbing activities, 'Absolutely just a job... It's soulless. It's hard work, got nothing whatsoever to do with anything of any value in your life.' He is clearly involved in this 'soulless' work as an economic means to an end.

Some participants were more ambiguous about having jobs in the climbing industry and the possibilities such work offered them. A man who was in his mid-thirties, a climber of much repute and the manager of an indoor climbing wall, on being asked if he had chosen his job because it allowed him time to climb, responded, 'I definitely chose … I mean, I see it as a career, and I work within the outdoor and climbing industry, rather than say as a teacher, and, it's taken just as much effort as well. People look at you and think … It's not actually that easy, you have to work at it.' However, as he got older, he has questioned his career choice, 'Crikey, should I have been doing some career where I'm now headmaster of a school, or something like that?' A traditional occupation, such as teaching, would have afforded him more status and financial security. As well, his frustration partially arises out of people seeing his job as an extension of his sporting 'hobby', as opposed to his chosen career path. His female partner, also in her thirties, who is involved in a more secure occupation in education, speculates that he has doubts because, 'It's a money thing, linked to a male thing about the breadwinner kind of status … I'm the main salary earner.' However, she also asserted that the situation, '… very much suits us. You know he's looked at different things to do and one day he might do it, but I think he'll do it when he wants to. There's no pressure from me. Now, he can take an afternoon off and go climbing.' Therefore, through working together as a couple they are able to have a relationship which goes against traditional gendered and economic stereotypes, and which currently suits them both, despite some drawbacks.

In comparison, a climber, in his late thirties, explained the fact that he only climbed at lower grades, by stating emphatically, 'If I'd have started earlier, I think that would have been different. But, I've got a successful business and lots of other things, and you think about things more, starting late.' His status derives from his work, and not his climbing reputation. However, this sentiment was expressed vehemently and, more than once during the interview, as he felt it important that I realize how well he had done in his job. Later on in the interview, he said, 'I've noticed that with climbers where that's all they've done … younger ones coming along, fitter, they're stronger, they're doing better climbing, and of course, the older ones are frustrated. They've got no job prospects.' A number of the climbers did support his view that they were frustrated because of a lack of options, given that their youth had been spent climbing and not obtaining qualifications, for example. In this way, they illustrate how over-reliance on an extreme sport can affect their choices in a broader, everyday context. Others, however, were not dissatisfied with their life choices. Some of these climbers, even when older, still valued the freedom that temporary employment such as roped access work, gave them. Moreover, they were not all overly concerned with earning a huge salary, choosing freedom to travel, for example, over material wealth. The 40-year-old, Ben Moon, described in an introduction to a recent interview as being one of Britain's most-well known and successful climbers, has managed to organize a lifestyle that has allowed him to set up his own climbing company. In this way, he can proclaim, 'What I do after breakfast depends on what I'm doing climbing wise at the time ... If I'm climbing hard and I have some project on the go then that will take priority over work and stuff' (Kirkpatrick 2007: 90). However, this option is open to him because of his past reputation in the climbing world as an elite climber. Such celebrity can have a negative side in that the success of the business depends on his name, so he often feels 'pressured to do stuff' (Kirkpatrick 2007: 90). But he also feels the rewards outweigh the negative aspects, given he has never had a 'proper' job since leaving school at 17, 'Plus, when I'm bouldering, technically I'm still at work' (Kirkpatrick 2007: 90).

Another view on extreme sports participants is provided by Maria Coffey (2003) who writes about her wish to accompany her partner Joe Tasker, the elite British mountaineer, on a trip to Tibet. She documents her partner's response to this request, thus: '"But why?" he said. "It's just like anywhere else. I'd just as soon stay here. I'm going there to do a job, you know"' (Coffey 2003: 17). For him, in this instance at least, climbing is seen as just a mundane way to earn a living. Further, what would be considered an extreme pursuit by mainstream society, is just a 'job'. Whilst for others still, climbing-related work is not considered to be routine and boring as it allows them to do what they love best. In this way, an oppositional dichotomy of the extreme and the mundane is blurred and the concept of 'mundane extremities' can be seen to have resonance for the climbers' everyday experiences of negotiating, and balancing, paid work and an extreme leisure pursuit. The climbers' responses also revealed that the everyday and the extraordinary are involved in a shifting, symbiotic relationship, as this 44 year old demonstrated when asked if there was a connection between his business acumen and his climbing, 'Yeah, I've thought about that a bit ... my dad just thought, "Well, if you're a good climber, eventually you'd put your hand to something you wanted to do, and, hopefully, be good at it."' In building up a successful business, he had used some of the attributes also needed for climbing: intense concentration and single-minded focus and perseverance, for example. In this way, the extraordinary aspects of an extreme sport had informed the mundane.

Conversely, for this mountain guide, in his thirties, it was the mundaneness associated with his previous job as a miner, which sparked off a climbing career: 'That is really when I started climbing, during the miner's strike. And, when I went back after the strike, a lot of people's lungs were cleared out.' The expression, 'a lot of people's lungs were cleared out' can be taken in a literal sense, when striking miners had a taste of the fresh air, but also in a metaphorical sense. Some miners, including this man, saw things differently when not underground. The mundane rhythms of a regular job did not accommodate his new-found love of climbing, specifically mountaineering, which demanded long periods of time away from paid employment. In addition, as a working-class man and one without any qualifications, the world of education also became that of the extraordinary, leading to his eventually gaining a PhD. In this way, an extreme sport can be seen to destabilize the 'mundane' elements of paid employment. However, as with the earlier example of the climber turned business man, for another climber in his early forties, confidence gained through extreme climbing translated into a resource in his mundane, working life:

> Being a climber adds lots of things in terms of travelling to unusual places, but, also confidence in some areas of my job. When I come across a situation that I think is a bit scary, I just think, 'Well, it can't be as scary as climbing, so don't worry about that.'

## Conclusion

The data concerning families, work and relationships and the sport of rock climbing, reveals how the extreme influences and effects the mundane in a number of ways. For instance, across all the subgroups, engaging in an extreme leisure pursuit can provide relief from the stresses of modernity, the rush and realities of everyday life, and the boredom and frustrations of unsatisfying, or low-paid work. However, it can also impoverish the mundane world by causing tension in relationships, as well as narrowing job prospects and life chances more generally. Further, it can, for some of the climbers who are engaged in climbing related work, actually financially fund their desire to take part in an extreme sport. This interactive relationship between the mundane and extreme shifts over time, that is, a person's biographical time, but also in the context of social and historical change.

Additionally, men's agency can be seen in this shifting interaction, through their undergoing life changes in middle age, through partner's influences and through a changing awareness of the body (which I go on to look at in the next chapter). Importantly, though, men are sometimes afforded agency in these transitions between the sporting world and the private, heterosexual sphere of the family, because of female partners' willingness (or sometimes a lack of choice) to negotiate – for instance, in the sharing of family responsibilities. Thus, any mobility of masculine identity between sporting and other sites is, at least partially, dependent on traditional, gendered power relations. Yet, within this context, there was evidence of heterosexual coupledom being transformed by a mutual desire to 'make things work'. This was apparent with the example of the male climber who was prepared not to have the status of main-breadwinner, to enable him to climb. However, this also shows that men must be willing to forgo certain privileges, which are bestowed by conforming to a model of hegemonic masculinity, if their everyday heterosexual relationships are to become more equal.

**CHAPTER 8**

# Everyday Bodies and Sport

## Introduction

In relation to bodies, embodiment and everyday cultures, Nettleton and Watson (1998: 2) argue that it is surprising, given the centrality of the body in relation to everyday life, that there has been little empirical research into how humans experience their body, particularly research which prioritises '… engaging ordinary men and women in talk about their personal bodily experiences'. At the same time, we need more empirical evidence of how people experience their bodies in different ways according to their gender. A central finding of my empirical study was the importance of the fit and 'working' body for the participants, which is understandable, given that it is the body which has perhaps captured the imagination of those writing on men, masculinities and sport more than anything else (Klein 1990; Messner 1992; McKay et al. 2000). Meanwhile, Connell (1995) places an acknowledgement of men's bodies and their relationship to masculinity central to social analysis. In later work, he observes:

> In historically recent times, sport has come to be the leading definer of masculinity in mass culture. Sport provides a continuous display of men's bodies in motion. Elaborate and carefully monitored rules bring these bodies into stylized contests with each other. In these contests, a combination of superior force (provided by size, fitness, teamwork) and superior skill (provided by planning, practice and intuition) will enable one side to win. The body, I would conclude, is inescapable in the construction of masculinity, but what is inescapable is not fixed. (Connell 1997: 233)

Further, Connell's (2005: 71) argument that gender needs to be understood as a structure of practice leads to a focus on embodiment, for, as he argues, 'gender is a social practice that constantly refers to bodies and what bodies do … it is not social practice reduced to the body'.

Therefore, some theorists have preferred the term 'male embodiment' to 'men's bodies' as this incorporates the corporeality and sociality of people's bodies over the gendered life course (Monaghan 2005). Monaghan argues that Connell (1995) and Watson (2000) are amongst the few sociologists who have researched male bodies using an embodied perspective but also asserts that Watson's work, although grounding men's experiences in relational and proces- sual bodies simultaneously, does not consider more positive attempts by men at constructing plural masculinities and sexualities. This compares to work done on sporting men within a masculinity studies framework, where, often, the body has not been seen in positive ways but as illustrative of men's capacity to take pain, or sustain injuries, sometimes in order to gain acceptance in sporting circles. Further, gendered practices and images of the body become embodied for people and effect, consciously or not, people's participation in sport over the life course. Woodward (1997) uses Connell's approach as an 'antidote' to the theoretical problems of both social constructionism and biological essentialism. She argues that it is a notion of embodiment that can expand on studies of the sporting body, which have hitherto limited this analysis by not examining the corporeal, or by downplaying the possibility of positive male identifications with the body when seen over the life course. I would add to this observation by noting that a previous focus on the male sporting body has, in general, not con- sidered men's bodies outside of the sporting arena by placing them in the broader context of men's everyday milieus.

This chapter will examine how male embodiment has been conceptualized in the area of sporting studies and, more generally in sociological work on the con- nections between bodies, gender and masculinities. Some of these debates will be carried through into a discussion on how men manage pain and injury in the context of an extreme sport. The chapter will then raise issues initially consid- ered in Chapter 5 on sporting gendered relations, particularly in respect of how ideological assumptions about women's and men's physicality have implications for everyday sporting practices. It will also consider how men embody their sporting identities by exploring the male climbers' experiences of their bodies in terms of training regimes and other body practices, such as dieting. The ageing male sporting body will be discussed to see if everyday sporting practices, and the way these may shift over the life course, enable us to see if, and how 'extreme' and 'mundane' masculinities are changing in any way.

## Embodied Sporting Bodies

The male climbers I interviewed illustrated the need for a focus on embodiment to be able to examine their subjective thoughts about participating in sport. When asked about the joy of using his body, one young climber in his early twenties said, 'I generally go indoor bouldering most days in the week. And, I do find that if I get home, I'm like, just sort of imagining. Which is quite sad really. Imagining the sort of movements and stuff.' Even when not physically in a sporting context, in other everyday locations he imagines making climbing moves which then give him a sense of embodied satisfaction, as others in the study have also shown. Another climber, in his forties, thought about physical sporting movements in a different way when he compared traditional climbing to the less risky practice of sport climbing and other, related practices:

> There's nothing prepared about trad climbing, whereas bridge jumping, rope access, sport climbing, I put them in the same group. I like sport climbing but I'm using it as a way of remembering body movements. Interesting, but it don't grab you, don't grab my heart.

In this way, he dislocates the actual physical moves made in sporting contexts from the emotional, even passionate experience that climbing is for him.

In contrast, an elite climber, in his early forties, participated in the sport to actually submerge his embodied self. He did this specifically to lose any sense of ego through the intense focus needed on all-absorbing climbing routes. He reflected:

> It's like to have any ego actually involved means failure, because your ego, you might be positive, or you might be worrying, you know got to get, a bit tight that sort of thing. Now that amount of effort, engaging that thought process, is already distracting you from what you need to be doing. You need to be completely absorbed in the movement, and by being like that, you're not actually that absorbed.

Le Breton (2000) has theorized extreme sports by seeing participation in them as characterized by an escape back into the body, through, for example, a necessary engagement with risk and danger. And thus, extreme pursuits, such as rock climbing, are not necessarily seen as 'balanced' kinds of activity, ones that can be seen to facilitate 'flow' – that is, the rather pleasurable loss of self (Harris 2005). However, this man here can be seen to refute this idea, in that he seeks to escape the body, and thus, lose his sense of embodied identity.

Through these examples, we can see how climbers remember their embodied sporting experiences in different ways, illustrating that the physical is always related to something beyond the act itself. For example, the young climber's recollection, of imagining climbing moves when he is outside of the sporting sphere, therefore, challenges a mind/body dualism in that, as he remembers his embodied experiences, he experiences bodily sensations. Using Merleau-Ponty's (1962) ideas in relation to male boxers' sporting identities, Woodward (2006) explores how his challenge to the Cartesian dualism of a mind and body split allows the sporting participant to actively construct their identity, as these male climbers are doing here. Further, she argues that this construction needs also to be located in terms of bodies and their connection to social structures, as I go on to discuss. Firstly, however, the concept of embodiment needs to be considered in more detail, as is useful here to consider why these men, and others in the study, are not reflecting on their bodies as if they were somehow outside of themselves, but they are all actually living the body.

In exploring the relationship between workplace identities and the body, with Hall et al. (2007) I draw on a distinction between 'the body', as it has figured within the social sciences, from feminist theory to medical sociology and 'embodiment'. Much of the work on the body is about the body we have, the object body that we might alter in some way, whether via diet and exercise or piercing and cosmetic surgery. It is the body through which identities may be claimed or imposed, through the materialities of clothing, or body modification. It is also the body which is open to the scrutiny of others – colleagues, employers or partners, as well as of the state, the media and, for my purposes here, other sporting peers (see Nettleton 1992, for example). The concept of embodiment, however, takes us towards the body that we are and, as such, provides a fruitful starting point from which to investigate processes of male sporting identification (see Nettleton and Watson 1998 and Williams and Bendelow 1998).

Woodward (2008) observes that feminist critiques have argued that a Western, post-Enlightenment split between mind and body has meshed with a gender hierarchy that links culture and the intellect with masculinity and nature and the body with femininity. This has often resulted in reductionist associations between women and bodily functions such as menstruation, reproduction and breast feeding (see Firestone 1970). In response, theorists as Butler (1990) and Grosz (1994) have used Foucauldian perspectives to highlight the social 'production' of bodies through discursive practices such as medicine. Within these debates, however, the body as the material site of human experience was felt to have been marginalized. Theorists such as Moi (1999) have sought to address this issue by offering a feminist development of theories of embodiment grounded in the work of Merleau Ponty (1962), focusing on the lived body as the analytic starting point. This is an approach that is also adopted by cultural phenomenologist, Csordas (2002: 241) who argues that, 'embodiment can be understood as an indeterminate methodological field defined by perceptual experience and the mode of presence and engagement in the world.' His perspective is reflected in the work of medical sociologist, Watson, who views embodiment as a site at which the personal and the social interweave, citing Giddens' view that identity is sustained through 'practical immersion in the interactions of day-to-day life' (Giddens 1991: 99, cited in Watson 2000: 111). If we view identity as 'the interface between subjective positions and social and cultural situations' (Woodward 1997: 1), then human embodiment is core to this interface. Does this mean that the notion of the body as an object can be dismissed?

What I suggest, with Hall et al. (2007), is that the body as objectified, scrutinized or mediatized remains an important aspect of embodied subjectivity in that particular kinds of male bodies play a part in who men think they are. In this sense, men's bodies when engaged in sport are constantly under scrutiny from others and from themselves. Male climbers, for example, are often consciously or not, performing for an audience of onlookers which range from other male climbers keen to see how well they mange on a route, to female, non-climbing partners and, potentially, the (hidden) male gay gaze. They all look upon the male climbing body and sometimes as an object of desire. Such scrutiny can bring identities into self-doubt and insecurity, for instance, as older men's sporting performances are watched by younger, up-and-coming climbers and who possess more youthful and fitter bodies, which are often more suited to climbing success. This demonstrates Morgan et al.'s (2005) observation, that an individual is the site of numerous bodies, for instance, here, the sexual and the sporting body. In this way, performances of masculinity through these 'bodies' are complex and interactive.

Seen in this generational context, Whitehead (2002: 19) has argued that while 'many men fail to achieve a seamless, constant, symbiotic relationship between their bodies and dominant discourses of masculinity', they may still attempt to do so and their masculine subjectivity is bound up in these attempts. Moreover, whilst feminists such as Delphy (1984) have argued that bodily differences are made to ground 'gender' via what Connell (2005) later described as 'gender projects', these projects are enacted in local contexts. This means that different kinds of masculinities emerge from what Connell (2005: 81) refers to as 'configurations of practice generated in particular situations in a changing structure of relationships'. Thus, for example, historical location and class-based position provide contexts for these specific practices. In relation to sporting men's bodies and their subjective relationship to those bodies, then, I have already posed the question in Chapter 4, as to whether non-mainstream sports allow men a space to 'do things differently', for instance in allowing them new forms of male identities in the context of body practices. In Chapter 6, I explored whether being in a situation such as on a dangerous climb afforded men new possibilities of relating to others, in part, as a consequence of being forced to display characteristics of fear and vulnerability about their bodies. Further, as Csordas (2002) and Young (2005) argue, a body-based phenomenological starting point should not exclude wider cultural and structural dimensions of subjective experience. Indeed, with Hall et al. (2007), I suggested that it is through particular variables – class, age, historical location – as well as the agency of individual men that 'restrictively normative conceptions of sexual and gendered life' (Butler 2004: 1) might be both done and undone. What, for instance, as I explore later in this chapter, is the relationship between men's ageing bodies and their shifting masculine (sporting) subjectivities? Such questions point to the potential fluidity and changing disruptions of masculinities and male subjectivities in the context of the everyday.

This discussion raises empirical questions about how embodiment can be investigated. Leder (1990) argued that the human body is a vehicle for perceiving the surrounding environment and it is primarily during illness that the body makes itself felt. This argument suggests that, in investigating embodiment, we are interrogating something that may lie beyond the individual's notice for much of the time. Morgan suggests that in modern society some men are seen as embodied while others are not: 'Many images of men in sport, at war and in doing sex are highly embodied or, to be more exact, we are encouraged to read these representations in this way. Pictures of stockbrokers, bishops or dons might not seem as embodied as images of sportsmen or warriors' (Morgan 2002: 407). He concludes with the warning that 'if we fail to see their bodies in these cases this may be because of a prior framework of understanding that links men, bodies and action' (Morgan 2002: 407).

Such arguments return us to the notion of 'particular situations' and 'changing structure[s] of relationships' (Connell 2002: 81). If some men's bodies disappear from the gaze of others, this reflects a traditional tendency towards privileging and rendering visible those male bodies that conform with notions of hardness, domination and physical competence. If we accept Morgan's problematization of particular men being somehow less embodied than those who conform to dominant ideas of the masculine body, how much more is this a paradox for 'extreme' sporting men? The rock climbers in my study certainly, at one level, embodied a dominant conception of the hard, strong and muscle-bound body which men in traditional sports have to strive for, unless injured, for example. However, at another, they are engaged in a sport where more traditionally feminine characteristics, such as grace and balletic movement are required on some types of climb.

As I have already indicated, much of the work on sport, men and the body has been concerned with how men deal with pain and injury, which is part of a process often seen as masculinizing. Messner (1992: 121) has largely conceptualized the male sporting body as a 'tool' or 'weapon' with the result that male athletes are seen to become alienated from their own bodies by 'brushing aside' injuries, or taking drugs to cover them up. For athletes (and manual workers), Williams and Bendelow (1998: 166) argue that pain for such groups is a familiar feature of their 'normal' everyday lives (their emphasis). A number of the climbers, particularly the elite ones, persisted in continuing to climb, even when in some pain from previous sporting injuries. Others recounted climbing 'till their hands bled' or until they shredded their hands 'to bits'. Athletes, therefore, risk injury and pain through competition and have to weigh up the social costs and benefits of admitting pain, for example, before any decision is taken to disclose this publicly. This is confirmed by Watson (2000: 101) who documents how men conceal injury from professionals and manage any pain in the course of their everyday lives. More recently, Lilleaas (2007) in her work on handball players and their reactions to their embodied selves, found that they accepted pain as part of the sporting experience. They also used physical activity to enable them to deal with difficult feelings, as their training regimes had become embodied. I discuss some of these issues around pain and injury further in Chapter 9.

Woodward (2006) observes that Bourdieu's concept of 'illusio' has been used by different theorists to explain why sporting participants engage routinely with sporting practices, such as boxing, when violence and distress, not to mention punishing training routines, are integral to the experience (Wacquant 1995). She further cites Wacquant to show that illusio is defined as 'the shared belief in, and collectively manufactured illusion of the value of the games (real) men play becomes progressively instilled and inscribed in a particular biological individual' (Wacquant 1995: 173). As Woodward (2006) notes, illusio operates at the level of the unconscious and the concept also allows for an explanation of how gender identities are both experienced and enacted through the embodied self. However, she also points out that the way the concept has been used has often been gender specific. Furthermore, when masculinity has been theorized in this framework it has been seen to offer no opportunities for ambivalence or resistance. Moreover, by gendering the concept of illusio, it enables us to consider the broader context in which gendered meanings for sporting participants are created. Therefore, as I noted earlier in this chapter, how individuals deal with aspects of physical pain and injury or mental anguish, which then becomes embodied, has a wider social context.

Studies such as Kotarba's (1983) have highlighted that social and cultural factors surround how pain is managed. Conversely, Williams and Bendelow (1998) also point out that such perspectives tend to downplay the active and reflective role of the individual, who can call on their own beliefs and knowledge systems in their own responses to pain. However, in addition, gender, age, class and ethnicity are seen as fundamental to the meaning of pain for people. In relation to gender, Bendelow (1993) found that with her respondents, men were more disposed to use a mind/body split when discussing pain, whereas women were more likely to have a holistic approach to pain. Moreover, for women, this viewpoint also incorporated an acknowledgement of emotional aspects. Of relevance, therefore, to this acknowledgement of how pain is both subjectively experienced and socially structured is Williams and Bendelow's (1998) statement: '… what is really needed is an approach that recognizes the dialectical interplay of freedom and constraint in contemporary society and accords equal weight to both in the constitution of the body, self and lifestyles' (Williams and Bendelow 1998: 79). Specifically, in relation to masculinities, Watson (2000) also argues that we need to adopt a theoretical view where bodies are 'seen as sharing in social agency, in generating and shaping courses of conduct. The body is not a finished product, pace Descartes, it is a process and its meanings and capacities will varying (sic) according to its context' (Watson 2000: 38). And, if the body is not a finished product, social changes to the sport of rock climbing, which include women's greater participation, can also effect both men's and women's embodied sense of themselves. I proceed to suggest this in the next section, through an analysis of my data which illustrates the subjective and reflexive accounts, of gendered sporting participants.

## 'Sticky Boot' Syndrome: Gendered Physicalities

When you think of a woman climbing, you wouldn't think of them on some grue-some overhang, would you? Like, you know, with blood pouring out of their hands. You think of them executing a fabulous sequence on something. Climbing, especially in my era, was a lot to do with hurling yourself at really steep over hanging crags, like lacerating yourself and real struggles. And you've got that kind of, all that energy or stuff, testosterone, and it's better than going out and drinking pints and having a scrap. (Male climber in the study, early forties)

Theorists looking at reasons for women's under-participation in sport, and for the prejudice they sometimes face in different sporting contexts, have focused on perceptions of biological differences, or what Bryson (1990: 176) has defined as 'the myth of male superiority through the inferiorisation of women'. Cashmore (2000) states that it is an issue of convention that we organize women's and men's sports separately. He asserts that biological differences exist between women and men but they are of much less importance than our conceptions about those differences, given that the body is a process – constantly changing in both physical and cultural terms. Additionally, the position of women in the outside world is reflected in their sporting experiences and the discrimination and inequality they subsequently face. Bryson goes so far as to say, 'Women's experience has been one of denial: they simply have not been allowed to enter sports, again on the basis of a mistaken belief in their natural predisposition' (Bryson 1990: 179). He feels that in open competition, women would be able to achieve parity with men in nearly all events, except where 'the rawest of muscle power' is called for. For women, he adds, 'Their only disadvantage is what men believe about them' (Bryson 1990: 179). And, importantly, I would add, what women believe about themselves (see Kiewa 2001 and Dilley 2002).

These assumed biological differences can be seen in the gendered assumptions and expectations about women's different physical attributes and abilities in relation to men across a range of new, and mainstream, sports. Hasbrook and Harris (2000: 14) argue that, 'Physical skill, strength, size, gesture, and posture provide us with gendered identities and communicate our gender to others.' Moreover, Kane and Greendorfer (1994) define sport as a medium where bio-logical differences interface with both social and cultural interpretations of gender role expectations. Sport is seen as a site where the physicality of the male body represents power and dominance, and the female body represents sub-servience, frailty and weakness. They conclude with the view that '… it is not difficult to understand how sexual (physical) difference, gender difference and gender hierarchy are taken to extreme cultural forms in athletics and physical activity …' (Kane and Greendorfer 1994: 32). Meanwhile, Dilley (2007) uses the term 'physicality' to suggest a person's embodiment and physical engage-ment specifically with the world of rock climbing, despite it being problematized as a term by some feminist writers (for instance, Hargreaves 2000). Instead, she argues that it is a concept that can be seen to incorporate women's embodied state, as well as men's, if a specific context is specified. Physicality, for Dilley, is therefore concerned with the subjective experience of having a body, living in it, as well as through it, and with physical perception and experience. This definition has been useful for thinking through the differences in how women's and men's climbing styles are often perceived in the climbing community.

It could be argued that climbing is a sport where women can compete on virtually equal terms with men and where the lack of brute strength, for example, in either sex, can often be compensated for by technique. Further, that women's achievements in the sport, in comparison to men, over the last decade has been phenomenal. It could be assumed because of these changes, that physical differences between the sexes are not an issue in rock climbing, and certainly not in a way which upholds a gender hierarchy. However, an examination of female climbers' experiences reveals this not to be the case. Ryan (2005c) notes how the American climber Lynne Hill's successful first ascent of the infamous US El Caps 'Nose' route, was put down to her having 'small fingers' which allowed her to climb the route. In this sense, it could be argued that her achievement was devalued by this gendered conception of her sporting skills. In relation to the sport of climbing, Lewis (2000) has examined the climbing body in detail, specifically the hands of a climber. However, he does not differentiate the climbing body or body parts, in gendered terms, or theorize the implications of this for sporting gendered relationships more generally. Starting to analyse the climbing body in terms of what are perceived as 'masculine' or 'feminine' climbing styles, movements and skills and how this connects to a gendered sense of self, can reveal how gendered expectations about climbing ability, physicality and technique still exist, and inform everyday practices.

As Plate (2007) points out, research exists to show that sports are usually considered to be either masculine, gender neutral or feminine. This research demonstrated that feminine sports are seen to indicate nonaggression and grace, whereas masculine sports are seen as those incorporating more risk and strength (see Koivula 2001). As I discussed in Chapter 4, I revealed that some male climbers particularly associated women as being more suited to 'slab climbing', where the style of climbing calls for balance and nimbleness. Men, in comparison, were seen to favour, and be better, at more 'thuggy' climbing on steep overhanging rock, as the male climber cited at the start of this section clearly believed. One female climber, in her thirties, spoke about this phenomenon in terms of her own experience of noticing how some men viewed female climbers:

I've heard men say it about women before they climb a particularly hard problem, 'Oh well, she's the right shape for it' or 'Oh well, she's small', or 'She wore sticky boots.' Like they wear clogs or something when they climb! I'm thinking, 'Are you wearing roller skates? What are you talking about?'

Indeed, one male interviewee who was a rock climber and mountaineer, aged in his late fifties, typified such views:

> I climb better with women, because we've probably complemented each other on different climbs. I'm sort of fairly big and strong, a lot of muscle tone perhaps. I don't want to generalize, but a lot of women I've climbed with in the past, I've always felt, er, perhaps subconsciously, were a little bit less physical and brutal, probably quite rightly. But, as a consequence, I think they climb neater and with the better footwork.

Another man, aged 71, further illustrated this view: 'I would say that women will climb, er, slab and, er, stuff like that. I think laybacks and, er, overhangs and stuff like that, you can virtually forget, you know?' Although these examples do not fully support Hargreaves's (1994) argument that biological differences between the sexes are assumed, which then serve to exclude women from some competitive sports, they do indicate that women's participation in climbing can be seen as limited to certain practices and styles.

In contrast, a male climber in his late thirties, when asked if particular styles of climbing could be seen as either masculine or feminine, said, 'I don't think there are any particular styles of climbing. I mean people joke about it, saying those are girl moves, make them easier, but that's just rubbish. In reality, women achieve and climb at the same level on a whole variety of climbs.' These contrasting opinions could be accounted for by the age gap, indicative of a generational difference of opinion. However, later in the interview, the same 71 year old reflected:

> I don't think they're naturally that way, and they would build up with a specific aim to go at that, and they do, they get brilliant at it. Some of the outdoor overhangs, you know in mountains and things like that, absolutely fantastic the top lady climbers.

Such contradictory opinions can be at least partly be explained by the fact that more women coming into the sport have ensured some of the most technically proficient and elite climbers are now female. As I suggested in Chapter 5, this influx into the sport by women at the top levels of achievement has forced some men to reconsider their traditional views on women's sporting capabilities.

As well as these structural changes to an extreme sport such as climbing, in terms of the composition of participants, more everyday disruptions are also relevant to consider in relation to men's views on their own climbing techniques. For this male climber, in his twenties, it was a sporting accident which precipitated a change in 'gendered' climbing styles. He remembers:

> I had a fall in 98, that was on quite a bold route. Since then, I've been less bold and more careful and tended to choose better protected routes. I've slowed down and taken stock a bit more, and, worked on the control more and trying to build up my

courage. That was probably about the tip of the change really, when I started moving towards the more sort of flowing, er, stylish climbing, I suppose, and the less thuggy stuff. So, because I've now been climbing quite a long time, my technical skill has improved considerably. I now get more enjoyment out of that, out of performing several moves in a row, delicately and nicely, than I do out of getting up a really steep route that I can look at and go, 'Wow that was steep!'

Dilley's (2007) research is concerned with women for whom climbing has changed their sense of their own physicality, in that many of the female climbers she interviewed have greater upper body strength through climbing, as well as increased flexibility. For some women in her study this carried over into their everyday lives, as, for instance, with one of her interviewees whose handshake was no longer very 'ladylike'. Moreover, some of her interviewees did not see these 'unladylike' changes positively, feeling that their femininity was now compromised. In comparison, the male climber cited above associates 'feminine' ways of climbing as being more 'stylish', and he gets greater pleasure out of adopting such technical skills, moving as he puts it 'in a row, delicately and nicely'. In this way, a climbing accident was a catalyst for his adoption of these new techniques and he does not consider it a weakness, or a failure on his part, that he now prefers to climb in a way that many would see as more suited to women rock climbers. It may have taken an 'extreme' accident for the male climber to change his behaviour, but this does signify something of a shift in masculine, everyday sporting practices.

## Everyday Sporting Practices and Ageing Bodies

Watson (2000) concludes, after interviews with men about their bodies regarding their subjective feelings as they get older and move into adulthood, that most men eventually lose 'everyday experience of the lived body actively experienced through physical activity' (Watson 2000: 97). Consequently, on marriage and parenthood for instance, the 'taken-for-granted' body as they remember it is the dominant way of remembering their past body and there was also an inevitability felt about putting on weight, or not being as fit as they once were. Even the men in Watson's study who took some form of exercise were aware of the ageing process in terms of the body not recovering as quickly, when playing a game of squash, for instance. He also argues that the body becomes marginalized for men in the context of the demands of work and family. Likewise, Nettleton and Watson (1998), reflecting on the body and middle age feel that we become more aware of but are not always comfortable about our bodies in mid-life. However, the data from the male climbers I interviewed can be used to problematize some of these assumptions about the trajectory of male (sporting) bodies across the life course.

Jackson and Scott (2002: 370) point out, 'as well as criticising the all-pervasive pathologisation of women's bodies, feminists have called for the problematisation of men's bodies'. And, as Morgan argues, 'at least superficially, women tend to be more embodied and men less embodied in social scientific, popular and feminist writings and representations' (Morgan 2002: 407). As I have demonstrated, however, this is changing and more recent work has focused on men's bodies. For example, Grogan (1998) discusses the social pressures and cultural changes that create body dissatisfaction among both women and men, highlighting the increasing requirement that men be both slender and muscular. Whilst men have also been seen to be concerned with body modification through dieting and cosmetic surgery, as Monaghan (2005) notes. This invites for the questioning of Whitehead's (2002) assumption that the kind of bodily presence associated with dominant masculinities is all about force, hardness, toughness, physical competence and applying physicality to the world. For instance, many of the climbers I interviewed were openly obsessed with training regimes and body image, thus supporting arguments that men in general are becoming more body-conscious, some even anorexic, and that it is now more socially acceptable to voice such concerns (see Williams and Bendelow 1998). For example, one interviewee, in his late twenties, when asked how he responded to seeing photographs of himself in magazines, replied, 'The thing is, I'm never, ever, defined like some of the other people are, so I always think I look fat. There's only a couple of times when I've seen myself on photographs, where you think "God I'm thin and ripped."'

Horne et al. (1999) argue that men's sporting bodies are also becoming more sexualized, in ways that were previously reserved for the spectacle of women's bodies. Landesman (2000) also supports the view that men are more concerned with body appearance than ever before but argues this is not because of a crisis in masculinity or fear of women, but because people in general have more time, money and leisure to spend on themselves. He also sees this as due to the rigid distinctions between the categories of femininity/masculinity and hetero-sexual/homosexual, now not being so pronounced. In addition, the view that men can be seen to be more anxious than women over body image can be attributed, partly, to a loss of self esteem previously gained through the workplace. Certainly, a number of the climbers interviewed were concerned with weight gain in relation to their climbing. Many of them had dieted to different degrees. For some men, this body consciousness was due to a need to lose weight to be able to climb harder. For others, the fear of being fat was about wanting to maintain a self-image of a honed and 'fit' sporting male. There was even an element of covert competition in terms of who dieted the most extremely or effectively. One younger climber observed, 'The thing is. It's such a crucial thing. You lose sixteen pounds and you're 10 per cent stronger. It can be really obsessive, but it does work as well. I've been ridiculously obsessive at times. I used to weigh potatoes. I'd go on a 1,000 calories a day diet.'

This climber was an elite sportsman and so it could be argued that such practices could be seen as 'normal' in being able to attain the high level that he had achieved in the sport. His behaviour could also be seen as indicative of men now becoming more feminized through consumption practices and media pressure, for example. However, the climbers interviewed revealed very different views on their attitudes to training and the everyday routines associated with that: dieting and other body practices such as fitness regimes, for instance. Individual decisions on whether and how much to train can also be seen in a generational perspective, which can then be used to interpret trends and fashions in training as this climber, aged 44, recalls:

> The period that I was sort of, most known for climbing, like in the seventies, you didn't, people didn't really train then, and it was still seen as a little bit uncool. You know, you were supposed to drink beer and have a fag as you leave and then stumble out the pub, you know what I mean? [laughter]. And then, I suppose, everyone started training and it became a big deal and people saw that it worked. Everyone was mad on training then in the eighties. I did do some training, just weight training at home with a friend.

Such generational shifts can, at least partly, be attributed to a greater number of climbers trying to get more sponsorship deals and, therefore, to an increasing mainstreaming of the sport. An additional reason for these different attitudes to training for a sport can be linked to changes in masculinity more generally, in society. Increasingly, men have more images to choose from than the hard, beer-drinking, macho stereotype of old, as softer, more feminized and caring attributes become more acceptable to adopt and, increasingly, more openly. The same man goes on to say:

> I've altered my diet recently, 'cause I was getting really badly overweight, which has crept up on me over the past four years. I feel a bit more enthusiastic now about going climbing. Obviously, if you've been good at something and then you're not that good, that's not great. But if you've been good at something and then you're absolutely appalling!

Thus, he reveals that he has adopted, to some extent at least, a more modern attitude to training, through dieting, to improve his sporting performance. However, he also states, 'I suppose modern climbers, now they'll actually have a training regime. Then go out and do a climb, and then, like, train three days a week and then have a rest. I mean, it seems a bit strange to me.' His comments reveal that the newer, everyday practices of a younger generation of climbers have not been fully adopted by all older climbers. And, moreover, he shows that participants can have a contradictory approach to these shifts. Conversely, however, not all the younger climbers I interviewed had adopted a rigorous and self-disciplined training regime, as this man, in his late twenties, revealed:

> I've never trained as such. I've only ever climbed for climbing sake. I climb 'cause I enjoy it, that's all. I've never trained to get better, I've never aimed for certain grades. I've got routes out there that I'd like to do, but I'm not prepared to go out

and train hard to be able to do them. The only time that I've thought about my weight is when I came back from Nepal and I'd spent four months sitting on my arse and eating [laughter]. I had a right belly – so I just started eating more healthily and cycling. But it was more with the aim of getting fit again, rather than with the aim of getting thin again.

Whereas, another young climber, in his early twenties, when asked if he had been concerned about his weight, or if he had ever dieted, replied, 'It's not something that I'm massively concerned about. I suppose I probably would be if I was overweight.' This perhaps reflects the fact that, at his age, weight gain was not even an issue.

Though interviewees in mid-life often spoke about having to diet or train more excessively than they used to do, to be able to continue to climb at the level they still desired, not all of them, however, were concerned with seeing the body as a 'project', something that needed to be worked on as they aged, as this climber, in his fifties demonstrated:

When you're a young climber, you're not really sure of what you're capable of and your body's much better than your technique. Whereas, now, I know exactly what I can pull off or not pull up, I know exactly what techniques I'm capable of. When you're my age, experience and a lot of stamina are far better.

He later said, 'If you climb well, climb properly, steadily, then you can choose the grade to suit your body. If necessary I'll just drop me grade down to V. Diffs (very easy climbs). Most of my friends, now, will appreciate any grade of climb.'

In his refusal to accept that youth necessarily entailed one being able to climb better, getting older was here seen as a resource – body strength could, for this climber, be compensated for by technique and self-knowledge of his own body's capabilities and limits. Likewise, this older man, in his seventies, spoke positively about getting older: 'But I think if you push yourself in anything – rock climbing, walking, mountaineering, even in skiing – it does help your health in old age. You get the other extremes where you get couch potatoes that go to work, do their eight hours. They'll come back, have a big tea, sit down and not even move out the chair.' His comments reveal that the ageing process threatens the body and what it has been capable of but also that fitness in old age changes the nature of the ageing process itself. Physical changes to the body were not the only concern of some of the participants, as the comments of a 42-year-old climber, showed:

I was starting to believe, until quite recently, that getting older meant that you got physically weaker, but, recently read a few articles about climbers a lot older than me, like in their fifties. I mean there's a French climber. He's 52. I mean he quite literally is one of the best boulderers ever. Just recently, in a world cup competition, you know, which is all youngsters, he came sixth. He's an absolute machine. He's really into meditation. He says that the thing about climbing is it's all in the head anyway and his body's obviously not in bad shape. So, hey, I'm 42, he's 52. There's plenty of time left there for that sort of thing if I wanted to. But, for most of us, it's actually how much we really want to, you know?

This early middle-aged climber does not stress technique as a way of dealing with the body's fragilities in later life but rather, as he further states in the interview, the importance of 'the mental side of things'. In this way, he demonstrates that men are all, more or less, embodied, and that for him, agency was an integral part of how he experienced his body.

## Conclusion

Connell (1987) conceives of men's power thus, 'The social definition of men as holders of power is translated not only into mental body images and fantasies, but into muscle tensions, postures, the feel and texture of the body. This is one of the main ways in which the power of men becomes "naturalized", i.e. seen as part of the order of nature' (Connell 1987: 85). At one level, this conception of men's power as shown in, and produced through the body, has resonance with the male climbing bodies that I have explored in this chapter, as well as being of relevance for how men conceptualized women's sporting bodies. This could be seen in men's accounts of training routines that could be defined as excessive and often undertaken by elite climbers to enable them to climb harder routes, whatever the cost to themselves. It could also be seen in some male climbers' views that women's bodies were 'naturally' more suited to less physical and so 'easier' climbs, than men's. However, Rowe et al. (2000) see masculinity and the male body as a contested site and, therefore, fraught with contradictions. They assert that, 'Sporting bodies, then, are produced under sociopolitical conditions that simultaneously re-inforce and subvert existing structures of power in a manner that militates against secure and consistent gender identities' (Rowe et al. 2000: 248–9). Therefore, they conclude that, 'any acquaintance with such politics of the body cannot ignore the crucial role of sport in relaying and problematizing the meanings of gender, sexuality and race' (Rowe et al. 2000: 262). Current sporting studies, such as Atkinson, (2007) bear out these assertions regarding men's anxieties and fears about secure gender identities. In a study of Canadian men who take sport supplements, including growth hormones, he concludes that whilst middle class, white males, 'by no means have unfettered power chances across the social landscape' (Atkinson 2007: 184), their power chances relative to women, for example, are still greater. However, '...the men who supplement with sports products genuinely express fear, doubt and anxiety about what constitutes masculinity in Canada, and their embodied performances of gender and class are evidently affected' (Atkinson 2007: 184). The question that arises here, therefore, is how do such anxieties effect men's conduct with other men and women, as well as inform any shifting sense of self?

As Woodward (2006: 23) argues: 'The material body and the economic, social and cultural structures which shape experiences and set the parameters of the self are crucial elements in the reconstruction of gender identities.' Taken collectively, the comments of the individual elite and non-elite male climbers discussed in this chapter reflect their subjective accounts of their experiences of changing bodies. This chapter has, therefore, focused on the gendered body as a means of exploring whether masculinities can be seen to be shifting when the body undergoes change. In doing so, the chapter has pointed to the fluidity and attendant disruptions of masculinities and male subjectivities. These narratives have been recounted through pain and injury or, in dealing with the process of an ageing body, in relation to the body's shifting capabilities. Furthermore, the vulnerability of the body, as well as being a source of consternation or anxiety for some interviewees when it affected their climbing, and so their sense of self, also allowed some men to reflect on themselves in new ways. Others' experiences can also illustrate these changing and embodied subjectivities, for example, Guiton (2004) contemplates an accident in Bolivia, which put him in a wheelchair. When powerless to intervene in a son's party that got out of hand, he observes, 'I have reflected long and hard upon this metamorphosis from "he who is in control" to "he who must be protected". Women must feel as vulnerable as this most of their lives, while men can live with the illusion of invulnerability, sporting the odd trophy black eye to demonstrate their toughness' (Guiton 2004: 10). Though his assumption of women's inherent vulnerability is debatable, it is his reflection on this new self-awareness that has emerged out of a forced and so changed relationship to his body, which is of interest here.

Specifically, in my study, this was also seen when men's experience of their own bodies altered, for example, after 'extreme' events, such as a climbing accident, which made one man alter his previous (and gendered) climbing style. It was also seen in the accounts of older men, who defied stereotypical images of necessarily ageing and failing male bodies, and who continued to accrue body capital through keeping fit and active into their seventies. These examples drawn from my research support Robertson's (2003) findings that, in disciplining and pushing at the corporeal limits of the body, men risk bodily impairment. However, as Robertson also concludes, through such experiences, any subsequent renegotiations of masculinity can entail the emergence of new subjectivities, ironically, achieved through sport itself. Thus, through evolving body practices and a greater and more reflexive awareness of their changing bodies, the rock climbers embodied sense of who they were was apparent. With these findings in mind, the last chapter explores if male subjectivities and practices, can also be seen to be changing in relation to 'risk'.

# CHAPTER 9

# Risking It

## Introduction

The concept of risk has, relatively recently, become central to the social sciences. Also, as high-risk 'extreme' sports have grown in popularity, as Stranger (1999) has documented, there remains a lack of empirical work on the meanings people give to voluntary risk-taking. Tulloch and Lupton (2003) illustrate this with the example of people taking part in activities that society in general perceives as risky, but the participants themselves do not, as evidenced by the climbers in my study. A study on Australian surfers (Stranger 1999) has shown that voluntary risk-taking is done for a variety of reasons. These can range from the need for thrills and excitement, to overcoming personal fears and to exercise personal agency as well as for emotional engagement, control and self-improvement. Meanwhile, Tulloch and Lupton (2003), in a discussion of risk and the everyday, cite the importance of Lash's (1993, 2000) call for an investigation into how members of cultural subgroups respond to risk in aesthetic and emotional ways. Of relevance also, is Lash's view that contradiction, complexity and ambivalence are a greater part of people's responses to risk than has been previously allowed. Such 'risk cultures' Tulloch and Lupton feel, afford more chances of fluid and interchanging ways of viewing risk, which also draw on embodied and affective judgements. They argue that 'fine grained empirical analysis, which is able to explore people's ideas and experiences of risk' (Tulloch and Lupton 2003: 7), can be used to explore where and how the reflexivity that challenges modernity occurs and how it is expressed. Further, they argue that Lash, like Mary Douglas (1992), is concerned with how risk judgements that are made are never neutral, but are shaped through shared understandings and anxieties which go beyond the rubric of 'risk'. For Lash, this is the fear of the 'terrible sublime' of death.

Risk sports and other activities have also been conceptualized by the term 'edgework'. For example, Milovanovic (2005) argues that in modern society, it is in the spaces of 'edgework' where the expression of the emotions can be found. This is particularly because of our present focus on rationality and reason, which can be seen as features of a post-Enlightenment society. Lyng (2005), in discussing the concept of 'edgework', observes:

The question – why would anyone risk their lives when there are no material rewards for doing so? – can be answered simply. What draws people to "extreme sports", dangerous occupations, and other edgework activities is the intensely seductive character of the experience itself. As the participants themselves report, they do it because "it's fun!" The challenge – to explain how life-threatening experiences come to acquire a seductively appealing character in the contemporary social context – requires a complex sociological theory of structure and agency in late modernity. (Lyng 2005: 5)

Lyng (2005: 5) further observes that risk-taking experiences are best understood as undertaken to escape diverse aspects of contemporary life, including institutionalized routines, or as 'an especially pure expression of the central institutional and cultural imperatives of the emerging social order.' Whilst Bennett and Silva (2004) argue that in contemporary society, there is a contradictory move towards both risk and choice, and it is in the sphere of the everyday where these complexities are best able to be observed.

With the notion of voluntary risk-taking and the term 'edgework' in mind, in this chapter, I will look at the concept of 'mundane extremities' in a related way to risk. The idea of 'authentic' risk-taking practices, which was meaningful for some of the participants in this study, in terms of their own rock climbing and other experiences, will be explored. I will also investigate injury and risk in relation to everyday masculine practices, with reference to some of the ideas explored in earlier chapters, for instance, in Chapter 8 in relation to the body. I will also examine whether different kinds of masculinity emerge across the life course through risk-taking activities. In so doing, I will again be concerned with sporting masculinities in a framework of men's everyday roles and identities. Finally, I will consider women climbers and gendered differences in risk-taking to further investigate potentially shifting masculinities.

## Mundane Extremities and Risk

As I have referred to in a number of the chapters, some of the climbers refused the label of 'the extreme' in relation to the sport of rock climbing and, in doing so, were reflecting on the meaning of an 'extreme' sport across diverse sporting contexts. I have argued that the idea of a 'continuum' of the extreme, in relation to different sports, is useful to be able to assess what a notion of the extreme means for individuals and for cultural perceptions of climbing as a dangerous and risk activity. The male rock climbers interviewed for this study can be seen, at one level, to be courting Lash's 'terrible sublime' of death by engaging in risky sporting activities. However, as I revealed in earlier chapters, though climbers can be seen to be obvious risk-takers, for many, the point was to minimize any risk involved, to live to climb another day as it were. This was revealed in the comments of one climber, aged 50, who, when I asked if he regretted not pushing himself harder to achieve higher climbing grades, replied:

No, I mean, I sometimes think if I was, if I'd been born 30 years later, I could have climbed much, much harder than I did, or do now because I'm wearing protection. [In] my day when you started, the hard part wasn't the physical aspect of the climbing, it was making it safe, building control.

It is precisely because traditional climbing can be made so much safer nowadays, with the risks, to some extent at least minimized, that this man can climb much harder than he did in the past, when safety was more of an issue. The climber, Simon Yates (2002) argues that in his experience of working as a roped access worker (see Chapter 7), the safest workers were those who were also climbers and cavers. According to Yates, these workers had rope skills to protect themselves, and, as well, they could assess danger as well as rationalize fear. They were also unafraid of heights in the course of their work and cool under pressure, while other workers on roped access sites were either, Yates argues, not aware of the dangers or stupidly and actively courted risk. Furthermore, statistics for steeplejacks or scaffolders, for instance, show more deaths in those professions than for roped access workers. He also contrasts the example of long-distance truck drivers who are encouraged because of profit motives to operate in a way dangerous to both the public and themselves, with climbers, who usually risk only their own or their partner's life, but are often represented in the media as needless risk-takers. There have even been occasional calls to ban climbing since its inception, most famously from Queen Victoria, following the Matterhorn disaster of 1865.

However, it could be argued that the climbers Yates refers to do not take risks in their working environment precisely because their livelihood depends on their safety. Whilst, in the actual everyday practices of rock climbing they may be more inclined not to be rational or safety conscious, given that risk for some climbers may be the point, and not a side effect, of the activity. The view that risk is actively sought by climbers and other extreme sports enthusiasts is upheld by theorists who are concerned with analysing people's behaviour across a range of risk activities. For instance, Smith (2005) when discussing financial trading as a high risk activity, compares this to risk sports, which are conceptualized as those where the people involved in them maximize, rather than minimize, risk activity. He states: 'Most skydivers ... and other leisure risk-takers fervently embrace the risk factors of their sport' (Smith 2005: 188). Thus, though few of the climbers I interviewed actively admitted to courting risk, it was clear that some climbers, especially the elite young men took risks to achieve the sporting success they desired. This could be seen in their occasional, boastful responses to my questions. Further evidence of risk-taking is given by Coffey (2003), who, when discussing male mountaineers, writes: 'These men did fit the stereotype to some degree: They were fit, strong, determined, often bearded and usually dressed in comfortable outdoor clothes. But some of them also had a remarkable capacity for enjoyment, as if the danger inherent in their sport made them anxious to savour fully all of life's pleasures' (Coffey 2003: 65). For these mountaineers, putting themselves in risky situations honed their perceptions and so a heightened love of life. Indeed, many of my interviewees knew another rock climber, or a mountaineer, who had died, or been seriously injured.

Moreover, in my study, a climber, in his forties, when comparing rock climbing to mountaineering said:

> You've got more control over rock, multi pitch rock climbing, even moderate Alpine routes or hard routes, there's control elements in there ... but if it's dependent on the weather or a chunk of ice, or, somebody's left an old rope in place, you know, you die doing fuck all. With rock climbing, you don't.

He later goes on to say, 'It must be safer climbing on big walls when you know what you're doing, than walking down a street in London – so it's a balance of risk – you know?' Not only does he make a distinction between the risks that are potentially faced in different aspects of the same extreme sport, he also feels that it is everyday life itself 'walking down a street', that holds more dangers than the sport of rock climbing. A view which was echoed by this man, in his thirties, who distinguished between climbing and other activities around the idea of risk management:

> It's all about risk management, or risk-taking. You see, for me, the thing that I do, which is the most dangerous thing I do, is go motorbike riding, which is far more dangerous than climbing. Go to the hospitals. It's just ludicrous. But, then again, I have put myself in quite a few positions climbing, where you think, 'Ah, you've blown this' or, 'You're going to die or break your legs', or, 'Oh, what am I doing here?' So, yeah, you can injure yourself quite badly in a very short fall, and you can be really unlucky. But, because I know it, you don't think of it as being that dangerous.

Here, the everyday activity of riding a motorbike was seen to be much riskier than the pursuit of rock climbing. However, he qualifies this when he admits that he has taken risks in his own climbing, which are then rationalized because of his everyday familiarity with risk-taking, and the dangerous aspects of the sport. The view that everyday life is itself 'risky' is also echoed by Coffey (2003) who compares the risks mountaineers take to those of us who lead more normal, mundane lives, 'But it is the same for all of us, really. Everything can change in an instant, even though we try to lead the safest of lives' (Coffey 2003: 230). In this, she complicates further a division between extreme sporting participants, and those people engaged in 'normal' and non-risky everyday activities.

Furthermore, a male climber, in his late 30s, challenged a number of conceptions about an assumed similarity between different sports defined as 'extreme', when he said, 'I mean, yes, it's an extreme sport, but no more so than canoeing is. You can kill yourself canoeing'. He also implied that whether a sport is defined as extreme or not, is, at least partially, down to how the individual approaches that sport and her or his level of competency, 'Climbing is not that risky, if you've got a vague idea of what you're doing and you approach it in a sensible manner.' Gifford (2004: 9) problematizes the distinction between the notion of extreme and the not-so-extreme, when he writes: 'Some of the contexts in which we climb can be disturbing or problematic. You don't have to be a hard climber to have to deal with death- if there's no risk, there's no climbing.' He, therefore, argues that it is not only the elite climbers who face dangerous situations when climbing. Climbers who would not be defined thus can find themselves unexpectedly in an 'extreme' environment. Indeed, if there is no risk, there is no authentic climbing for him. Thus, a climber in the study, aged 43, distinguished, in terms of 'risk', between what he feels are 'authentic' climbing practices from the falsity of related sporting practices such as bungee jumping:

> There's a lot of things I don't understand with climbing and say rope access. I have felt quite offended by things like bridge jumping and bungee jumping. Set up some bridge, 50 metre bridge swings and they're so excited and they think it's the most radical thing in the world, and I'm just thinking 'Fucking hell, I could tie my mum on there and throw her off.'

He also makes a comparison between different climbing practices which other climbers, though clearly not him, *would* consider to be authentic:

> So many things in life are fairground rides, and I don't think climbing is. Sport climbing is a fairground ride, but I think on-sight climbing is something that can kill you, whereas bridge jumping, rope access, sport climbing, I put them in the same group.

For this man, accepted climbing activities, such as sport climbing, are judged on the same terms as bungee jumping, even though other climbers would not class these together. Others, still, would see sport climbing as a legitimate and respectable climbing activity, but class bungee jumping as an activity that non-climbers, or indeed, climbers, would participate in for a quick, but relatively non-risky, thrill. However, for him, 'real', and so in his eyes, authentic types of climbing, are not 'fairground rides' where one can seemingly experience danger but what is in reality a carefully staged and so, false, experience of risk. What is more, these inauthentic activities are not viewed as practices that can cause injury, or death.

## Injury and Risk

As I began, in part, to explore in the previous chapter, issues of risk, competition, violence in sport and injury have all been looked at in relation to masculinity and identity (see, for example; Curry and Strauss 1994; Young et al. 1994; Dyck 2000). Young and White (2000: 126) argue that: '... the cultures of some sports continue systematically to produce high injury rates not only because of the financially driven emphasis on winning but also because of the connection between aggression and the process of masculinization'. But how is risk of injury negotiated in individualistic and (supposedly) non-competitive sports like climbing for example? More specifically, if it is common, as Young et al. (1994) assert regarding male-defined sports such as athletics, that willingness to risk injury is as highly valued as demonstrating pure skill, how does this translate into more individualistic sports? Young and White's (2000) conclusion that men expose themselves to injury because the rewards of hegemonic masculinity remain meaningful for them despite the attendant dangers attached to this, needs to be investigated in diverse sporting contexts to assess whether the potential/actual/symbolic rewards are the same for all men. In relation to skateboarding, for instance, Borden (2001) discusses young male skateboarders talking about the risk of pain, danger and bodily injury involved in a new sport and links this to the '... competitively collective nature of the group ...' (Borden 2001: 53). This is seen to be created by an extreme set of individual attitudes and actions. Male bonding is, therefore, created by such injuries through an aggressive masculinity.

Some of the reactions of the rock climbers I interviewed to their sporting injuries did, indeed, support Young et al.'s (1994) argument, that privileging forceful notions of masculinity is highly valued, and the risk of serious injury is framed as a masculinizing experience. One man, aged in his 30s, who had never been able to climb consistently for more than nine months in a year without having an injury which then stopped him climbing for up to 6–8 weeks, said, 'I probably take risks with what I do ... It's one of those sports where you learn by your mistakes ... But also I don't give up. So I keep trying something, trying something, keep trying something until I either do it or my body's falling apart ... till your fingers are bleeding whatever. I just keep going. I like being obsessive.' He eventually gave up the sport completely. This was partially because of repeated risk-taking and injury but it was clear that he had taken both pleasure and pride in keeping on taking risks to the extent of chronic, bodily damage. An older ex-climber, in his sixties, looking back to a period when he was younger and having suffered a brain haemorrhage, reflected on his reaction to being told to give up climbing by medical staff:

> I can remember I was in the [hospital], I had the cot sides up and my parents were there and this doctor came. He started telling me about, 'You're gonna have to do this and you'll be here for while. But, your're gonna have to give up climbing.' And, at the time I said that I wouldn't, you know? I could tell my parents were upset and my brother made a very, er, significant remark. He made some comment about, 'You're far more likely to live now than you were before.' Because, it would stop me climbing [laughter]. I don't think I was dangerous climbing or too reckless, but you know, I did feel that I forever want to try something a bit harder, a bit more dangerous.

So, despite serious illness he was still intent on climbing and even wanted to do something more risky than his last climb. This could be seen as due to a number of reasons: the pleasure he gained from being obsessive about rock climbing, the risk itself involved, or because it enhanced his masculine identity. In addition, it has been argued that with mountaineering it is even more likely to be the case that, 'Caution in mountaineering is rarely celebrated, or even seen as heroic' (Coffey 2004: 86). The climbers detailed here can be seen to reflect a lack of caution or self regard for their own bodies, in respect of their risk-taking practices, when danger was sought for its own end. However, when his own son took up climbing, the same man's attitude was somewhat different:

> I believe very much in encouraging kids to do whatever takes their fancy and to be honest with you I mean, I think I would have treated girls exactly the same. What I'm talking about with my boys, I, introduced them to the outdoors ... wasn't specifically to climbing, it was to the environment and, in actual fact, Henry first launched into when he was about fourteen. He started to get this mad interest in mountain bikes and I was actually keener for him to do that than climb, because I felt it was less dangerous. I was a bit put out, perturbed, I think that's the right word, when he started showing an interest in mountains and climbing and the bike stayed in the garage a lot more. But it wasn't me that pushed him into climbing.

Viewed from one perspective, this attitude towards his son taking up climbing can be seen as paternalistic. But, from another, it can be seen as indicative of his taking responsibility for his son in his role as a father, given that he afforded his son agency by not stopping him from climbing. Further, as an ex-climber, he was more aware of the potential risks his son might take. Another climber, in his fifties, had been sensitive, when younger, to the effect that his potential risk-taking might have on others, specifically his family. He reflected, 'When I first started, you know, like most young lads, your parents either let you do it or stop you, or try to. Although you might feel safe and think you're in control they obviously look on the worse side of it. So, you'd just say, "Oh, I had a great day you know", then you might not mention the minor scrape.'

The risks that climbers take can be conceptualized in diverse ways. For instance, by risking injury, these men take a gamble on, potentially, not being able to climb for some time. Thus, they confirm Harris's (2005) contention that extreme sports participants knowingly gamble with their bodies. Alternatively, they can risk their lives and/or their family's wellbeing. Or, they face the dilemma of having to decide whether or not to control, in some way, their risk-taking behaviour. Though I felt in the interview that the man cited above was, perhaps, downplaying the risks he took in his climbing, his concern for his family was clearly evident in his attempts to shield them from his risk-taking activities. Such concerns illustrate Tulloch and Lupton's (2003) findings, which document people starting to take less physical risks in sporting activities, when starting a family. Later in the interview, the same climber said

I mean, I'm lucky in that I've never been seriously injured. I think I pulled one little tendon, slowed me down for a few weeks, but other than that I've never had to back off from my climbing. But, I never go mad. You know, when I was young I made a decision – that I wasn't gonna bum around climbing for several years – for my parents. I was gonna do something useful straight away and climbing was just a recreation.

Further, as I have noted, Gifford (2006) identifies a paradox, in that climbers may often think of themselves as risk-takers but are actually inhibited by open and uncontrolled displays of emotion. When discussing this issue he argues, 'The key concept here is "control". It is a word that touches the heart of the sport. Testing the edge of control is what climbing is about...Between control and risk is the field of personal action, a matter of degrees of judgement for each climber based upon ability, experience, the conditions, her judgement of him and his judgment of her' (Gifford 2006: 160). This, of course, includes decisions made about the safety of a climb and the weather conditions, whether a route is within the limits of the technical skills and experience of a particular climber, and so on, as this 40-year-old man demonstrates:

I solo a lot. But it doesn't feel risk-taking though, because everything's so well wired, I guess, with what I do. I suppose you look around and think, 'Well I could slip here, I might fall off.' But it's enjoyable the risk element because it is part of the identity of climbing. It's partly why you do it.

However, an individual's assessment of the risk involved extends beyond the specifics of the act of climbing itself. The earlier interviewee's decision to conceal the riskier side of the sport from his parents needs to be seen in relation to his overall feelings of responsibility to them, to make something of his life, not as he put it in the interview, to be a 'climbing bum'. Therefore, men's relationship to risk-taking and their decision making in this context, can be placed in the wider framework of their everyday lives and identities as sons, or as fathers. Further, there is also a random element involved in risk-taking in climbing (most accidents in rock climbing, for example, take place not on the climb itself, but from descending down the cliff afterwards). Thus, even when taking care to minimize risks, the consequences are still arbitrarily experienced (Yates 2002). However, even so, such decisions exercised about the level of risk involved, or to be con-trolled, are not made in an ethical vacuum. This can be seen when individual climbers decide not to bolt certain types of rock, such as gritstone, due to local, regional ethics that forbid this. To go against such a tradition entails risking the disapproval of the climbing community. In addition, given that many of the inter-viewees' risk assessments were taken with an acknowledgement of the implica-tions of their practices for others, this necessitates looking at men's risk practices and behaviours over the life course, in more depth.

## Risk and the Life Course

Earlier in this work, through the data, I identified that the concept of what is extreme is not fixed and is rather a relational concept in regard to (shifting) subject positions and particular everyday practices when engaging in the sport. This was evident by some of the participants taking greater risks, or by their deliberately seeking out new climbing practices. Lyng's (2005) assertion that such activities can be regarded as undertaken to escape the routines of everyday life holds true for some climbers, certainly. However, the mundane world of the private sphere can be seen to become 'risky' when men embark, for instance, on a new relationship and so their participation in the extraordinary world of climbing may be effected. Furthermore, such extraordinary moments can be fleeting.

One, 35-year-old climber, spoke about always wanting to be 'chasing a moment':

Trad [traditional] climbing is about overcoming fear, and it's just about being out there, and hoping you get that thing. I've talked to a few people about this, and a lot of people say the same thing, It's probably that you're chasing one moment all the time. And, you get it maybe two or three times in a year, where you're absolutely on form and you're just not scared at all, and you're just flowing and the whole thing is a joy. The rest of the time, you're in that nether world of like, one minute you're having a great time, next minute you're shit scared and not enjoying it.

In this way, he illustrates Csikszentmihalyi's (1975) point that certain leisure pursuits, including climbing, can produce a sense of flow, through a person becoming detached and so, objective, about the activity in hand. Furthermore, this provides a space that is not characterized by everyday anxieties. Such a state also sometimes grants people a significant glimpse into themselves (Harris 2005). However, these chased moments of transcendence occur infrequently and are only a small part of the extreme activity, which consists mostly of practices and feelings that are mundane in that context. Further, any transcendence is only achieved through controlling and managing both elements of risk and fear. Thus, transcendence can also be seen to be gendered in that achieving those moments for this very competent and skilled climber, is dependent on a traditional masculine control of an extreme situation.

This study of the extreme sport of rock climbing can be seen to address Tulloch and Lupton's (2003: 134) argument, that more work needs to be done which identifies the shifting and multiple risk cultures that make up 'risk modernity'. I would also argue that we need to pay more attention to both the gendered and life course aspects of such 'thrill seeking' for us to be able to examine issues around Lash's 'lure of death' and, indeed, the reasons why people indulge in such voluntary risk-taking. Tulloch and Lupton start to incorporate the life course in that they view their interviewees' experiences of risk as changing over time, in terms of years or even days. The views of some of the climbers interviewed supported their findings in that many of their participants constructed a view of themselves as being risk-takers in their youth or early adulthood, then, perhaps on entering middle age became more risk averse, as this climber, in his late thirties, reveals:

> In the past I've always climbed some very dangerous stuff, but I don't want to do that forever. Because, it's a numbers game, and then you're going to get injured, or killed. I don't want that to happen. I've been lucky and never been injured, but I don't want to continue doing that. But, I think there's a lot of other things that you can do that are equally rewarding. Because I'm in relationship where I don't want to take risks. Yes, age and relationships I think.

The fact of growing older and of being in a relationship had made him reflect on and rethink the randomness of the risk-taking element in his climbing. Moreover, a consideration of risk-taking in the context of an extreme sport can also reveal the need to consider changes over the life course in a climber's individual biography, in interaction with the different kinds of everyday climbing activity undertaken. Implicitly for this climber, in his early forties, life course changes have had an impact on the decisions he makes around risk-taking:

> I mean I did some serious routes then that I was convinced that I had little chance or I was gonna die on. I think since, sort of '95, '96, '97, I was getting more and more out of doing long climbs, quickly, efficiently and getting to weird and wonderful places and doing the travel bit with it. I had a lovely girlfriend then … that made me think that I didn't particularly like the thought of random life and death. Rock climbing has a control factor in it – Himalayan climbing or Alpine climbing, you've got a big random element in there of life and death. Flick a coin and away you go.

Though his 'lovely girlfriend' caused him to reassess his risk-taking behaviour, his decision whether or not to take up different types of climbing such as mountaineering, or to decide to continue with these particular climbing pursuits as he got older, is based on an assessment of the different kinds of risks involved in specific climbing practices, which I have referred to earlier in this chapter. However, getting older and being in an established relationship did not influence the risk-taking decisions of all the climbers interviewed, as this male climber and his female partner, both in their seventies, illustrated. When asked if he felt he had grown more cautious on climbs, as he got older, his view was that he hadn't. His partner verified this:

I mean now, you go somewhere, to that big castle and there was jaggedy rocks, you used to walk on. It was a sheer drop and he just walks on them, 'For god's sake! Will you come off, because I'm getting shivers.' He just thinks he's still young but he's not.

But he retaliates, and brushes off her fears, saying, 'I think the confidence never leaves you.'

As I have also commented on in Chapter 6, a climber, in his thirties, reported taking more risk for its own sake, specifically because he felt trapped by both his heterosexual relationship and increased material wealth. Further evidence of climbers not being content with decreasing their level of risk-taking pursuits as they aged is revealed in the account of this 44-year-old climber, who expresses regret at no longer taking the risks he took when he considered himself, as a young climber, to be untouchable:

> You just think 'I'm invincible and I'm gonna do it', so when you get older, I suppose you realize you're actually not. It just don't seem as important, as I'm not obsessed with it. I suppose, I must have been obsessed with it really, so you get a bit of a funny perspective on things, don't you? But sadly you don't, you never quite get that buzz you do out of something when you are obsessed with it. I sort of miss it really in that sense.

In their own empirical research with interviews with Australians and Britons, a central question for Tulloch and Lupton (2003) was, 'Is risk perceived as "democratizing" in its universal effects, as Beck sees it, or do the old, "modernist" categories of age, gender, social class and so on still play an important role in the ways people understand and deal with risk?' (Tulloch and Lupton 2003: 11). Clearly, as I have demonstrated, a (reflexive) masculine identity can be seen to have been constructed across the life course by the climbers in my study, in relation to some of these categories. This illustrates that these modernist categories are still of relevance in attempting to explain how sporting participants understand and deal with risk in an extreme sport. And, in dealing with risk, as well as sometimes not being in full control of their risk-taking experiences, they have been able to exercise agency by taking decisions about when to 'risk it', or not. Moreover, though, control exercised in a sporting context may not always cross over into wider everyday life, where control is ceded to institutions, or technology, for example.

## Social Contexts to Gendered Risk-taking

In the previous section, I began to consider how gender and age informs risk-taking decisions. As I have already suggested in this chapter, in relation to the sport of rock climbing, a pertinent question to consider is how does risk-taking, and so the potential death of those involved, take on meaning in relation to masculine identities. Lewis (2000) explores the experience of the 'marginal situation of death' in relation to rock climbing and argues that adventure rock climbing embodies the possibility of witnessing the death of others and anticipating one's own death in real life and in the imagination. Although he does not ask this question in a gendered sense, the possibility of serious injury, or death were reasons a number of the climbers I interviewed gave for giving up specific kinds of climbing activity. In contrast, Kay and Laberge (2003) note, in the sport of extreme skiing, some skiers think that taking increased risks will avenge those who have already died, 'It apparently gives solace to those left alive that death is noble in the name of freedom ... or a steeper descent' (Kay and Laberge 2003: 392). Such motivations for increased risk-taking can, therefore, be seen as complex. Further, risk-taking does not always have noble intentions behind it. Recent deaths on Everest, which, it has been argued, could have been avoided if those mountaineers passing others not yet dead were not so focused on summiting (Malley 2006), show that risky pursuits, far from being either ethical or noble can be seen to be individualistic and selfish in the extreme. So much so that Beaumont and Douglas (2006) feel that Everest has been reduced to a 'playground'. It is only by locating the concept of risk and how it shifts in terms of what is considered a 'risky pursuit', in a wider social, economic and political framework, that we can begin to see how such actions by climbers and mountaineers might be at least partially understood.

For both sexes, however, who engage with rock climbing or other extreme sports, the social and political context of risk in society affects how they pursue, and experience, their chosen sport. This can be seen in a number of ways. In a British context (Brindle and Lewis 2006), official government reports state that we have become a risk averse nation. The present culture, it is argued, can eliminate our national urge to explore and seek out adventure because of more and more regulation. Conversely, Reith (2005) argues that voluntary or recreational risk-taking becomes more tolerated, or even encouraged in society, as public organizations strive to make modern life safer. However, as Douglas (1999) notes, adventure package tour operators do everything they can to minimize risks as it is in their interests to do so. He also argues that the outdoors is not an extended leisure centre and, therefore, risk cannot be fully eliminated. Moreover, whilst there is a fear that, for example, insurance costs and child protection legislation will stop climbing clubs taking young people out to climb, rescue teams do not want to legislate for people going out in bad weather (Douglas 2007). Such restrictions would inevitably take away an integral part of risk-taking activities. Instead, rescue workers suggest that learning survival skills from older people, as part of an apprenticeship where individuals learn over a period of time what to do if the weather turns nasty, or vital equipment is lost, is vital, but is also seen as no longer being the custom.

However, Stranger (1999) is critical of attempts which explain people's participation in extreme sports as reflecting some of the social changes I have just outlined, for instance, the notion that increased regulation in society fuels a need to seek out excitement, which may be missing in our everyday lives. Such views, he feels, cannot adequately account for the fact that there is real danger inherent in such sports, or explain why climbers, for instance, do not need an audience to perform. Furthermore, Lewis (2004) argues, in relation to British traditional, 'adventure' climbing, that commercialization and rationalization have not changed the fact that doubt, risk and danger are an integral part of this practice. It has also been seen as important not to let marketing, peer pressure or bravado influence our own personal threshold of acceptable risk, for 'Once the fanfare is stripped away, these activities are real – real enough to kill people' (Watters 2003: 266).

Therefore, for some theorists, individuals, in response to these social contexts, engage with a range of extreme sports and so enter, according to Lyng (1990), a world based on the transgression of boundaries which are conceived as 'life versus death, consciousness versus unconsciousness, sanity versus insanity, ordered sense of self and environment versus disordered sense of self and environment' (Lyng 1990: 864). However, I would ask how much of this 'transgressing of boundaries', as well as a perceived need for authenticity and self-realization is something that is specifically masculine? Indeed, in the context of climbing, this is something that women have not, till relatively recently, largely been part of, except as the documented, isolated women explorers, mountaineers and adventurers of the past (Loomis 2005).

What are the gendered differences between women and men climbers in taking calculated risks in their everyday sporting practices and routines to achieve a sporting goal? Tulloch and Lupton (2003) found, in their study, that men tended to talk of risk-taking in relation to things like sport or 'daring deeds' or foreign travel whereas women were more liable to define risks for themselves in terms of crime or violence. Specifically in relation to climbing, Palmer (2004) when discussing adventure sports, cites the example of female mountaineer, Alison Hargreaves, who died on K2 in 1998 and the subsequent media reaction to her as a mother, due to placing herself at risk. When men take risks with their lives on mountains, Palmer argues, they are seen as heroic and brave, but female adventurers are perceived in the media as selfish, driven and egocentric. She concludes that, 'where women are involved in dangerous pursuits, all sorts of cultural definitions and limitations are placed upon their behaviour' (Palmer 2004: 65). Whilst, Rose and Douglas (2000) in a biography of Hargreaves, detail her need to mesh the roles of motherhood and mountaineer and report that apparently, her deepest fear on an expedition was getting frostbite and not being able to hold her children. Indeed, for this reason, she had turned back from her first attempt at climbing Everest. Similarly, Summers (2007) in discussing mountaineers who are also parents, explores the notion that women and men take the decision to place themselves in risk situations on mountains from different positions. For instance, it is usually female climbers who have to consider issues of childcare and whether to take children to base camp, on an expedition, as they are most likely to be the primary care giver. Summers concludes that gender inequalities are still present in the climbing community and come into sharp focus if climbers are parents, especially if they are mothers.

Further evidence of gender inequality is provided by Arlene Blum. An American and pioneering mountaineer, now in her sixties, she explores the dilemmas of being a mother and mountaineer, in her book *Breaking Trail*

(2005). In this work she examines the paradox that she needs to climb for herself to be a woman but was not seen as a woman if she was also a climber, especially regarding the spectacular risk-taking mountaineering for which she was known. In a discussion with her, at a UK International Festival of Mountaineering Literature (Robinson 2006), I asked her if she found scaling some of the world's highest mountains, or being a mother more difficult and/or more fulfilling. She replied, much to the amusement of an audience of international climbers, that it had to be motherhood, on both counts. Such reaction to a renowned, female mountaineer daring to suggest that the trials and tribulations of motherhood might be more daunting than reaching a previously unexplored mountain peak, can be understood by the devaluing of the mundane (represented here by motherhood and the family) by those (usually male) participants of extreme sporting activities.

On the other hand, Coffey (2003) asserts that the calculated risks that men take as mountaineers has far reaching consequences for their loved ones. Yet still they take them. Therefore, as well as women's involvement in sporting risk activities being judged differently than men's, men's risk-taking also effects the world of the mundane for women. Coffey (2003: 43), again writing about her relationship with the mountaineer, Tasker, relates, 'Joe was the adventurer, the risk-taker, and his life was compartmentalized into "expedition" and "at home".' This affected her by making her feel she had to take on a nurturing role, despite years of feminism, by 'keeping a place warm and dry and comfortable for him to return to' (Coffey 2003: 43). Thus, Robert's view, that, 'The risk brings no material gain but it offers something ... It is a demonstration that man is not wholly tied to grubbing for his food, not wholly tied by family and social loyalties; that there are states of mind and spirit that he values more highly than life itself on any lower level' (Roberts 1939, cited in Coffey 2004: 95), can be seen as further evidence that the mundane, and traditionally the world of women, has been conceived of as less than the extreme and extraordinary sphere, historically viewed as the domain of men.

## Conclusion

In conclusion, therefore, what masculine identities are emerging, or can be glimpsed from this changing context of risk? Or, to put it another way, how might such different attitudes to risk vary amongst different kinds of masculinities? For some men, in this study, the risk sport of climbing is intimately wrapped up in a masculine image and identity in very traditional ways, as this man makes clear when expressing why climbing eventually became important to him. He reflected, 'So it was definitely danger, that was the excitement of it, and also the bit where I felt able to control danger. I suppose it was, you were hoping for admiration from others, you know?' Whilst Coffey, (2004) discussing the views of a male mountaineer who has made a conscious decision to take less risks in the mountains after taking on a new family, concludes:

The need for adventure, he believes, is hard-wired into some human beings, part of our natural evolution. 'That's why risk-takers have to go out on the hunt,' he said, 'but they're not hunting animals anymore, they're not providing game for the table, they're going out and proving themselves against a challenge. It goes right to the ego of men.' (Coffey 2004: 11)

In this way, it can be seen that men receive admiration for managing danger, especially, in public discourse, the elite climbers. However, women are not accorded the same accolade. Indeed, women risk-takers, as I have noted, have been seen as unfeminine, and 'abnormal', especially if their families are seen as having been put at 'risk', which then threatens a popular conception of motherhood. Conversely, instead of putting the everyday world of women on a higher plane, by glorifying motherhood, for example, male climbers can also devalue the mundane world of family and relationships, by advocating an 'ethical' stance that places the male need for risk and adventure above the material ties of families and relationships.

However, in contrast to those participants who actively courted danger, despite the risk of injury, or others who refused to wear a helmet, even when the particular climbing activity necessitated this for safety reasons, there was evidence in my study of climbers dealing with risk that challenged traditional assumptions of the link between a successful, or hegemonic masculinity, with dangerous risk-taking. This climber, in his seventies, said, 'Once you get to an impasse and you know that you can't do a certain move, You've got the ability to climb back down. If you go above that, you're pushing it, you know? In fact, you're being foolhardy aren't you?' In this way, though there is a kudos to be gained from avoiding risks, and from being able to control them, it is more important to 'risk' potentially losing face in front of others, than be 'foolhardy'. Risks, therefore, do not have to be actually taken, for them to be controlled. Furthermore, a 50-year-old man, considering his own risk-taking practices said, 'I'm fairly chicken, you know, fairly safe. I put in lots of protection. I'll hang around forever, rather than carry on regardless.' Therefore, as well as being able to reflect on their vulnerabilities as these men can, other male climbers, as I have noted in this chapter, also protect loved ones in the mundane world of the everyday by concealing, minimising or even giving up their extreme, risk-taking activities. This could be seen when life course changes allowed them to view the world differently, as I have also explored in Chapter 7. As Lyng (2005) argues, the spectacle of people engaging in 'edgework' can be indicative of their need to escape the everyday, particularly the structural conditions which underpin alienation and oversocialization. It is also, I would contend, borne of a desire to both embrace and to resist and transform traditional ways of 'doing' masculinity.

# Conclusion: A Different Kind of Hard?

Mountains should not serve as an escape from reality. They are surely an escape back to reality.

D. Cook, 'Running on Empty'

In this research, the notion of the everyday has allowed me to tie together arguments around masculinities and invest the idea of the 'mundane' and the 'extreme' with theoretical and political significance. For, as Gardiner (2000) realizes, the point of studying the everyday is not only to describe it, but, also, to change lived experience. Indeed, through the idea of 'mundane extremities', I have been able to investigate whether both the landscape of sporting masculinities and the boundaries of the mundane and extreme, can be reconfigured.

Lefebvre (1991) argues that leisure can provide a space for critically examining everyday life. Thus, for Chaney (2002) the everyday acts as a space for envisioning 'other ways of being' and, to trace the significance of that change, he argues that we need to look at everyday life and represent what is orderly or disorderly about it. The common experience of normality he sees as giving our lives order and stability and can be considered to be what makes our experiences meaningful. But what, my work has asked, is a 'common experience' of the normal and everyday if normality means soloing a rock face without ropes or protection or sometimes climbing in hazardous and potentially life-threatening conditions?

As Highmore (2000: 3) argues, the exceptional is 'there to be found at the heart of the everyday', going on to show that understanding the mysterious and the bizarre involves scrutinizing the everyday, for that is precisely its site. This paradox at the heart of the mundane has been addressed, here, in relation to an extreme sport. In 'making strange' the everyday in order to understand it we make it more governable but also more alien. What then, when we render the extreme or exceptional mundane, does this tell us about the complex interaction of the extraordinary and the routine of the everyday?

In order to address this question, I asked, in Chapter 7, what is an 'uncommon experience' if the extraordinary world becomes entangled and inseparable from the rhythms and familiarity of the private sphere, or the routinization of work? Thus, a problematizing of both the mundane and the extreme to consider the different subgroups of extreme sporting masculinities has provided new empirical evidence of, for example, men's emotional and intimate territories as in Chapter 6, and their embodied selves as explored in Chapter 8, or, as examined in Chapter 9, regarding a 'common experience' of gendered risk. Moreover, although differences could be seen across subgroups in these areas, for instance, in relation to body practices, the importance of finding similarities of experience across these groups was also apparent. This was evident when it became clear that non-elite climbers could be fiercely competitive, whereas the elite could sometimes put more value on friendships or relationships rather than on sporting achievement. In effect, through these examples, the mundane and the extreme became enmeshed and inseparable and, thus, the theoretical and empirical separation of the ordinary from the extraordinary became problematic and unworkable.

Lefebvre's (1971) notion that there are moments of intense emotion or heightened social involvement that would transcend the everyday, therefore allowing people to be more 'truly' themselves, can be seen in terms of how some of the climbers perceived their climbing activities as enabling them to feel 'truly alive' or where the 'real' self could be realized. However, as Cook (1994: 11) writes, in discussing this very issue with regard to climbing: 'Is not this definition, so common in writing about our sport, somewhat limiting? In what other form of human activity means being cut off from family, friends, work? These things are usually considered to be enhancers of sensibility, not a hindrance.'

With this in mind, the concept of 'masculinities in transition' has been employed to account for the mobility of masculine identity, both across separate spheres, and within the same individual. A concept of the 'heroic male project' (Whitehead 2002: 118–19), although helpful in being able to analyse men's hegemonic behaviour, requires a more detailed perspective that takes account of men's capacity to move between residual identities – such as the emotionless and needlessly risk-taking extreme sports participant – as opposed to the one who can reveal vulnerability, or maintain meaningful and intimate links with other men and women. Analysis of the data also revealed that exploring men's identities in relation to how they inhabit public sporting spheres, the private world of families and relationships, as well as working environments, can provide unexpected glimpses into men's practices and subjectivities. Therefore, as Woodward (2006) notes, routine and pre-emptive masculinities combine in different sites where identities are, indeed, re-drawn, if in ambivalent and contradictory ways, to which I would add, also, across sites.

In Chapter 3, I raised the question of whether the sport of rock climbing enables the formation of a 'new macho', where, under the guise of individualism in an alternative sport, older, traditional masculine characteristics of competitiveness and aggressiveness can be altered, or disguised but can still be very much present. Or, conversely, whether extreme sports allow a 'different kind of hard' to surface, where men, through participating in the everyday practices of an extreme sport, are able to reflect on and change past and sometimes disturbing, masculine behaviours, or, consider how they may conduct more equal relationships with women. As the analysis of the data has attested, there are no simple answers to these questions. Perhaps, it is more helpful to continue to bear in mind, as a number of theorists have done, the complexity and diversity of sporting masculinities, while also acknowledging that men's efforts to fashion new ways of being in an extreme sport can be done for many reasons. These can range from the strategic, having learnt to 'do' different types of masculinity to their advantage, to a genuine wish to transform intimate, and other relations. Moreover, not only are these masculinities ambivalent and contradictory within and across different sites – they alter at different stages in the life course.

This raises the interesting if thorny question for theorists of masculinity, concerning which points in men's lives are to be judged the most meaningful in terms of assessing any shifts in masculine identity. I have suggested that an investigation of the interaction between the extreme and mundane sites of everyday life can be useful in any refusal to simplify such potential transformations. Moreover, the urge to seek and find change in men and masculinities can be overwhelming, given the investments people have, from their different positions, in doing this. Therefore, a feminist critical position on any perceived shifts in masculine identities and gender relations continues to be theoretically, and politically, necessary.

Men can be seen to want to climb rocks and mountains, not simply 'because they are there' but for a number of reasons. These include, as Abramson and Fletcher (2007) note, both because of reasons of science, empire and nationalism as well as a desire for freedom and self-realization, which can be seen in the sport's 'playful' status. I would also argue that men climb because sporting masculinities are sutured into the very fabric of the everyday, through blood, skin and grit (stone). However, when the top of a climb is reached the climber can choose to look backward, to survey the terrain recently travelled, or look upwards and out across the horizon and beyond. If, therefore, as Bennett and Silva (2004: 16) argue, '[t]he attention to research on everyday life identifies a range of small changes, and implies that these can have significant cumulative effects', then Gardiner's (2000: 208) view that daily life contains '[r]edemptive moments that point towards a transfigured and liberated social existence ...' can generate new forms of personal relations and identities.

These 'cumulative effects' and such 'redemptive moments' can be explored through analysis of men's (and women's) need to scale rocks and mountains and through their own very different stories of why they do something that seems extraordinary, as well as unfathomable, to most people.

# Bibliography

Abdel-Shehid, G. (2005), *Who Da Man? Black Masculinities and Sporting Cultures*, Toronto: Canadian Scholars' Press.

Abramson, A. and Fletcher, R. (2007), 'Recreating the Vertical: Rock-Climbing as Epic and Deep Eco-play', *Anthropology Today*, 23(6): 3–7.

Allin, L., West, A. and Ibbetson, A. (2003), 'Social Climbing', in A. Ibbetson, B. Watson and M. Ferguson (eds), *Sport, Leisure and Social Inclusion*, Eastbourne: LSA Publications.

Anderson, E. (2002), 'Openly Gay Athletes: Contesting Hegemonic Masculinity in a Homophobic Environment', *Gender and Society*, 16(6): 860–77.

Anderson, K. (1999), 'Snowboarding: The Construction of Gender in an Emerging Sport', *Journal of Sport and Social Issues*, 23: 55–79.

Andrews, D.L. (2002), 'Coming to Terms with Cultural Studies', *Journal of Sport and Social Issues*, 26(1): 110–17.

Appleby, K.M. and Fisher, L.A. (2005), '"Female Energy at the Rock" A Feminist Exploration of Female Rock Climbers', *Women in Sport and Physical Activity Journal*, 14(2): 10–23.

Armstrong, G. and Giulianotti, R. (1997), *Fear and Loathing in World Football*, Oxford: Berg.

Atkinson, M. (2007), 'Playing with Fire: Masculinity and Exercise Supplements', *Sociology of Sport Journal*, 24(2): 165–86.

Backett-Milburn, K. and McKie, L. (eds) (2001), *Constructing Gendered Bodies*, Basingstoke: Palgrave.

Barker, C. (1999), *Television, Globalization and Cultural Identities*, Buckingham: Open University Press.

Barkham, P. (2006), 'A Bigger Splash, a Lot More Cash', *Guardian*, 17 July, pp. 6–9.

Bartky, S. (1998), 'Foucault, Femininity, and the Modernization of Patriarchal Power', in R. Weitz (ed.), *The Politics of Women's Bodies: Sexuality, Appearance and Behaviour*, Oxford: Oxford University Press.

Bauman, Z. (1992), *Intimations of Postmodernity*, London: Routledge.

Bayers, P.L. (2003), *Imperial Ascent: Mountaineering, Masculinity and Empire*, Boulder, CO: University Press of Colorado.

Beal, B. (1995), 'Disqualifying the Official: An Exploration of Social Resistance Through the Subculture of Skateboarding', *Sociology of Sport Journal*, 12, (3): 252–67.

Beal, B. (1996), 'Alternative Masculinity and its Effects on Gender Relations in the Subculture of Skateboarding', *Journal of Sport Behaviour*, 19: 204–20.

Beal, B. (1999), 'Skateboarding: An Alternative to Mainstream Sports' in J. Coakly and P. Donnelly (eds), *Inside Sports*, London: Routledge.

Beal, B. and Weidman, L. (2003), 'Authenticity in the Skateboarding World', in R. Rinehart and S. Sydnor (eds), *To the Extreme: Alternative Sports Inside and Out*, Albany, NY: State University of New York Press.

Beal, B. and Wilson, C. (2004), '"Chicks Dig Scars": Commercialisation and the transformations of skateboarders' identities', in B. Wheaton, (ed.), *Understanding Lifestyle Sports: Consumption, Identity and Difference*, London: Routledge.

Beaumont, P. and Douglas, E. (2006), 'Has Mighty Everest been Reduced to a Playground?', *Observer*, 21 May, pp. 24–5.

Beck, U. (1992), *Risk Society: Towards a New Modernity*, New Delhi: Sage. (Translated from the German Risikogesellschaft [1] published in 1986.)

Beck, U. (1994), The Reinvention of Politics: Towards a Theory of Reflexive Modernization, in U. Beck, A. Giddens and S. Lash (eds), *Reflexive Modernization: Politics, Tradition and Aesthetics in the Modern Social Order*, Cambridge: Polity Press.

Beck, U. (1999), *World Risk Society*, Malden, MA: Polity Press.

Beck, U. (2006), *Cosmopolitan Vision*, Cambridge: Polity Press.

Beck, U. and Beck-Gernsheim, E. (1995), *The Normal Chaos of Love*, Cambridge: Polity Press.

Bell, M. (2003), 'Adventure Racing and Epic Expeditions' in R. Rinehart and S. Sydnor (eds), *To the Extreme: Alternative Sports Inside and Out*, Albany, NY: State University of New York Press.

Bendelow, G. (1993), 'Pain Perceptions, Gender and Emotions', *Sociology of Health and Illness*, 15 (3): 273–94.

Bennett, T. and Silva, E. (2004), 'Everyday Life in Contemporary Culture', in E. Silva and T. Bennett (eds), *Contemporary Culture and Everyday Life*, Mill Valley, CA: Sociology Press.

Bennett, T. and Watson, D. (eds), (2002), *Understanding Everyday Life*, Oxford: Blackwell.

Benson, S. (1997), 'The Body, Health and Eating Disorders' in Woodward, K. (ed.), *Identity and Difference*, London: Sage.

Benyon, J. (2002), *Masculinities and Culture*, Buckinghamshire: Open University Press.

Birrell, S. (2000), 'Feminist Theories for Sport', in J. Coakley and E. Dunning (eds), *Handbook of Sports Studies*, London: Sage.

Birrell, S. and Richter, D (1987), 'Is a Diamond Forever? Feminist Transformations of Sport', *Women's Studies International Forum*, 10: 395–409.

Blum, A. (1980), *Annapurna: A Woman's Place*, San Francisco: Sierra Club Books.

Blum, A. (2005), *Breaking Trail: A Climbing Life*, New York: Scribner.

BMC (2006), 'Equity Survey Results'. Available at: www.thebmc.co.uk/News.aspx?id=1030.

BMC (2007), 'Climbing in the UK – Popularity and Participation. Available at: www.thebmc.co.uk/Feature.aspx?id=1422.

Booth, D. (2004), 'Surfing: from One (Cultural) Extreme to Another', in B. Wheaton, (ed.), *Understanding Lifestyle Sports: Consumption, Identity and Difference*, London: Routledge.

Booth, R. (2008), 'Water Sports', *Guardian*, 10 January, p. 11.

Borden, I. (2001), *Skateboarding, Space and the City: Architecture and the Body*, Oxford: Berg.

Bordo, S. (1989), 'The Body and the Reproduction of Femininity: A Feminist Appropriation of Foucault', in S. Bordo and A. Jaggar (eds), *Gender/Body/ Knowledge: Feminist Reconstructions of Being and Knowing*, London: Rutgers.

Boscagli, M. (1992), '"A Moving Story": Masculine Tears and the Humanity of Televised Emotion', *Discourse*, 15(2): 64–79.

Bourdieu, P. (1977), *Outline of a Theory of Practice*, Cambridge: Polity Press.

Bourdieu, P. (1986), *Distinction: A Social Critique of the Judgement of Taste*, London: Routledge.

Brannen, J. and Nilsen, A. (2002), 'Young People's Time Perspectives: From Youth to Adulthood', *Sociology*, 36(3): 513–37.

Bridel, W. and Rail, G. (2007), ' Sport, Sexuality and the Production of (Resistant) Bodies: De/Re-Constructing the Meanings of Gay Male Marathon Corporeality', *Sociology of Sport Journal*, 24: 127–44.

Brindle, D. and Lewis, P. (2006), 'Safety Last: Britons Urged to Cut Off the Cotton Wool and Rediscover their Spirit of Adventure', *Guardian*, 18 October, p. 3.

Brod, H. (1987), *The Making of Masculinities: The New Men's Studies*. Boston: Allen & Unwin.

Browne, D. (2004), *Amped: How Big Air, Big Dollars, and a New Generation Took Sports to the Extreme*, London: Bloomsbury.

Bryson, L. (1990), 'Challenges to Male Hegemony in Sport', in M. Messner and D. Sabo (eds), *Sport, Men and the Gender Order*, Champaign, IL: Human Kinetics.

Butler, J. (1990), *Gender Trouble. Feminism and the Subversion of Identity*, New York: Routledge.

Butler, J. (1993), *Bodies that Matter: on the Discursive Limits of 'Sex'*, London: Routledge.

Butler, J. (1997), *Excitable Speech: A Politics of the Performative*, London: Routledge.

Butler, J. (2004), *Undoing Gender*. New York: Routledge.

Calasanti, T. (2003), 'Masculinities and Care Work in Old Age', in S. Arber, K., Davidson and J. Ginn (eds), *Gender and Aging: Changing Roles and Relationships*, Buckinghamshire: Open University Press.

Campbell, E. (2003), 'Interviewing Men in Uniform: A Feminist Approach', *International Journal of Social Research Methodology*, 6 (4): 285–304.

Carrigan, T., Connell, R.W. and Lee, J. (1985), 'Toward a Sociology of Masculinity', *Theory and Society*, 14: 551–604.

Carrington, B. (1998), 'Sport, Masculinity and Black Cultural Resistance', *Journal of Sport and Social Issues*, 22(3): 275–98.

Cashmore, E. (2000), *Making Sense of Sports*, 3rd edn, London: Routledge.

Cashmore, E. (2004), *Beckham*, Cambridge: Polity.

Caudwell, J. (1999), 'Women's Football in the United Kingdom: Theorizing Gender and Unpacking the Butch Lesbian Image', *Journal of Sport and Social Issues*, 23(4): 390–402.

Cave, A. (2005), *Learning to Breathe*, London: Hutchinson.

Chaney, D. (2002), *Cultural Change and Everyday Life*. Basingstoke: Palgrave.

Choi, P. (2000), *Femininity and the Physically Active Woman*, London: Routledge.

Clough, P. (1992), *The End(s) of Ethnography from Realism to Social Criticism*, London: Sage.

Coakley, J. and Donnelly, P. (eds) (1999), *Inside Sports*, London: Routledge.

Coffey, M. (2003), *Fragile Edge: Loss On Everest*, London: Arrow Books. (First published 1989, Chatto & Windus.)

Coffey, M. (2004), *Where the Mountain Casts Its Shadow: The Personal Costs of Climbing*, London: Arrow Books. (First published in the UK, 2003, Hutchinson.)

Cole, C. (1998), 'Addiction, Exercise and Cyborgs', in G. Rail (ed.), *Sport and Post-Modern Times*, New York: State University of New York Press.

Collinson, D.L. and Hearn, J. (eds) (1996), *Men as Managers, Managers as Men: Critical Perspectives on Men, Masculinities and Managements*, London: Sage.

Connell, R.W. (1987), *Gender and Power: Society, the Person and Sexual Politics*. Cambridge: Polity Press.

Connell, R.W. (1995), *Masculinities*. Cambridge: Polity Press.

Connell, R.W. (1997), 'Men's Bodies', in K. Woodward (ed.), *Identity and Difference*, London: Sage.

Connell, R.W. (2000), *The Men and the Boys*, London: Polity Press.

Connell, R.W. (2005), *Masculinities*, 2nd edn, Cambridge: Polity Press.

Connell, R.W. (2007), 'Foreword', in L. Segal, *Slow Motion: Changing Masculinities, Changing Men*, 3rd edn, London: Palgrave.

Cook, D. (1994), 'Running on Empty: Climbing Literature in the '80s', in T. Gifford and R. Smith (eds), *Orogenic Zones*, Wakefield: Bretton Hall College of the University of Leeds.

Cooper, T. (2005),'The Taxman Cometh', in *Daily Telegraph*, 9 July, p. 2.

Cornwall, A.. and Lindisfarne, N. (eds) (1994), *Dislocating Masculinity: Comparative Ethnographies*, London: Routledge.

Cox, B. and Thompson, S. (2000), 'Multiple Bodies: Sportswomen, Soccer and Sexuality', *International Review for the Sociology of Sport*, 35(1): 5–20.

Craig, D. (1988), *Native Stones: A Book About Climbing*, London: Fontana.

Creedon, Pamela J. (ed.) (1994), *Women, Media and Sport: Challenging Gender Values*, London: Sage.

Csikszentmihalyi, M. (1975), *Beyond Boredom and Anxiety*, San Francisco: Jossey-Bass.

Csordas, T. (2002), *Body/Meaning/Healing*, Basingstoke: Palgrave Macmillan.

Curry, T.J. and Strauss, R.H. (1994), 'A Little Pain Never Hurt Anybody: A Photo-Essay on the Normalization of Sport Injuries', *Society of Sport Journal*, 11: 195–208.

Dant, T. and Wheaton, B. (2007), 'Windsurfing: An Extreme Form of Material and Embodied Interaction', *Anthropology Today*, 23(6): 8–12.

Da Silva, R. (ed.) (1992), *Leading out: Women Climbers Reaching for the Top*, Seal Press: Seattle.

Davidson, K., Daly, T. and Arber, S. (2003), 'Exploring the Social Worlds of Older Men' in S. Arber, K. Davidson and J. Ginn (eds), *Gender and Aging: Changing Roles and Relationships*, Buckinghamshire: Open University Press.

De Garis, L. (2000), '"Be a Buddy to Your Buddy" : Male Identity, Aggression, and Intimacy in a Boxing Gym', in J. McKay, M. Messner and D. Sabo (eds), *Masculinities, Gender Relations and Sport*, London: Sage.

Delphy, C. (1984), *Close to Home: A Materialist Analysis of Women's Oppression*, London: Hutchinson.

Dilley, R. (2002), 'Women and Climbing: An Exploration of Resistance, Collusion and the Embodied Self', unpublished MSc dissertation, Edinburgh University.

Dilley, R (2007), 'Women's Climbing Physicalities: Bodies, Experience and Representation', in V. Robinson, (ed.), Special Issue of *Sheffield Online Papers in Social Research*, Gender and Extreme Sports: The Case of Climbing, August, Issue 10.

Donnelly, P. (2003), 'Sports Climbing vs. Adventure Climbing', in R.E. Rinehart and S. Sydnor (eds), *To the Extreme: Alternative Sports, Inside and Out*, Albany, NY: State University of New York Press.

Donnelly, P. (2003), 'The Great Divide: Sport Climbing vs. Adventure Climbing' in Rinehart, R.E. and Sydnor, S. (eds), *To The Extreme: Alternative Sports, Inside and Out*, Albany, NY: State University of New York Press.

Donnelly, P. and Young, K. (1988), 'The Construction and Confirmation of Identity in Sports Subcultures', *Sociology of Sport Journal*, 5: 223–40.

Donnelly, P. and Young, K. (1999), 'Rock Climbers and Rugby Players: Identity Construction and Confirmation', in J. Coakly and P. Donnelly (eds), *Inside Sports*, London/New York: Routledge.

Dornian, D. (2003), 'Xtreem', in Rinehart, R.E. and Sydnor, S. (eds), *To The Extreme: Alternative Sports, Inside and Out*, Albany, NY: State University of New York Press.

Douglas, E. (1998), 'Women, Freedom, and Risk', *Climber*, June 1998.

Douglas, E. (1999), 'Packaged and Regulated, but Still Dangerous', *Guardian*, 29 July, p. 3.

Douglas, E. (2007), 'Death in the Snow: Why have Five Climbers been Killed on One Peak?' *Guardian*, 3 February, p. 9.

Du Gay, P., Hall, S., Janes, L., Mackay, H. and Negus, K. (eds) (1997), *Doing Cultural Studies: The Story of the Sony Walkman*, London: Sage /The Open University.

Dunning, E. (1999), *Sport Matters: Sociological Studies of Sport, Violence and Civilization*, London: Routledge.

Dyck, N. (ed.) (2000), *Games, Sports and Cultures*, Oxford: Berg.

Edley, N. and Wetherell, M. (1995), *Men in Perspective: Practice, Power and Identity*, London: Prentice-Hall.

Edwards, T. (2006), *Cultural Masculinities*, London: Routledge.

Eng, H. (2003), 'Sporting Se/xuality: Doing Sex and Sexuality in a Norwegian Sport Context', published dissertation, Oslo: The Norwegian University of Sport and Physical Education.

Erickson, B. (2005), 'Style Matters: Explorations of Bodies, Whiteness, and Identity in Rock Climbing', *Sociology of Sport Journal*, 22(3): 373–96.

Farrell, E. (2007), 'Into Blue', in *Holland Herald*, KLM, November, pp. 30–9.

Felski, R. (1999–2000), 'The Invention of Everyday Life', *New Formations*, 39(Winter): 15, 26–8, 30–1. Reprinted in Bernett, T. and Watson, D. (2002) *Understanding Everyday Life*, Oxford: Blackwell, pp. 351–4.

Ferrante, K. (1994), 'Baseball and the Social Construction of Gender' In P.J. Creedon (ed.), *Women, Media and Sport: Challenging Gender Values*, London: Sage.

Fillion, K. (1996), *Lip Service: The Myth of Female Virtue in Love, Sex and Friendship*, Sydney: HarperCollins.

Firestone, S. (1970), *The Dialectic of Sex: The Case for Feminist Revolution*, London: Jonathan Cape.

Fitzclarence, L. and Hickey, C. (2001), 'Real Footballers Don't Eat Quiche: Old Narratives in New Times', *Men and Masculinities*, 4(2): 118–39.

Foucault, M. (1987), *The History of Sex and Sexuality: An introduction*, London: Penguin.

Foucault, M. (1995), *Discipline and Punish*, 2nd edn. New York: Vintage Books.

Gardiner, M.E. (2000), *Critiques of Everyday Life*, London: Routledge.

Giddens, A. (1991), *Modernity and Self Identity*, Cambridge: Polity.

Giddens, A. (1992), *The Transformation of Intimacy: Sexuality, Love and Eroticism in Modern Societies*, Cambridge: Polity.

Gifford, T. (2004), *The Joy of Climbing: Terry Gifford's Classic Climbs*, Dunbeath: Whittles Publishing Ltd.

Gifford, T. (2006), *Reconnecting with John Muir: Essays in Post-Pastoral Practice*, Athens, GA: University of Georgia Press.

Gilchrist, P. (2007), 'Reality TV on the Rock Face: Climbing the Old Man of Hoy', *Journal of Sport in History*, 27(1): 44–63.

Gill, F. (2007), 'Violent' Femininity: Women Rugby Players and Gender Negotiation, *Women's Studies International Forum*, 30(5): 416–26.

Gill, R. (2003), 'Power and the Production of Subjects: A Genealogy of the New Man and the New Lad', in B. Benwell (ed.), *Masculinity and Man's Lifestyle Magazines*, Oxford: Blackwell.

Gilroy, S. (1997), 'Working on the Body: Links between Physical Activity and Social Power', in G. Clarke and B. Humberstone (eds), *Researching Women and Sport*, London: Macmillan.

Giulianotti, R. (1999), *Football: A Sociology of the Global Game*, Cambridge: Polity.

Giulianotti, R. (ed.) (2004), *Sport and Modern Social Theorists*, London: Palgrave.

Goffman, E. (1967), *Interaction Ritual*, New York: Anchor Books.

Green, E., Hebron, S. and Woodward, D. (1990), *Women's Leisure, What Leisure?* London: Macmillan.

Grogan, S. (1998), *Body Image: Understanding Body Dissatisfaction in Men, Women and Children*, London: Routledge.

Grosz, E. (1994), *Volatile Bodies: Toward a Corporeal Feminism*, Indianapolis: Indiana University Press.

*Guardian*, 2006, Advert for NISSAN x-Trail, 9 June.

*Guardian Jobs*, 2007, 1 October, p. 11.

Guiton, E. (2004), 'Life Goes On', *Guardian*, 19 August, p. 10.

Guiton, E. (2005), 'Life Goes On', *Guardian*, 5 February, p. 9.

Hall, A. (1994), 'Gender and Sport in the 1990s: Feminism Culture and Politics', *Sport Science Review*, 2: 48–68.

Hall, A., Hockey, J. and Robinson, V. (2007), 'Occupational Cultures and the Embodiment of Masculinity: Hairdressing, Estate Agency and Firefighting', *Gender, Work and Organization*, 14(6): 534–51.

Hall, M.A. (1990), How Should We Theorize Gender in the Context of Sport? in D. Sabo and M. Messner (eds), *Sport, Men and the Gender Order*, Champaign, IL: Human Kinetics.

Hall, M.A. (2002), 'The Discourse of Gender and Sport: From Femininity to Feminism', in S. Scraton and A. Flintoff (eds), *Gender and Sport: A Reader*, London: Routledge.

Hall, S. (1996), 'Introduction: Who Needs Identity?' in P. du Gay, S. Hall, L. Janes, H. Mackay and K. Negus (eds), *Doing Cultural Studies: The Story of the Sony Walkman*, London: Sage/The Open University.

Hareven, T.K. (2000), *Families, History and Social Change: Life-course and Cross-cultural Perspectives*, Boulder, CO: Westview Press.

Hargreaves, J. (1994), *Sporting Females: Critical Issues in the History and Sociology of Women's Sports*, London: Routledge.

Hargreaves, J. (2000), *Heroines of Sport: The Politics of Difference*, London: Routledge.

Hargreaves, J. (2004), 'Querying Sport Feminism: Personal or Political?' in R. Giulianotti (ed.), *Sport and Modern Social Theorists*, London: Palgrave.

Hargreaves, J. and McDonald, I. (2004), Series Editors' Foreword, in B. Wheaton (ed.), *Understanding Lifestyle Sports: Consumption, Identity and Difference*, London: Routledge.

Harris, D. (2005), *Key Concepts in Leisure Studies*, London: Sage.

Harris, J. and Clayton, B. (2007), 'The First Meterosexual Rugby Star? Rugby Union, Masculinity and Celebrity in Contemporary Wales', *Sociology of Sport Journal*, 24(2): 145–64.

Harris, K.K. (2007), *Extreme Metal: Music and Culture on the Edge*, Oxford: Berg.

Hasbrook, C.A. and Harris, O. (2000), 'Wrestling with Gender: Physicality and Masculinities among Inner-City First and Second Graders', in J. McKay, M.A. Messner and D. Sabo (eds), *Masculinities, Gender Relations and Sport*, London: Sage.

Haywood, C. and Mac An Ghaill, M. (2003), *Men and Masculinities*, Buckingham: Open University Press.

Hearn, J. (1993), 'Emotive Subjects: Organizational Men, Organizational Masculinities and the (De) construction of "Emotions"', in S. Fineman (ed.), *Emotion in Organizations*, London: Sage.

Hearn, J. (1998), 'Theorizing Men and Men's Theorizing: Varieties of Discursive Practices in Men's Theorizing of Men', *Theory and Society*, 27: 781–816.

Hearn, J. (2004), 'From Hegemonic Masculinity to the Hegemony of Men', *Feminist Theory*, 5(1): 49–72.

Hearn, J. and Morgan, D. (eds) (1990), *Men, Masculinities and Social Theory*, London: Unwin Hyman.

Heywood, I. (2002), 'Urgent Dreams: Climbing, Rationalization, and Ambivalence', in G. Ritzer (ed.), *McDonaldization: The Reader*, Pine Forge Press.

Heywood, I. (2006), 'Climbing Monsters: Excess and Restraint in Contemporary Rock Climbing', *Leisure Studies*, 25(4): 455–67.

Highmore, B. (2002), *Everyday Life and Cultural Theory*, London: Routledge.

Hockey, J. and James, A. (2003), *Social Identities across the Life Course*, Basingstoke: Palgrave Macmillan.

Hockey, J., Meah, A. and Robinson, V. (2007), *Mundane Heterosexualities: From Theory to Practices*, London: Palgrave.

Hockey, J., Robinson, V. and Meah, A. (2002), '"For Better or Worse?" Heterosexuality

Reinvented', *Sociological Research Online* 7, www.socresonline.org.uk/7/2/hockey.html.

Holland, S. (2004), *Alternative Femininities: Body, Age and Identity*, Oxford: Berg.

Horne, J., Tomlinson, A. and Whannel, G. (1999), *Understanding Sport: An Introduction to the Sociological and Cultural Analysis of Sport*, London: Routledge.

Ingraham, C. (1999), *White Weddings: Romancing Heterosexuality in Popular Culture*, London: Routledge.

Jackson, S. (1999), *Heterosexuality in Question*, London: Sage.

Jackson, S. and Scott, S. (2002), 'Introduction to Part 6, Gendered Embodiment', in S. Jackson and S. Scott (eds), *Gender: A Sociological Reader*, London: Routledge.

Jamieson, L. (1998), *Intimacy: Personal Relationships in Modern Societies*, Cambridge: Polity.

Jamieson, L. (2002), 'Contextualising Friendship and Relationships Across the Life Course' (unpublished paper), *Research on Families and Relationships Conference*, University of Edinburgh, November.

Jenkins, R. (2004), *Social Identity*, 2nd edn, London: Routledge.

Kane, M.J. and Greendorfer, S.L. (1994), 'The Media's Role in Accommodating and Resisting Stereotyped Images of Women in Sport', in P.J. Creedon (ed.), *Women, Media and Sport: Challenging Gender Values*, London: Sage.

Kay, J. and Laberge, S. (2003), 'Imperialistic Construction of Freedom in Warren Miller's *Freeriders*', in R. Rinehart and S. Sydnor (eds), *To the Extreme: Alternative Sports, Inside and Out*, Albany, NY: State University of New York Press.

Kay, J. and Laberge, S. (2004), '"Mandatory Equipment": Women in Adventure Racing', in B. Wheaton. (ed.), *Understanding Lifestyle Sports: Consumption, Identity and Difference*, London: Routledge.

Kerfoot, D. (1999), 'The Organization of Intimacy: Managerialism, Masculinity and the Masculine Subject', in S. Whitehead and R. Moodely (eds), *Transforming Managers: Gendering Change in the Public Sector*, London: University College London.

Kerfoot, D. (2001), 'Managing the "Professional" Man', in M. Dent and S. Whitehead (eds), *Managing Professional Identities: Knowledge, Performativity and the 'New' Professional*, London: Routledge.

Kiewa, J. (2001), '"Stepping Around Things": Gender Relationships in Climbing', *Australian Journal of Outdoor Education*, 5(2): 4–12.

King, C.R., Leonard, D.J. and Kusz, K.W. (2007), 'White Power and Sport: An Introduction', *Journal of Sport and Social Issues*, 31(1): 3–10.

King, S.J. and McDonald, M.G. (2007), '(Post) Identity and Sporting Cultures: An Introduction and Overview', *Sociology of Sport Journal*, 24: 1–19.

Kirkpatrick, A. (2007), 'My Life Led Up to This', *Climb*, 24: 90.

Kivel, B.D. and Kleiber, D.A. (2000), 'Leisure in the Identity Formation of Lesbian /Gay Youth: Personal, but Not Social', *Leisure Sciences*, 22(4): 215–32.

Klein, A.M. (1990), 'Little Big Man: Hustling, Gender Narcissism and Bodybuilding Subculture', in M.A. Messner and D. Sabo (eds), *Sport, Men and the Gender Order: Critical Feminist Perspectives*, Champaign, IL: Human Kinetics.

Koivula, N. (2001), 'Perceived Characteristics of Sports Categorized as Gender-Neutral, Feminine and Masculine', *Journal of Sport Behavior*, 24(4): 377–94.

Kotarba, J. (1983), *Chronic Pain: Its Social Dimensions*, Beverley Hills, CA: Sage.

Krane, V. (2001), 'We Can Be Athletic and Feminine, But Do We Want To? Challenging Hegemonic Femininity in Women's Sport', *Quest*, 53(1): 115–19.

Kusz, K. (2003), 'BMX, Extreme Sports, and the White Male Backlash', in R. Rinehart, and S. Sydnor (eds), *To the Extreme: Alternative Sports Inside and Out*, Albany, NY: State University of New York Press.

Kusz, K. (2004), 'Extreme America: The Cultural Politics of Extreme Sports in 1990s America', in B. Wheaton (ed.), *Understanding Lifestyle Sports: Consumption, Identity and*

*Difference*, London: Routledge.

Laberge, S. and Albert, M. (1999), 'Conceptions of Masculinity and of Gender Transgressions in Sport among Adolescent Boys', *Men and Masculinities*, 1(3): 243–67.

Landesman, C. (2000), 'Gym'll Fix It', *Guardian*, 20 April, pp. 6–7.

Lash, S. (1993), 'Reflexive Modernization: The Aesthetic Dimension', *Theory, Culture and Society*, 10: 1–23.

Lash, S. (2000), 'Risk Culture' in B. Adams, U. Beck and J. van Loon (eds), *The Risk Society and Beyond*, London: Sage.

Laviolette, P. (2007), 'Hazardous Sport?', *Anthropology Today*, 23(6): 1–2.

Lawrence, J. (1994), 'Women and Climbing Writing', in T. Gifford and R. Smith (eds), *Orogenic Zones*, Wakefield: Bretton Hall College of the University of Leeds.

Le Breton, D. (2000), 'Playing Symbolically with Death in Extreme Sports', *Body and Society*, 6 (1): 1–11.

Leder, D. (1990), *The Absent Body*, Chicago: University of Chicago Press.

Lefebvre, H. (1971), *Everyday Life in the Modern World*, (S. Rabinovitch, trans.), New York: Harper Torchbooks.

Lefebvre, H. (1991), *The Critique of Everyday Life*, Volume 1, (J. Moore, trans.), London: Verso. First published in France, 1947.

Lewis, N. (2000), 'The Climbing Body, Nature and the Experience of Modernity', *Body and Society Journal*, 6(3–4): 58–80.

Lewis, N. (2004), Sustainable Adventure: Embodied Experiences and Ecological Practices within British Climbing', in B. Wheaton (ed.), *Understanding Lifestyle Sports: Consumption, Identity and Difference*. London: Routledge.

Lilleaas, U. (2007), 'Masculinities, Sport and Emotions', *Men and Masculinities*, 10(1): 39–53.

Lindsay Fitzclarence, L. and Hickey, C. (2001), 'Real Footballers Don' t Eat Quiche: Old Narratives in New Times', *Men and Masculinities*, 4(2): 118–39.

Loomis, M (2005), 'Going Manless', *The American Alpine Journal*, 47: 3–19.

Lupton, D. (1998), *The Emotional Self*, London: Sage.

Lyng, S. (1990), 'Edgework: A Social Psychological Analysis of Voluntary Risk-taking', *American Journal of Sociology*, 95: 851–86.

Lyng, S. (2005), 'Edgework and the Risk-Taking Experience', in S. Lyng (ed.), *Edgework: The Sociology of Risk–Taking*, London: Routledge.

Mac an Ghaill, M. (ed.) (1996), *Understanding Masculinities*, Buckingham: Open University Press.

MacClancy, J. (1996), *Sport, Identity and Ethnicity*, Oxford: Berg.

Mackinnon, C. (1987), 'Women, Self Possession and Sport', in C. Mackinnon, *Feminism Unmodified: Discourse on Life and Law*, Cambridge, MA: Harvard University Press.

Macnaghten, P. and Urry, J. (2000), 'Bodies of Nature: Introduction', *Body and Society*, 6(3–4): 1–11.

Maffesoli, M. (1996), *The Time of the Tribes: The Decline of Individualism in Mass Society*, London: Sage.

Maguire, J. (1999), *Global Sport: Identities, Societies, Civilizations*, Cambridge: Polity.

Maley, J. (2006), 'Italians Passed Us By, Says Everest Rescuer', *Guardian*, 9 June.

Martin, G. (2002), 'Conceptualizing Cultural Politics in Subcultural and Social Movement Studies', 1(1): 73–88.

Martin, R. and Miller, T. (1999), 'Fielding Sport: A Preface to Politics?' In R. Martin and T. Miller (eds), *SportCult*, Minneapolis, MN: University of Minnesota Press.

McKay, J. Messner, M. and Sabo, D. (eds) (2000), *Masculinities, Gender Relations and Sport*, London: Sage.

McDermott, L. (1996), 'Toward a Feminist Understanding of Physicality within the Context of Women's Physically Active and Sporting Lives', *Sociology of Sport Journal*, 13: 12–29.

McKay J. and Rowe, D. (2001), 'Panic Sports and the Racialized Male Body', in T. Miller (ed.), *Sportsex*, Philadelphia, PA: Temple University Press.

McRobbie, A. (1994), *Feminism and Youth Culture: from 'Jackie' to 'Just Seventeen'*, Basingstoke: Macmillan.

Mead, G.H. (1934), *Mind, Self and Society from the Standpoint of a Social Behaviourist* (ed. C.W. Morris), Chicago, IL: University of Chicago Press.

Mennessen, C. (2000), '"Hard" Women and "Soft" Women: The Social Construction of Identities Among Female Boxers', *International Review for the Sociology of Sport*, 35: 21–33.

Merleau-Ponty, M. (1962), *The Phenomenology of Perception*, New York: Routledge.

Messner, M. (1987), 'The Meaning of Success: The Athletic Experience and the Development of Male Identity', in H. Brod (ed.), *The Making of Masculinities: The New Men's Studies*, Boston: Allen & Unwin.

Messner, M. (1992), *Power at Play: Sports and the Problem of Masculinity*, Boston, MA: Beacon Press.

Messner, M. (2001), 'Friendship, Intimacy and Sexuality', in S.M. Whitehead and F.J. Barrett (eds), *The Masculinities Reader*, Cambridge: Polity.

Messner, M. and Sabo, D. (eds) (1990), *Sport, Men and the Gender Order*, Champaign, IL: Kinetics Publishers.

Messner, M. and Sabo, D. (eds) (1994), *Sex, Violence and Power in Sports: Rethinking Masculinity*, Freedom, CA: Crossing.Hart.

Middleton, P. (1992), *The Inward Gaze: Masculinity and Subjectivity in Modern Culture*, London: Routledge.

Midol, N. and Broyer, G. (1995), 'Toward an Anthropological Analysis of New Sport Cultures: The Case of Whiz sports in France', *Society of Sport Journal*, 12: 204–12.

Miller, S. (1983), *Men and Friendship*, San Leandro, CA: Gateway Books.

Miller, T., Lawrence, G., McKay, J. and Rowe, D. (2001), *Globalization and Sport: Playing the World*, London: Sage.

Milovanovic, D. (2005), 'Edgework: A Subjective and Structural Model of Negotiating Boundaries', in S. Lyng (ed.), *Edgework: The Sociology of Risk-Taking*, London: Routledge.

Moi, T. (1999), *What is a Woman?: And Other Essays*, Oxford: Oxford University Press.

Moller, M. (2007), 'Exploiting Patterns: A Critique of Hegemonic Masculinity', *Journal of Gender Studies*, 16(3): 263–76.

Monaghan, L. (2005), 'Big Handsome Men, Bears and Others: Virtual Constructions of "Fat Male Embodiment"', *Body and Society*, 11(2): 81–111.

Morgan, D. (1992), *Discovering Men*, London: Routledge.

Morgan, D. (1999), 'Risk and Family Practices: Accounting for Change and Fluidity in Family Life' in E. Silva and C. Smart (eds), *The New Family?* London: Sage.

Morgan, D. (2002), 'You Too Can Have a Body Like Mine', in S. Jackson and S. Scott (eds), *Gender: A Sociological Reader*, London: Routledge.

Morgan, D., Brandth, B. and Kvande, E. (eds) (2005), *Gender, Bodies and Work*, Aldershot: Ashgate.

Muggleton, D. (2000), *Inside Subculture*, Oxford: Berg.

Nettleton, S. (1992), *Power, Pain and Dentistry*, Buckingham: Open University Press.

Nettleton, S. and Watson, J. (1998), *The Body in Everyday Life*, London: Routledge.

Pahl, R. (2000), *On Friendship*, Cambridge: Polity.

Palmer, C. (2004), 'Death, Danger and the Selling of Risk in Adventure Sports', in B. Wheaton (ed.), *Understanding Lifestyle Sports: Consumption, Identity and Difference*, London: Routledge.

Perrin, J. (2005), *The Villain: The Life of Don Whillans*, London: Hutchinson.

Plate, K.R. (2007), 'Rock Climbing is a Masculine Sport? Understanding the Complex Gendered Subculture of Rock Climbing', in V. Robinson (ed.), special issue of *Sheffield*

*Online Papers in Social Research*, Gender and Extreme Sports: The Case of Climbing, August, Issue 10.

Poole, S. (2005), 'Double-plus Good', *Guardian Arts Section*, 25 June, p. 15.

Powter, G. (2007), *We Cannot Fail: The Dark Psychology of Heroic Adventure*, London: Robinson Publishing.

Pritchard, P. (1999), *The Totem Pole*, London: The Constable Press.

Pronger, B. (1998), 'Post-Sport', in G. Rail (ed.), *Sport and Post-Modern Times*, New York: State University of New York Press.

Pronger, B. (2000), 'Homosexuality and Sport: Who's Winning?' in J. McKay, M. Messner and D. Sabo (eds), *Masculinities, Gender Relations and Sport*, London: Sage.

Raban, J. (1999), 'Worlds Apart', *Guardian*, 23 October, pp. 1 and 3.

Rapport, N. (1997), *Transcendent Individual: Towards a Literary and Liberal Anthropology*, London: Routledge.

Reith, G. (2005), 'On the Edge: Drugs and the Consumption of Risk in Late Modernity', in S. Lyng (ed.), *Edgework: The Sociology of Risk-Taking*, London: Routledge.

Rinehart, R. (2005), '"Babes" and Boards: Opportunities in New Millennium Sport?' *Journal of Sport and Social Issues*, 29(3): 232–55.

Rinehart, R. and Sydnor, S. (2003), 'Proem', in R. Rinehart and S. Sydnor (eds), *To the Extreme: Alternative Sports, Inside and Out*, Albany, NY: State University of New York Press.

Roberts, K. (1997), 'Same Activities, Different Meanings: British Youth Cultures on the 1990s', *Leisure Studies*, 16(1): 1–16.

Robertson, S. (2003), '"If I Let a Goal In, I'll Get Beat Up": Contradictions in Masculinity, Sport and Health', *Health Education Research*, 18(6): 706–16.

Robinson, V. (1996), 'Heterosexuality and Masculinity: Theorising Male Power or the Male Wounded Psyche?', in D. Richardson (ed.), *Theorising Heterosexuality*, Buckingham: Open University Press.

Robinson, V. (2002), 'Men, Masculinities and Rock Climbing', *Pavis Papers in Social and Cultural Research*, Buckingham: The Open University.

Robinson, V. (2003), 'Everyday Heterosexualities and Everyday Masculinities: The Mundane and the Extreme', PhD thesis, University of Manchester, UK.

Robinson, V. (2004) 'Taking Risks: Identity, Masculinities, and Rock Climbing', in B. Wheaton (ed.), *Understanding Lifestyle Sports: Consumption, Identity and Difference*, London: Routledge.

Robinson, V. (2006), 'In Conversation with Arlene Blum', *The Nineteenth International Festival of Mountaineering Literature*, Bretton Hall Campus, The University of Leeds, 25 March.

Robinson, V. (ed.) (2007), Introduction, Special Issue of *Sheffield Online Papers in Social Research*, Gender and Extreme Sports: The Case of Climbing, August, Issue 10.

Robinson, V. (2008), 'Men, Masculinities and Feminism', in D. Richardson and V. Robinson (eds), *Introducing Gender and Women's Studies*, Basingstoke: Palgrave Macmillan.

Robinson, V. and Hockey, J. (forthcoming), *Masculinities in Transition*, London: Palgrave.

Robinson, V., Hockey, J. and Hall, A. (2007), 'Negotiating Sexual and Gender Boundaries', in C. Beckett, O. Heathcote and M. Macey (eds), *Negotiating Boundaries: Identities, Sexualities, Diversities*, Newcastle: Cambridge Scholars Publishing.

Rojek, C. and Turner, B.S. (2000), 'Decorative Sociology: A Critique of the Cultural Turn', *Sociological Review*, 48: 629–48.

Rose, D. and Douglas, E. (2000), *Regions of the Heart*, Washington, DC: National Geographic Society.

Roskelley, J. (1991), *Lost Days*, Harrisburg, PA: Stackpole Books.

Rowe, D., McKay, J. and Miller, T. (2000), 'Panic Sport and the Racialized Masculine

Body', in J. McKay, M. Messner and D. Sabo (eds), *Masculinities, Gender Relations and Sport*, London: Sage.

Rutherford, J. (1992), *Predicaments in Masculinity*, London: Routledge.

Ryan, M. (2005a), 'Climb Like a Girl. Part 1', UKC Articles, www.ukclimbing.com/articles/page.php?id=107.

Ryan, M. (2005b), 'Climb Like a Girl. Part 4', UKC Articles, www.ukclimbing.com/articles/page.php?id=114.

Ryan, M. (2005c), 'Climb Like a Girl. Part 2', UKC Articles, www.ukclimbing.com/articles/page.php?id=110.

Sabo, D. and Messner, M. (1994), 'Changing Men Through Changing Sports: An Eleven Point Strategy ', in M. Messner and D. Sabo (eds), *Sex, Violence and Power in Sports: Rethinking Masculinity*, Freedom, CA: Crossing.

Salisbury, J. and Jackson, D. (1996), *Challenging Macho Values: Practical Ways of Working With Adolescent Boys*, London: Falmer Press.

Schutz, A. (1973), 'Common-sense and Scientific Interpretation of Human Action', in A. Schutz (ed.), *Collected Papers: The Problem of Social Reality*, The Hague: Martin Nijhoff.

Scraton, S. (1992), *Shaping up to Womanhood: Gender and Girl's Physical Education*, Buckingham: Open University Press.

Scraton, S. and Flintoff, A. (2002), 'Sport Feminism: The Contribution of Feminist Thought to Our Understanding of Gender and Sport', in S. Scraton and A. Flintoff (eds), *Gender and Sport: A Reader*, London: Routledge.

Segal, L. (1990), *Slow Motion: Changing Masculinities, Changing Men*, London: Virago.

Segal, L. (2007), *Slow Motion: Changing Masculinities, Changing Men*, 3rd edn, London: Palgrave.

Seidler, V. (1989), *Rediscovering Masculinity: Reason, Language and Sexuality*, London: Routledge.

Seidler, V. (ed.) (1992), *Men, Sex and Relationships: Writings from Achilles Heel*, London: Routledge.

Seidler, V. (1994), *Unreasonable Men: Masculinity and Social Theory*, London: Routledge.

Seidler, V. (1998), 'Masculinity, Violence and Emotional Life', in G. Bendelow and S.J. Williams (eds), *Emotions in Social Life: Critical Themes and Contemporary Issues*, London: Routledge.

Seidler, V. (2006), *Transforming Masculinities*, London: Routledge.

Seidman, S. (1997), *Difference Troubles*, Cambridge: Cambridge University Press.

Sharp, B. (2001), 'Take Me to Your (Male) Leader', *Gender and Education*, 13(1): 75–86.

Silva, E. and Smart, C. (1999), 'The "New" Practices and Politics of Family Life', in E. Silva and C. Smart (eds), *The New Family?*, London: Sage.

Simpson, J. (1988), *Touching the Void*, London: Jonathan Cape.

Simpson, J. (1996), *Storms of Silence*, London: Jonathan Cape.

Skellington, R.S. (2006), 'What's Sport Got to Do With It?', *Society Matters*, 8: 9.

Smart, B. (2005), *The Sports Star: Modern Sport and the Cultural Economy of Sporting Celebrity*, London: Sage.

Smears, E.A. (2001), Physicality and Gender Our Body of Knowledge: An Exploration of Women's Experiences of Physicality, unpublished PhD thesis, Leeds Metropolitan University.

Smith, C.W. (2005), 'Financial Edgework: Trading in Market Currents', in S. Lyng (ed.), *Edgework: The Sociology of Risk-Taking*, London: Routledge.

Smith, D. (1987), *The Everyday World as Problematic: A Feminist Sociology*, Milton Keynes: The Open University Press.

Smith, S.L. (2000), 'British Nonelite Road Running and Masculinity: A Case of "Running Repairs"?' *Journal of Men and Masculinities*, 3(2): 187–208.

Soutar, I. (2005), 'Taxing High Adventure', *Sheffield Telegraph*, 29 July, p. 19.

Sparkes, A.C. (2002), *Telling Tales in Sport and Physical Activity: A Qualitative Journey*, Champaign, IL: Human Kinetics.

Spector-Mersel, G. (2006), 'Never-aging Stories: Western Hegemonic Masculinity Scripts', *Journal of Gender Studies*, 15(1): 67–82.

Spracklen, K. (2001), '"Black Pearl, Black Diamonds": Exploring Racial Identities in Rugby League', in B. Carrington and I. McDonald (eds), *'Race', Sport and British Society*, London: Routledge.

Stainforth, G. (2005), 'Jim Perrin's The Villain – Reviewed', www.uk.climbing.com/articles/page.php?id=105.

Stanley, L. (1997), 'Methodology Matters!' in V. Robinson and D. Richardson (eds), *Introducing Women's Studies: Feminist Theory and Practice*, Basingstoke: Palgrave Macmillan.

Stanley, L. and Wise, S. (2008), 'Feminist Methodology Matters!' in D. Richardson and V. Robinson (eds), *Introducing Gender and Women's Studies*, Basingstoke: Palgrave Macmillan.

Stranger, L. (1999), 'The Aesthetics of Risk': A Study of Surfing', *International Review for the Sociology of Sport*, 34(3): 265–76.

Summers, K. (2007), 'Unequal Genders: Mothers and Fathers on Mountains', in V. Robinson (ed.), Special Issue of *Sheffield Online Papers in Social Research*, Gender and Extreme Sports: The Case of Climbing, August, Issue 10.

Thornham, S. (2000), *Feminist Theory and Cultural Studies: Stories of Unsettled Relations*, London: Arnold.

Thorpe, H. (2006), 'Beyond "Decorative Sociology": Contextualising Female Surf, Skate and Snow Boarding', *Sociology of Sport Journal*, 23: 205–28.

Todhunter, A. (1998), cited in *Rock and Ice*, September.

Toffoletti, K. (2007), 'How is Gender-based Violence Covered in the Sporting News? An Account of the Football League Sex Scandal', *Women's Studies International Forum*, 30(5): 427–38.

*Touching the Void* (2003), Film. Director, Kevin Macdonald. Darlow Smithson Productions.

Tulloch, J. and Lupton, D. (2003), *Risk and Everyday Life*, London: Sage.

UKClimbing.com (2005), 'Topic – OU article on Male Climbers', available at: www.ukclimbing.com/forum/t.php?t=121519&v=1, accessed 18 March 2005.

Vincent, J. (1995), *Inequality and Old Age*. London: University College London Press.

Wacquant, L. (1995), 'Review Article, "Why Men Desire Muscles"', *Body and Society*, 1: 163–79.

Watson, A. (2005), 'You Don't Have to be Crazy', *Telegraph*, 28 May, p. 15.

Watson, J. (2000), *Male Bodies: Health, Culture and Identity*, Buckingham: Open University Press.

Watters, R. (2003), 'The Wrong Side of the Thin Edge', in R. Rinehart and S. Sydnor (eds), *To The Extreme: Alternative Sports, Inside and Out*, Albany, NY: State University of New York Press.

Webster, J. (1995), 'Age Differences in Reminiscence Functions', in B. Haight and J. Webster (eds), *The Art and Science of Reminiscing*, Washington, DC: Taylor & Francis.

Wells, C. (2002), *A Brief History of British Mountaineering*, West Didsbury: British Mountaineering Council.

Wetherell, M. and Griffin, C. (1991), 'Feminist Psychology and the Study of Men and Masculinity: Part 1: Assumptions and Perspectives', *Feminism and Psychology*, 1(3): 133–68.

Wheaton, B. (2000a), 'Just Do it: Consumption, Commitment and Identity in the Windsurfing Subculture', *Sociology of Sport Journal*, 17(3): 254–74.

Wheaton, B. (2000b), '"New Lads"? Masculinities and the "New Sport" Participant',

*Men and Masculinities Journal*, 2(4): 434–56.

Wheaton, B. (2004a), '"New Lads"? Competing Masculinities in the Windsurfing Culture', in B. Wheaton (ed.), *Understanding Lifestyle Sports: Consumption, Identity and Difference*, London: Routledge.

Wheaton, B. (ed.) (2004b), 'Introduction: Mapping the Lifestyle Sport-Scape', *Understanding Lifestyle Sports: Consumption, Identity and Difference*, London: Routledge.

Wheaton, B. (2005), 'Selling Out? The Commercialisation and Globalization of Lifestyle Sports', in L. Allison (ed.), *The Global Politics of Sport*, London: Routledge.

Wheaton, B. (2007), 'After Sport Culture: Rethinking Sport and Post-Subcultural Theory', *Journal of Sport and Social Issues*, 31(3): 283–307.

Wheaton, B. and A. Tomlinson (1998), 'The Changing Gender Order in Sport? The Case of Windsurfing', *Journal of Sport and Social Issues*, 22: 252–74.

Whitehead, S.M. (2002), *Men and Masculinities*, Cambridge: Polity.

Whitehead, S.M. and Barrett, F.J. (eds) (2001), *The Masculinities Reader*, Cambridge: Polity.

Whitson, D. (1990), 'Sport in the Social Construction of Masculinity', in D. Sabo and M. Messner (eds), *Sport, Men and the Gender Order*, Champaign, IL: Human Kinetics.

Williams, S.J. (2001), *Emotion and Social Theory: Corporeal Reflections on the (Ir)Rational*, London: Sage.

Williams, S.J. and Bendelow, G. (1998), *The Lived Body: Sociological Themes, Embodied Issues*, London: Routledge.

Wilson, B. (2002), 'The Canadian Race Scene and Five Theses on Youth Resistance', *Canadian Journal of Sociology*, 27(3): 373–412.

Winlow, S. (2001), *Badfellas: Crime, Tradition and New Masculinities*, Oxford: Berg.

Woodward, K. (ed.) (1997), *Identity and Difference*, London: Sage.

Woodward, K. (2002), *Understanding Identity*, London: Arnold.

Woodward, K. (2004), 'Rumbles in the Jungle: Boxing, Racialization and the Performance of Masculinity', *Leisure Studies*, 23(1): 5–17.

Woodward, K. (2006), *Boxing, Masculinity and Identity: The 'I' of the Tiger*, London: Routledge.

Woodward, K. (2008), 'Gendered Bodies: Gendered Lives', in D. Richardson and V. Robinson (eds), *Introducing Gender and Women's Studies*, Basingstoke: Palgrave Macmillan.

Wörsching, M. (2007), 'Race to the Top: Masculinity, Sport, and Nature in German Magazine Advertising', *Men and Masculinities*, 10(2): 197–221.

Yates, S. (2002), *The Flame of Adventure*, London: Vintage.

Young, I.M. (2005), *On Female Body Experience. "Throwing Like A Girl" and Other Essays*, Oxford: Oxford University Press.

Young, K. (1997), 'Women, Sport and Physicality: Preliminary Findings from a Canadian Study', *International Review for the Sociology of Sport*, 32: 297–305.

Young, K. and White, P. (2000), 'Researching Sports Injury: Reconstructing Dangerous Masculinities', in J. McKay, M. Messner and D. Sabo (eds), *Masculinities, Gender Relations and Sport*, London: Sage.

Young, K., White, P. and McTeer, W. (1994), 'Body Talk: Male Athletes Reflect on Sport, Injury and Pain', *Sociology of Sport Journal*, 11(2): 175–94.

# Index